THE LOST BELIEFS OF NORTHERN EUROPE

THE LOST BELIEFS OF NORTHERN EUROPE

Hilda Ellis Davidson

BARNES & NOBLE
BOOKS
NEW YORK

This edition published by Barnes & Noble, Inc.,
by arrangement with Routledge

1999 Barnes & Noble Books

ISBN 0-7607-1629-3

Printed and bound in the United States of America

99 00 01 02 MC 9 8 7 6 5 4 3 2 1

RRD-H

CONTENTS

Figures

Note: Figure sources are referenced in the Bibliography and individual artists accredited with each figure.

Every attempt has been made to obtain permission to reproduce copyright material. If there are any omissions, please contact Fiona Parker at Routledge's London office.

Introduction

> Stout men were we, but that passed by,
> Above our bones men tread.
>
> (attributed to Fland mac Lonain:
> trans. Robin Flower)

How should we approach a religion of the past when it has left no creed for us to study, no sacred books or descriptions of rituals, no life of its founder and, indeed, little trace of the religious leaders and thinking minds who contributed to its development? Sometimes it is only possible to put together a few fragments of recorded beliefs and practices, to study carved stones or to find traces of mythology in legends and folk traditions and the tentative interpretation of names of nearly forgotten deities. This is roughly the position with the beliefs of some of the peoples of northern Europe, such as the Finno-Ugrians (including the Saami or Lapps and the Estonians), the Balts (including the Lithuanians and the Letts) and the Slavs. Traces of their mythology survive in folklore and folk art, and archaic features of surviving Baltic languages make the names of supernatural beings of much interest to scholars. In Finland the material collected by Lönnrot in the early nineteenth century, found in the lays making up the *Kalevala*, indicates a fine heritage of mythological tradition, but after so long a space of time there is little definite evidence from which to reconstruct ritual and belief (Honko 1987). In the case of the Celtic and Germanic peoples, however, the position is different. In studying their religion we are faced with many problems and there are vast gaps in our knowledge, but we have evidence from early art and archaeology in many different regions, and in addition an extensive early literature from medieval Ireland and Iceland. Although this was recorded by Christian chroniclers and story-tellers, in most cases in monasteries, it has, nevertheless, preserved a good deal of information about pre-Christian traditions and myths. Antiquarian enthusiasm for the past and the lively spirit of many of the old tales have ensured their continued existence in manuscripts and popular oral tradition long after Christianity was firmly established. It should therefore be possible to build up at least a partial picture of the old religion of north-western Europe, provided we realize the possibilities and limitations of the sources available.

How much is known of these peoples whom we call the Celts and the Germans? The terms 'Keltoi' or 'Celti', and in some cases 'Galati' and 'Galli', were used by Greeks and Romans for the northern barbarians who at times posed a considerable threat to the Mediterranean countries and dominated much of western and central Europe. Such terms seem to have been first used by the Greeks of the people north of Massilia, a Greek colony in southern France, while the Latin term first occurs in a poem by Rufus Festus Avienus, *Ora Maritima*, in the fourth century BC (Rankin 1987:1 ff.). The Celts moved in many directions, invading Italy and Greece and sacking Rome and Delphi, settling in Spain and as far east as Turkey, where St Paul knew them as the 'Galatians'. However, those who spoke the Celtic language in Europe have left no literature, and only traces remain in inscriptions and the names of places and persons. At some time in the first millenium BC, although the date is much disputed, they reached the British Isles. The Gaelic form of their language was spoken in Ireland and taken into Scotland and the Isle of Man, while the Brittonic form spoken in southern Britain survived in Wales and Cornwall and also in Brittany, where it was probably taken by refugees from Britain. It is from traditions preserved in the literature of these countries that we are able to learn something of Celtic religion before the coming of Christianity.

It was after the discoveries made in the salt-mines at Hallstatt in Austria in 1846, and a few years later at La Tène in Switzerland, that the existence of Celtic art was recognized for the first time. At Hallstatt there were a number of rich burials, while weapons and other objects of metal had been thrown into the lake at La Tène, which apparently had been a place of offering. The term 'Hallstatt' was used for the styles of art of the early Celtic period, from about 700 to 500 BC, and 'La Tène' for the later period, during which the art became even more original and striking. The furnishing of rich graves showed that the Celts had traded with Etruria and Greece, but they had also produced their own works of art, impressive in their individuality. As more material became available for study, it grew clear that many of these were of symbolic and religious significance. There were powerful figures in stone, which might be gods or ancestors, rich graves where both men and women were buried with wagons or chariots under burial mounds, many heads carved in stone, and occasional ritual groups in metal, like the little Strettweg Wagon on which a group of men and women with two stags have been placed around what seems to be a goddess (p. 24). In the La Tène period the metalwork was particularly striking, with complex linear patterns, spirals and foliage, as well as human faces and naturalistic animals and birds, often suggesting deliberate symbolism. When this style of art died out on the continent, it continued in the British Isles, and its final expression can be recognized in the splendid illuminated manuscripts and carved crosses of the Christian period. Ireland never came under Roman rule, and not only did the art there develop freely from earlier Celtic traditions, but a rich literature grew up in the early Middle Ages which reflected in its heroic tales a life-style of kings and warriors very similar to that of the Celts as earlier Greek and Roman writers had described them. It is now becoming recognized to an increasing degree that these tales have evolved in a Christian setting, and were intended for sophisticated audiences of a very different kind, but this does not mean that some early traditions cannot be found in the tales, antiquarian prose works and poems (McCone 1990:3 ff.).

The most impressive study of the Celtic peoples in early times was that of Posidonius, a Syrian Greek who died about 50 BC. He went to considerable trouble to gather information about their customs and way of life, and although his original work is lost, it is so often quoted by later writers that it is possible to reconstruct much of what he wrote (Tierney 1959–60). He and later historians interested in the Celts all emphasize their reckless courage and ferocity in battle, where they often fought naked, as they are sometimes depicted in classical art. There is general agreement as to Celtic enthusiasm for fine clothes, ornaments and elaborate hair-styles. Apparently they spent much time in feasting and drinking, and set great value on magnificent and impulsive hospitality, expecting generous treatment from the leaders whom they followed into battle. Their less endearing qualities were boastfulness and vanity, with a tendency to flare up at some imagined insult. Celtic chiefs were notorious for independence and touchiness and constantly quarrelled among themselves; had it not been for this, they would have been a far more serious threat to their southern neighbours. Classical writers were shocked and fascinated by their ferocious treatment of defeated enemies, and by their passion for head-hunting and preserving the skulls of the slain. Celtic disregard for human life, on a different level from the cold inhumanity of the Romans when putting down insurrection, caught the imagination of historians and artists. They were further fascinated by rumours and theories concerning the learning and practices of the druids, whom some regarded as natural philosophers and others as savage priests encouraging resistance to Rome.

The Germanic peoples who also settled in the British Isles cannot be traced back as far as the Celts, and their origins prove elusive, although their language, like that of the Celts, belonged to the Indo-European group (Mallory 1989:84 ff.; 95 ff.). The Romans used the term 'Germania' for the area enclosed by the Rhine, the Vistula and the Danube, where tribes speaking an early form of Germanic caused much trouble to them in the Rhineland. According to Julius Caesar, the Germans were settled to the east of the Rhine in the first century BC, with the Celts on the other side, but this must be a misleading simplification of the confused situation that actually prevailed there. *Germani* in Latin means 'children of the same parent', and seems originally to have been a tribal name, possibly even the name of a Celtic tribe. It is often not possible to know whether the language of a certain tribe was Germanic or Celtic, but the earliest Germanic-speaking peoples were distributed fairly widely over northern Germany and southern Scandinavia, and then gradually spread through modern Holland, Denmark, Poland, Czechoslovakia and southern Russia, crossing into England in the fifth century AD. How early their language can be traced back is an unsettled question (Todd 1975:19; Mallory 1989:87). The earliest Germanic text is in Gothic – an East Germanic language that was spoken up to the sixteenth century – since parts of the Bible were translated into Gothic by Bishop Wulfilas in the fourth century AD.

The outstanding source for the life of the Germanic people at the end of the first century AD is the short monograph of Tacitus *On the Origin and Geography of Germania* (generally known as *Germania*). Tacitus was a close friend of the younger Pliny, whose father had served on both the Upper and the Lower Rhine and written twenty books on the Roman campaigns there, unhappily now lost. He could also have been in touch with soldiers and merchants who could give him information. His book shows the lively interest that educated Romans took in the northern barbarians, and he deliberately stresses the contrast between the tough upbringing of German youth and the luxury and corruption of Roman society. He praises their warrior ideals and their loyalty to their leaders, while noting that when not engaged in battle they spent much time in indolence, drinking and boasting of their exploits, while their wives and older folks did much of the hard everyday work. He realized that there were considerable local differences between the tribes, and recorded what he could find out of their religious practices; his picture of a warrior society is on the whole in agreement with that given in later Germanic heroic poetry. Although doubts have been cast on his reliability, the information he gives has been confirmed rather than disproved as archaeological evidence enables us to build up a fuller picture of life in Germania and in the Roman period.

Clearly Celts and Germans had much in common, and were in close touch with one another in the Rhineland in Roman times, again in Britain in the fifth century AD, and in the British Isles in the Viking Age, even though they might be fighting one another for dominion or territory. Their life-styles were similar, and it is often impossible to decide from burial customs or archaeological remains whether a particular settlement was Celtic or Germanic. But language, after all, was an essential difference (Evans 1982), and their literature, art and mythology developed in different ways. The tendency now is to see them as distinct cultures, and to ignore the strong links that undoubtedly existed between the thought-patterns and world-pictures on which the myths were based. In each case the culture was an oral one, since writing and the Roman alphabet only came in with the establishment of the Christian church. Before this the only permanent records were Germanic runic inscriptions from about the second century AD onwards, and a few in Ogam ceremonial script (Dillon and Chadwick 1967:207). Runic inscriptions were used for memorials of people or events, to record short poems, and to inscribe names of makers or owners on precious objects, as well as for spells or charms, but early inscriptions are unfortunately difficult to interpret. There has been much discussion as to how far runes were used for religious purposes (Flowers 1986). Writing is believed to have been known to the Celtic druids, but it was never widely practised or used for transmission of religious tradition, with the result that no collections of sacred writing survive (Guyonvarc'h and Le Roux 1982:263 ff.).

The Germanic peoples established areas of settlement as the power of the Roman Empire declined, in what is known as the Migration Period, from the third to the sixth century AD. The Franks moved into Gaul, and were converted to Christianity early; the Visigoths went into Spain, the Lombards and Ostrogoths into Italy, and the Alamanni into southern Germany and Switzerland. Angles and Saxons from the Danish peninsula and northern Germany arrived as military war-bands and also as settlers in southern and eastern England, and absorbed, overcame or drove westwards the Celtic peoples living there. The Christian church had already been established to a limited extent in Roman Britain, and some of the new settlers were in close touch with the Christian Franks, so that when Augustine came to Kent in 597 to establish the new faith, his mission proved successful. Christianity had also been established in Ireland by St Patrick and others, and monks from monasteries in the Celtic west helped to convert Anglo-Saxon kingdoms, and worked as missionaries in Frisia and Germany. Bede's account of the conversion, written in the eighth century, gives some glimpses of opposition to the new faith, as do also some of the early *Lives* of Christian saints; but information about the pre-Christian religion comes mainly from archaeological evidence gained from rich graves and extensive cemeteries of the early settlement, from place- and personal names, and fragments of literary and antiquarian material.

The position was very different in the Scandinavian countries, where the old religion was not given up until some centuries after the conversion of Britain. Scandinavia at this time consisted of many small kingdoms constantly fighting among themselves, with frequent changes of ruling dynasties. The northern peoples remained outside the Christian church, in spite of many contacts with Christians and attempts by St Anskar and others from Germany to win over the rulers and set up churches in the market-towns. Not until the second half of the tenth century did Denmark accept the new faith, and Norway a little later, as the result of the vigorous efforts of Olaf Tryggvason. Iceland made Christianity the official religion in the year 1000, while Sweden held out until well into the eleventh century. It is therefore mainly on Scandinavian material from the close of the pre-Christian period that we have to rely for knowledge of the earlier religions of north-west Europe, as will become clear in the course of this study.

Like the Celts and Germans, the Scandinavians began to expand in various directions from the eighth century onwards, in search of trade and plunder, and the period of their restless activities in Europe and beyond is known as the Viking Age. In some areas they seized land and established colonies, but their expansion differed from the earlier ones because they did not move as tribes from their homelands. They went out as individuals or in small local and family groups; many were young men in search of wealth and renown, together with farmers who left their homes for the summer to be run by their wives and slave labour, while others travelled as merchant-adventurers and hoped to return after years abroad to buy land with their profits. Viking warriors were largely organized in small bands or ships' crews, joining together in temporary alliances for military expeditions, trading voyages or piracy. They might serve under famous leaders for a while, and then break up again, although sometimes they built up extensive armies or large fleets of warships, like the forces that invaded England in 866 or those that attacked cities in Merovingian France. Their fine ships and expert seamanship gave them mastery of the northern seas, and enabled them to travel far. They moved westwards to the British Isles, the Faroes, Orkney and Shetland, Greenland and the western shores of North America, as well as southwards to Spain, southern France and the Mediterranean. They went eastwards from Sweden along the Russian rivers to markets such as Bulgar on the Volga, and ultimately down the Dnieper to the 'Great City', their name for Constantinople. They went in search of silver and goods, gaining what they wanted by trading, raiding, imposing tribute on weaker people like the Lapps and the Slavs, ransoming prisoners or selling them as slaves, and earning payment for fighting as mercenaries in foreign kingdoms. In pursuit of their aims they endured great hardships, embarking on long journeys through difficult terrain and bitter weather, risking organized resistance or attacks from savage tribes. While they came into contact with the Christian church in their wanderings, they were reluctant to pay it more than lip-service, and were prepared to rob and pillage rich monasteries and churches if the opportunity offered.

The Vikings in their turbulent adventuring displayed some of the same qualities and weaknesses as their predecessors had done. They fought with a terrible ferocity that shocked those who witnessed it, and yet we know that many of them were also able farmers and good family men, returning to the land after a few years of raiding. They were loyal to their leaders and comrades, although apt to be independent and quarrelsome, and seldom able to combine successfully under one supreme commander. They were opportunists, excelling in rapid attacks from the sea and escaping before any force could be organized to oppose them. They resembled the Celts in a love of fine clothes, well-groomed hair and showy ornaments, and also in their admiration for generosity and hospitality. The Vikings made few permanent settlements, but one outstanding achievement was the establishment of an independent colony or free state in the uninhabited island of Iceland, which lasted until the island came under Norwegian rule in the thirteenth century. Here the law was the supreme arbiter, and there was no single ruler at the head as in other medieval kingdoms. It is from Iceland that our most valuable material on early religion in the north is obtained, for when writing came in with Christianity in the eleventh century, the Icelanders recorded all they could about its settlement and early history, of which they were justifiably proud. The government and law system of Iceland was set up by men who were wholehearted supporters of the old religion of the northern gods, and thus we have a unique opportunity to observe how they went about it and where their priorities lay.

Since we are nearer in time to the Vikings than to the Celts and continental Germans before their conversion to Christianity, we have more hope of learning something of their religious beliefs and practices. However, their culture too was oral, and there is little literature recorded in the Viking Age itself by those who had not become Christian. We depend on memories of that period reflected mostly in Icelandic sources recorded after the conversion. There are valuable accounts of the settlement of Iceland and histories of the early kings of Norway, and also a rich collection of Icelandic Family Sagas. These consist of prose tales, varying from short stories to what might be regarded as novels, dealing with the exploits and relationships of leading Icelanders in the early days of the commonwealth. These are partly based on family traditions and historic events, and partly fictitious. Some are clumsily put together, but the finest, such as *Njáls Saga* and *Egils Saga*, may be regarded as historical novels of outstanding quality.

These sagas are of a very different nature from the heroic tales of Ireland, preserved mainly in manuscripts of the twelfth century, but in many cases judged to be considerably earlier than this. In both cases it appears that early motifs and traditions going back to pre-Christian times have been deliberately employed by skilful story-tellers and poets of Christian communities, familiar with the medieval learned literature of their own time. In the Irish prose tales, old gods and goddesses may appear as kings and queens in an heroic setting of struggles between neighbouring kingdoms, and mighty achievements and tragic losses are seen against a background of portents and marvels, while poets and druids comment on the inevitability of fate. A favourite theme is a journey to a supernatural world by entry into a fairy mound or by a voyage over the sea. The setting of the Icelandic sagas is more realistic, even though the main characters may be portrayed as far larger than life. Traditions about vengeance killings and dominant local characters, preserved in popular tales, have merged with influences from romance literature and heroic poetry from the Germanic past, and out of this fruitful combination outstanding works of tragic and comic narrative have come into being. The background is that of farmstead, pasture and dairy, and heroic combats take place over winter fodder, stranded whales or the burning of woodland, against the austere setting of a bleak island where constant hard work and good luck were necessary for survival, while battles in the lawcourts are as exciting as those in the countryside.

These Family Sagas do not contain a great deal of information about the early religion, since the past tends to be viewed through the eyes of thirteeenth-century antiquarians, and the idea that the tales are a faithfully preserved record of the early period has long been abandoned. On the other hand, family traditions could be long-lived, and some of the material is based on pre-Christian poetry. A little may be learned also from the legendary sagas, the Sagas of Old Times. These deal with the adventures of kings and princes in early Scandinavia and of daring Icelanders away from home, most of them imaginary characters of invincible strength and bravery, and again show the influence of the romances. However, in some cases earlier heroic poems have been used as a source, and there are scattered memories of the cults of the old gods in the Scandinavian homelands.

In their enthusiasm to preserve all they could of their past, even though it might be a pagan past, the Icelanders recorded much early poetry. Poems on mythological themes have been mostly preserved in a precious manuscript of the thirteenth century, the *Codex Regius*, copied from an earlier one, generally known as the Elder or Poetic Edda. These deal with adventures of the gods, and with wisdom-contests between supernatural beings, and some may date back to the pre-Christian period. There are also many short poems by Icelandic poets (skalds) whose names are known, which come under the general heading of Skaldic Verse. They are in a complex, artificial style, with much use of mythological imagery, and this forms an important source for our knowledge of the supernatural world, since a number of poems predate the conversion and some go back to the ninth century. In addition, we have the treatise known as the Prose Edda by Snorri Sturluson, a brilliant writer and master of Icelandic prose, as well as a poet in his own right. He was a member of one of the most powerful Icelandic families, who took a leading part in politics (resulting in his assassination in 1241), but who was also an historian with an intense interest in the past of Iceland and Norway. He set out in the Prose Edda to provide a guide to young poets in a Christian society by retelling the old myths and collecting information from early poetry about the gods and their world, illustrated by many quotations and ending with a treatise on metre. This work is a treasure-house of material, and it would be difficult to gain any coherent picture of Scandinavian mythology without it. Snorri was one of the few scholars working outside a monastery; he possessed true scholarly integrity, and an ardent curiosity about the past without any desire to draw moral lessons from it.

If we are to search out the nature of northern religion before the coming of Christianity, it is clearly necessary to be prepared to range over a wide field; evidence may come from historical records, early literature and language, place- and personal names, archaeological discoveries and iconography, as well as the comments of outsiders and the speculations of Christian scholars concerning past beliefs and practices. The Celts and Germans (including the northern Vikings in the latter class) shared a common heritage and way of life, in spite of considerable differences in date and background. Their societies were predominantly warrior ones, with many small kingdoms and restless war-bands, run by leaders who had to justify their authority by skill and courage and good fortune in battle if they were to hold the loyalty of their followers. Their religion had to be one suitable for a world of continual challenge and struggle for survival in a demanding environment. Much of the religious tradition that survives has to do with the obtaining of victory and good fortune in battle; another important element is the reliance on divine powers when choosing a king who will achieve prosperity for his people and maintain a good relationship with the Otherworld. The fruitfulness of the land and the achieving of good harvests was of tremendous importance in the treacherous northern regions, where both sunshine and rain might be denied to the farmers and the summer was short, giving way in the most arctic regions to the almost total darkness of winter. These needs were linked with regular sacrifice to the gods at certain turning-points in the year, ceremonies in which all men and women took part, and also with the importance of the central place of assembly, the holy centre for every district where contact might be made with the divine world.

The link between religion and traditional wisdom was also a powerful one, and sufficient memory of seers and seeresses, poets and druids and lawmen has survived in the written sources to indicate a rich store of oral lore passed on to each new generation. Much of this has disappeared for ever, but still the impression left behind is strong. Skill in words was valued by these peoples as much as valour in battle; they all delighted in riddles, word-games, intricate poetic language and skill in argument. The Celts in the second century BC, according to Diodorus Siculus, made use of riddling speech and hinted at meanings, leaving much unsaid. We know that the Scandinavians took great pleasure in puns and complex riddles and the intricacies of skaldic verse. It is unlikely that they would display a childish naïvety in their myths, although one possible result of such subtlety in use of words might be that those who came into contact with them failed to understand their religious beliefs. Oratory, word-skills and inspiration were all seen as gifts from the gods, while the upholding of law was part of the divine order; it is essential to remember this and not to undervalue the significance of their myths or dismiss them as childish fantasies.

There is no doubt that the way back to a lost religion is not easy, and earlier attempts to interpret northern mythology should warn us how easy it is to start with preconceptions, insisting on one particular line of approach to the exclusion of all else. At one time legends of the supernatural world were explained as varieties of sun myths, and sun gods and sun weapons identified in the early tales and legends. In the early twentieth century Mogk made dogmatic statements rejecting Snorri's picture of the supernatural world as without any firm foundation, while – as an example of the opposite approach – the Swedish scholar Rydborg accepted everything in Old Norse literature as trusty and reliable, weaving an ingenious tapestry into which every strange detail in the poems and tales was fitted. Among other problems, we have to distinguish between the mythological material composed in a Christian society for purposes of entertainment and the conceptions that have been passed down from the pre-Christian period. Most of our evidence comes from the period immediately before the conversion, but the religion of the Celts and Germans stretches far back into the darkness of earlier centuries. It must have developed in different ways over the wide area of north-western Europe in the process of time. Moreover, the religions of neighbouring peoples, the various cults of the Roman Empire, and the teachings of the Christian church in surrounding countries were bound to have influence on it. We must avoid picturing one clear-cut and easily defined religious faith, seeing it rather as a general world-picture or a group of prevailing assumptions and beliefs, reflected in imagery and practice that were shared by the Celtic and German peoples before Christianity. It is for this reason that some Celtic and early Germanic material needs to be considered along with the later evidence from Scandinavia. In spite of the problems and frustrating gaps in our knowledge, we are surely fortunate to possess so much material of varying kinds on which to draw. The nature of this material and the problems and rewards encountered in interpreting it will be the subject of the following chapters.

It must be stressed that this will not be a straightforward account of the myths and beliefs of the peoples of north-west Europe. It is proposed instead to consider the differing kinds of evidence in turn, to see what particular problems each presents, and how each has been used to build up our understanding of the religious background. It is necessary also to realize that our interpretation of any past religion must be influenced to some extent by the thought-patterns of our own time and the prevailing fashions among scholars. Whenever the work of some outstanding thinker sets us on a new course in the interpretation of past religions, there is a period when the evidence is seen in a fresh light. Sometimes the exciting theories prove unreliable as time goes on and disciples of the master exaggerate this particular approach, but even when a reaction against them sets in, they may have contributed something to our better understanding. Various approaches towards the religion that preceded Christianity in north-west Europe will be considered therefore in the final chapter. The intention is to show both how complex and incomplete is the evidence on which we rely, so that a number of different conclusions may be drawn from it, and yet at the same time how the gradual building-up of the evidence over a wide field is making a fuller understanding possible. Popular books on mythology seldom reveal the sources of the theories on myths and cults and deities that they confidently present, and it seems therefore worth while to explore the sources of our information rather than to present it as a complete and reliable whole.

1

Help from Archaeology

Many such ancient treasures lay within that house of earth, the vast heritage of a noble race, hidden there by someone in times gone by, with deliberate intent.

(*Beowulf* 2231–6)

There is a good reason for starting with archaeological evidence for a lost religion: it is the only evidence that goes back to the early periods of Celtic and Germanic culture, far beyond that of the written sources in north-west Europe, while in later periods it may confirm or throw new light on conclusions drawn from written sources. There is much detailed evidence both from excavated sites and from cult objects that have been discovered accidentally, and this has contributed to our knowledge and also to our problems over the years. Some of the most important finds, like the Gallehus gold horns and the Gundestrup Cauldron, were found before the twentieth century began; much valuable evidence from graves was destroyed in the past, by both grave-robbers and irresponsible excavators, while the provenance of important early finds often remains unknown. In more recent years there have been expert investigations of sites that would have attracted little interest earlier, like that of the Ango-Saxon centre at Yeavering in Northumberland. Now if a rich wagon-burial or ship-grave is discovered, it will be investigated and recorded with all the new skills available, while the exploration of early cemeteries goes far beyond the selection of valuable artefacts and destruction of anything else, which was once the pastime of many landowners. Work has also progressed on the iconography of carved stones from the pre-Christian or early Christian periods in the north.

To deal adequately with the archaeological finds that have some bearing on the pre-Christian religion would require a book in itself, and perhaps several volumes. Here only a small number of examples has been selected, of widely differing types, to give some idea of the way in which archaeological discoveries may contribute to our knowledge of the religious past, especially when they can be linked with evidence from literary sources. They show also how difficult it is to draw reliable conclusions about beliefs from material remains or early works of religious art alone, with no additional help from written records. The material has been taken from the early Celtic period and from Anglo-Saxon England at the close of the pre-Christian period, as well as from Scandinavia; the scattered examples illustrate the types of problem that may be presented by archaeological evidence.

SACRED SPACE

When we go back to the earliest phases of Celtic or Germanic culture, we are virtually restricted to the evidence that archaeology provides, from the excavation of cult centres, places of assembly, house sites, to objects recovered from the earth and from the water. Greek and Latin commentators on the religion of these peoples indicate that most of their ceremonies were conducted out of doors, and for centuries their holy places appear to have been in forest clearings, on hilltops, on the shores of lakes or on islands. Such sites can offer little chance of identification if there were no buildings or carved stones to mark them out. The kind of evidence we may hope for is a boundary ditch enclosing a *temenos* or sacred space, inside which there may be signs of burning, animal or human remains, post-holes, ritual pits, and occasionally altars or isolated finds.

One example of an early Celtic site is at Aulnay-aux-Planches (Marne) in France (Brisson and Hatt 1953). This is a group of three cemeteries excavated at various times between 1927 and 1951, and the site appears to have been in use for a period of over four centuries, from the end of the tenth to the sixth century BC. The earliest graves, probably those of a semi-nomadic people

(a)

(b)

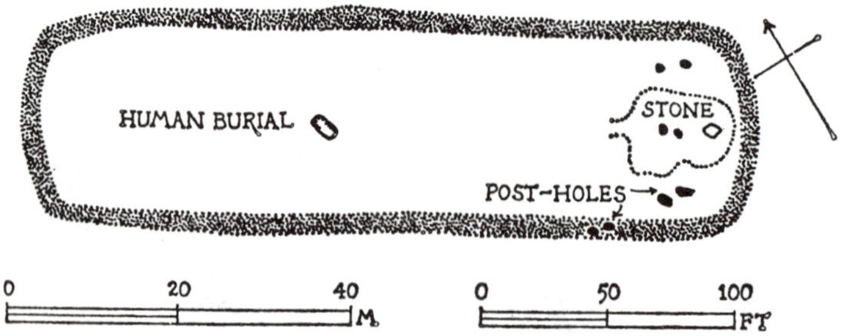

Figure 1 Plans of sacred sites at (a) Aulnay-aux-Planches (Marne), France and (b) Libenice, Czechoslovakia (after Piggort).

settling near the ancient highway, were flat cremation ones. The second cemetery seemed more organized, with the graves possibly protected by stones, and contained some examples of partial cremation; it was near this that a large ritual enclosure was found, thought to be of about the same date. The third group of graves included a number surrounded by circular ditches, thought to have been under small mounds, possibly the graves of new arrivals with different burial customs. Flat cremation graves continued at the same time. There were 28 mounds in all.

The enclosure by the second group of graves was about 89 m × 15 m, and surrounded by a ditch about 2 m in width. It contained a central grave, in which there was an urn holding bones, with some small pots around it. There were other cremation graves, together with an adult skeleton with no grave goods, and in another pit the bones of an infant. There were traces of marked or shaped stones which seemed originally to have been arranged in lines (Figure 1a).

This is an important site, indicating that some kind of ritual associated with the dead went on in the early Hallstatt period, inside a closed space. It evidently included animal sacrifice, since bones of various mammals were found, including dog, fox and young boar, and perhaps human sacrifice also. It is not easy, however, to establish the exact sequence of graves in the enclosure, and we can make no definite assumptions as to the kinds of rites that took place there, or to what supernatural powers those taking part may have addressed themselves. We cannot say whether the enclosure was in use at regular festivals or in times of crisis, or for the funerals of important people. We do not know if the graves it contained were those of people of high rank, or whether some represent human sacrifice. Here we are dependent on informed guesses, based on what the archaeological evidence suggests, and on what we expect of the religion of the early Celts.

Comparisons have been made between this site and another at Libenice near Kolin in Czechoslovakia, this time an oval enclosure surrounded by a ditch, excavated in 1959 (Filip 1976:83ff.; see Figure 1b). Inside, near the centre, was the grave of a woman, buried with elaborate jewellery of about the third century BC. At the eastern end were pits which seem to have been dug out more than once, possibly for libations, as well as pairs of post-holes. At the foot of what must have been two large posts were two neck-rings of bronze, which could have hung on these or been worn by wooden figures set up there. There were also animal bones, and the graves of four other people, including a child. In addition, there was a standing stone, roughly pyramidal in shape, a pit shaped rather like a keyhole, and stone blocks which may have formed an altar. This has led to suggestions that here we have the grave of a priestess of the La Tène period, that idols with torcs round their necks stood in the enclosure, and that human and animal sacrifices took place there, while a skull among the finds was used for libations.

Once again, however, there are extensive gaps in our knowledge. It is difficult to decide on the date of the enclosure, or how long it was in use; an existing sacred place may have been utilized by those who buried the woman there with careful funeral rites. We suffer from the lack of other excavated sites for comparison, although a considerable number of possible ritual enclosures in Celtic territory are now known, and one can hardly make a direct link with the site at Aulnay-aux-Planches when so many centuries divide the two. All that may be safely concluded is that there were enclosed places – and often the position of these is worth studying – where some kind of ritual activity and animal sacrifices took place which may have been associated with the dead. The hope is always that such scattered sites may be matched with further discoveries of a similar kind, so that the gaps in the puzzle grow smaller.

THE BURIAL AT VIX

The Celts as we encounter them in the literature seem to be dominated by powerful and energetic leaders, both men and women. It seems possible therefore that something might be learned of their ideas about the Otherworld from the way in which leading members of society were disposed of after death. One of the most dramatic discoveries of this century was that of a grave at Vix in the upper valley of the Seine, containing a woman of about 35 years of age, buried with considerable pomp. This was discovered in 1953 and excavated by Joffroy (Joffroy 1962). The tumulus that originally covered the burial chamber had disappeared, and the chamber had escaped discovery because it was dug out below ground level. The original mound must have been enormous, since the diameter of the base was about 42 m. In the burial chamber, which was almost square, there was a wagon with its wheels detached and propped against the east wall, with stones to wedge them in place. The wagon was in the centre of the chamber, and inside it the woman had been placed in a sitting position with her legs stretched out; Joffroy assumed that the wagon had been used as a litter supported by bearers to carry her to the tomb, and that horses had not been employed, since no harness was found.

The most striking object in the chamber was a crater, a type of vessel used at feasts for mixing wine and water (Figure 2). A number of such vessels, of Greek origin, have been recovered from Celtic graves, but this one was enormous, far larger than any other example known. It stood 1.64 m high (about 5′5″), and weighed 208 kg (about 470 lbs). Joffroy (1962:126) claimed it would have held about 1,200 litres of liquid. He concluded that it would have been impracticable for use at a feast because of the difficulties in serving wine from it, and that the wagon might have been used to transport it to the grave. It was of skilful and elaborate workmanship with splendid decoration. On each side of the handle was the familiar gorgon head usually found on craters, but in this case executed with unusual power and restraint. Round the neck was a frieze of warriors, some marching and others driving in four-horse chariots. On the lid was the figure of a woman resembling a seeress, wearing a veil over her head and shoulders and with one arm outstretched.

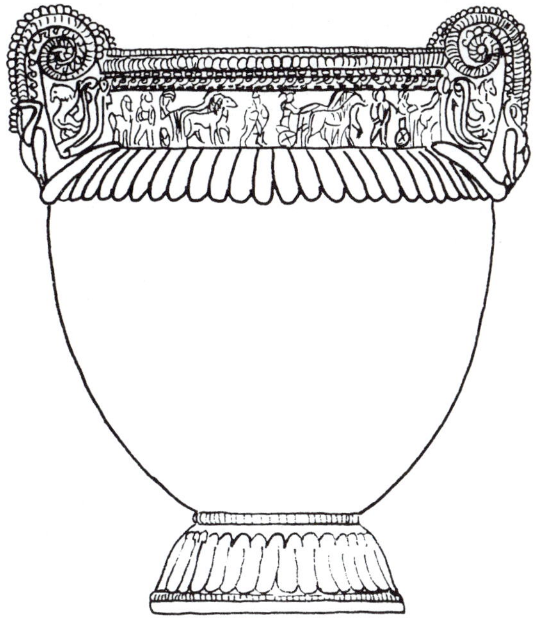

Figure 2 Crater from Vix grave. Drawing by Eileen Aldworth.

Other objects in the chamber included bowls, jugs and metal vessels of various kinds, as well as bowls in Greek figured ware. These, however, are not vessels associated with feasts, but rather suggest the dispensing of liquid in ceremonial rites, and one object found was thought to be an aspergill used for sprinkling. A large piece of red material, possibly leather, had been laid over the objects, which Joffroy thought might have been a tent. The dead woman was richly adorned with jewellery. A magnificent diadem of gold was still in place on her head, ending in two huge knobs of gold, with little winged horses at the points where these were joined to the curved headpiece. She wore brooches and necklaces, as well as bracelets on her wrists and ankles, while a large bronze torc lay upon her body. In spite of damage from the collapse of the ceiling and flooding of the chamber, it has proved possible to restore the crater, wagon and other pieces, so that the quality of their workmanship can be appreciated.

Not surprisingly, there has been much discussion concerning the contents of this tomb. One explanation for the enormous crater was that it was a diplomatic gift to a reigning queen, but this seems unlikely. The most interesting suggestion is that made by Bourriot (1965). He argued that this outsize vessel was probably a special offering made for a shrine, like the two huge craters mentioned by Herodotus (I, 51) as sent by Croesus to Delphi and placed in the temple there. He thought that it was never intended for mixing wine because of its size and weight, but that it might be used for sacrificial blood. There is a well-known passage from Strabo (*Geography* VII, 2.3) describing white-haired priestesses of the Cimbri climbing ladders to cut the throats of prisoners of war, who were suspended over enormous vessels of bronze (the term *krater* is used at one point) in order to judge from the flow of blood what the outcome of a campaign would be. This would suggest that the woman at Vix was a priestess or seeress, although she might also be a princess in her own right. The vessel would then have belonged to a local shrine, probably on Mount Lassois near the grave. If it was made as a gift, the choice of the procession of warriors with chariots, together with a sinister gorgon head and a figure on the lid resembling a seeress, would be appropriate for a vessel destined as an offering to a deity of war served by a priestess.

This is an attractive idea, in spite of difficulties that Bourriot himself acknowledges. There is a considerable gap between the Vix grave of the sixth century BC and the writings of Strabo, who died in AD 25, although he may be using information from an earlier source, and it is possible that such divination ceremonies associated with warfare were kept up for centuries. There is as yet no evidence for a sanctuary on Mount Lassois, although the possibility cannot be ruled out. White-haired priestesses such as Strabo mentions hardly accord with a woman in her thirties, but Bourriot claims that this expression may be used of fair-haired people typical of northern Europe. It is not certain that the Cimbri were a Celtic tribe, but this is a minor point. We are left with the problem of why the crater was deposited in the grave if it belonged to a temple: possibly a change of leadership might be the reason for this, or the death or incapacity of a famous seeress. The skull of the woman in the grave showed signs of a blow, although this is not thought to have caused her death.

The Vix tumulus is a good example of the problems and possibilities presented by a rich burial of the pre-Christian period. It is one of a series of wagon burials dated before 475 BC, the majority of which were in eastern Gaul; and all but one of the fifteen examples given by Joffroy were under tumuli. No others, however, were in as good condition as that at Vix, and many had been robbed. Where the sex could be determined, most of the dead were males, but there was at least one other woman. The body was usually placed in the wagon after the wheels had been removed, and when the vehicles survive, they seem to be of a type meant for processions or ceremonies rather than utilitarian use. The Vix burial stands out because of the size of the crater and what appear to be ritual vessels accompanying it. It seems unlikely that the wagons were chosen to symbolize a journey of the dead, particularly since the wheels were removed; they may have been included because they were used at the funeral, or as a status or cult symbol. The removal of the wheels can hardly be explained here by a desire to 'kill' the vehicle that had brought the dead to the grave, since they were carefully placed upright in the grave and no damage was done to the wagon. Bourriot's ingenious theory to account for the crater, it may be noted, was suggested by a passage from literature, and clues are needed from literature or art to help us to understand the significance of such archaeological finds. Since the early Celts left no literature behind, we have to rely largely on conjecture, and one theory may succeed another in the case of elaborate graves like that of Vix. Those that are well preserved and virtually intact are certain to provide surprises, and may give the impression that they are the result of exceptional circumstances. Consequently they alter our perspective and make us aware of fresh possibilities in the attitude of past communities towards their dead.

THE SHIP-BURIAL AT SUTTON HOO

Another illustration of the surprise element comes from Germanic territory, about a thousand years after the Vix burial, at the time when the pre-Christian religion was being abandoned in Anglo-Saxon England. Just before war broke out in the summer of 1939, a rich intact grave was discovered in Suffolk on heathland near Woodbridge. The treasures from this grave can now be seen in the British Museum, and the detailed report of the find was published by Bruce-Mitford (1975–83). There has been constant discussion and argument ever since the discovery as to the workmanship of the objects in the ship, their place of origin and their possible significance. They were found in what had been a wooden burial chamber, set up on the deck of a large sea-going ship, about 28 m in length; this had been dragged up from the river Deben on to the heath and lowered like a huge coffin into the place prepared for it, after which a mound was built above. The ship contained many grave-goods of outstanding workmanship and symbolic importance, but after fifty years of lively discussion we still do not know whether there was a body in the grave or not.

The grave was apparently prepared for a man, since it held weapons, shield, helmet and mailcoat, and these of such superb quality that the owner was presumed to be a warrior leader and probably an East Anglian king. All the accoutrements were of impressive workmanship, resplendent with gold and inlaid ornament, so that they suggest weapons and armour intended for ceremonial use rather than for battle. There was also a purse with an elaborate jewelled cover holding Merovingian gold coins, and a stone whetstone with a set of carved faces and a bronze stag at the top, thought to be a sceptre such as a king might hold on his lap on state occasions. There were rich jewelled shoulder-clasps to fasten a cloak, and a huge gold buckle with intricate interlacing patterns, unsurpassed by any previously found in Germanic graves. Indeed, many of the objects are without parallel as examples of intricate work in cloisonné, niello, garnets and glass, delicate cell-work and ingenious fastening devices. There were small belt-fittings, strap-ends and scabbard mounts of similar high quality, as well as a number of puzzling fragments like a set of delicate gold fittings that may have come from a slender wand of bone or ivory. A small lyre and a set of playing-pieces with a board were among the personal possessions arranged round the place where the body might be expected to lie.

It is possible that the body itself had simply disappeared in the acid soil. The first assumption, however, was that the grave was a cenotaph, and that the dead

?

man's body may have been lost in battle, as could have happened to at least one East Anglian king of the seventh century, if he drowned in a river with many of his warriors (Bede, *Ecclesiastical History* III, 24). A less convincing suggestion was that the dead received Christian burial, while the royal treasure was carefully placed in the mound because of associations with the old religion, in the transition period between the old faith and the new. Another theory was that the body was originally in a wooden coffin inside the burial chamber (Evison 1979), but convincing arguments against this have been put forward by East (1984). It has also been claimed that the body was cremated, since burnt remains were noted in a great silver dish in the centre of the chamber (Vierck 1979). Other mounds at Sutton Hoo were found to have held cremated remains, those in Mound 2, for instance, being placed on a wooden tray, while there are some examples in rich Anglo-Saxon graves of ashes of the dead being buried with unburnt grave-goods. As to whose the grave might be, the suggestion made by H.M. Chadwick (1940) at the outset has proved on the whole the most acceptable; he claimed that it was the grave of Redwald of East Anglia, who died about 625. This seemed impossible when the coins in the purse were dated by numismatists to the second half of the seventh century, but a revised dating, although not fully accepted, was 625–30. Redwald was a powerful and successful king, said to be the leading Anglo-Saxon ruler of his time, and although he accepted Christianity, Bede (II, 15) tells us that he slipped back into paganism, setting up an altar to the devil alongside that of Christ, and that his queen and some of his counsellors were opposed to the Christian church. Such a background might account for a ship-burial, perhaps with cremation of the body according to family tradition, even though some of the objects buried in the graves, such as a set of silver bowls with equal-armed crosses, are in the Christian tradition.

We have to bear these problems in mind in considering what may be learned from Sutton Hoo of the pre-Christian religion in East Anglia. First, the chosen rite was ship-burial, and this on an ambitious scale. The provision of a ship that could hold 40 oarsmen indicates that this symbol was felt to be sufficiently important to justify the expense and effort involved. Traces of another ship-burial, although of a smaller vessel, were found at Snape, 9 miles away, in 1862; unfortunately, this grave had been robbed, but one elaborate gold ring and fragments of a blue glass vessel indicate that this also was a rich burial (Bruce-Mitford 1955). In excavations in the same cemetery in 1988, a burial in what appears to be a log-boat was found, indicating that the ship was a familiar funeral symbol in this part of East Anglia (Filmer-Sankey 1992). The body, unfortunately poorly preserved, may have been that of a child, and the only surviving grave-goods were a knife, a buckle and stud, and a pair of drinking horns placed at the foot of the grave (Filmer-Sankey 1990). In 1991 a further find was made of a burial in a boat 3 m in length; this contained a body, not well preserved, with a sword, three spears, a shield, a knife and a spindle whorl. A horse's head with bridle and bit was found in a pit near the grave (Filmer-Sankey forthcoming). Mound 2 at Sutton Hoo also contained a ship-burial of an unusual type, with the boat laid across the top of the burial chamber; a parallel to this is known from Hedeby in Denmark.

Clearly, then, the main ship-grave at Sutton Hoo cannot be regarded as an isolated instance. The problems it presents serve as a good illustration of the limitations of archaeology as a means of interpreting burial customs. The use of boats or boat-like coffins for the dead, as well as the making of ship outlines in stones round graves or sacred places, is known in Scandinavia from early times. Ship-burial came into general use about the sixth century AD, and continued throughout the Viking Age, while ships and boats were also used in cremation funerals, and there are additional instances of ship-graves in regions of Viking settlement such as the Isle of Man and Russia. Altogether hundreds of ship-graves are known, although they only represent a small fraction of the number of Viking Age graves recorded (Müller-Wille 1968–9:87). Vessels were provided for both men and women, and varied from simple boats or parts of boats to the magnificent ships found at Gokstad and Oseberg in southern Norway. The Oseberg ship was about 21 m in length and had held the bodies of two women, with a richly carved processional wagon and many other splendid objects of carved wood which were preserved along with the ship itself in the blue clay of the burial place. Ships and boats or parts of boats may be buried under mounds or in flat graves, or burnt as part of a funeral pyre, where they are recognizable from the large number of metal rivets found among the ashes. There may be a series of ship-graves in one cemetery, as at Vendel and Valsgärde in Sweden, varying in date so as to suggest that members of the same family had been buried in this way over several generations. In one site at Kaupang in south Norway a number of men and women had been buried in boats in graves crowded together on a small headland, giving the impression that this particular spot was sacred.

Often the prow of a buried ship points towards the sea or a river, and there is equipment that suggests preparation for a voyage. In the graves at Vendel, of sixth-century date onwards, the dead were placed sitting upright in their vessels, as if they were intended to steer them into the Otherworld. The Oseberg ship, on the contrary, was weighed down by stones, as if it were essential to keep it fast in the grave. When only parts of ships were used, or the outline of a ship made over a grave in stones, it would seem that the symbol of a vessel was in itself of importance. The use of this funeral symbol may have been restricted to certain families, since in many cases there are no more than one or two ship-burials in a cemetery (Müller-Wille 1968–9:75). The practice is not limited to rich graves, and so can hardly be explained as the provision of a status symbol, nor does it seem simply to symbolize the journey to another world, athough such associations may well have increased the popularity of ship-funeral. One possibility is that the funeral ship was used by those who worshipped the Vanir, the powers of fertility, associated with seas and lakes and also with places of burial under the earth, since the ship is known to have been among their symbols. If the lady in the Oseberg ship with her attendant was a priestess of the Vanir cult, the ship and the wagon found with her might have been used on her progress from one community to another to bring blessing and fertility, as suggested by some accounts in the literature (p. 133).

These are possibilities, but the ship may well have had different meanings for the various families who found it appropriate as part of the funeral setting. It has always been used as a fitting symbol for departure, and from a purely practical point of view made a convenient framework for a funeral pyre, while it was also one of the most precious possessions of a Viking leader renowned for his exploits on the sea. The fact that a number of ships have been found in Anglo-Saxon graves in the period before the Viking Age introduces problems of the relationship between the royal dynasty of East Anglia and the Scandinavian kingdoms and so brings in new complications to the vexed question of ship-funeral.

A further source of possible evidence concerning religious beliefs is the collection of objects in the burial chamber of the ship in Mound 1 at Sutton Hoo. There were personal possessions of great beauty and value and possible symbols of royal power (Davidson 1992b:30), but also others that seem to represent life in a king's hall. There were a number of bowls, cups, dishes and drinking-horns, including two huge aurochs horns set with silver, such as could be passed round the hall at a feast. The lyre found in the chamber might be one used by the king himself, or by the king's poet who sang his praises, while playing-pieces might also symbolize the king's power and the skill and luck which brought him victory, since they are often included in lists of royal or even divine treasures (Davidson 1988:164). There are striking parallels between these grave-goods and those in two other outstanding graves from the early Anglo-Saxon period, the mounds at Taplow and Broomfield, unfortunately never properly excavated and recorded (East and Webster, forthcoming). Symbols of feasting are found in many Germanic graves, sometimes on a lavish scale and sometimes on a homely one, and it is possible to regard this as religious symbolism, since the sacrificial feast in honour of the gods was of major importance for both Celts and Germans as a link between the human and divine worlds (p. 89). At Sutton Hoo there were provided not only the means of serving food and drink but also vessels for its preparation, including three large cauldrons, one with a chain of elaborate workmanship for suspension over a fire, three buckets and a tub. The largest cauldron, made from a single sheet of bronze, would have held about 100 litres, and may have come from the same workshop as one in the Taplow grave.

Another point worth noting is the decoration of various objects. An analysis of significant motifs in the Sutton Hoo treasure was made by Hauck (1954), and he emphasized those associated with the cult of the Anglo-Saxon Woden, such as dancing warriors and battle scenes on the plates on the helmet, the eagle and dragon on the great shield, and even knots and chains, because of Woden's power to bind warriors and render them helpless. Other symbols might be linked with other cults; the boars on the shoulder-clasps are a motif widely associated with the fertility deities, while the mysterious faces on the stone sceptre might represent royal or divine ancestors (Enright 1983). The stag on the top of the sceptre as well as the trout in the centre of one of the hanging bowls are symbols of Otherworld powers in Irish literature. Such decorations are unlikely to be meaningless exercises in attractive ornamentation; there is no doubt that protective, threatening or lucky motifs were deliberately chosen for ceremonial treasures of this kind, associated with traditional lore and divine power.

If we ask why such a brilliant assortment of beautiful and valuable objects was left in the earth, we can give no clear answer. Some of them might be felt unsuitable for use once the old religion was abandoned, but there are also pieces with Christian decoration included in the treasure. Other rich graves of this period show that the Germanic peoples were accustomed to sacrifice much wealth at the death of a king, but the sheer richness of this grave is another of the surprises that an archaeological find can produce, contradicting our previous assumptions and theories. We have to seek to discover, if we can, the attitude to kings and to the supernatural world that rendered this natural and desirable (p. 135).

A further problem is the relationship between the various mounds in the cemetery, now thought to be a small one, used for a relatively brief period and restricted to wealthy and privileged members of society, probably from the reigning dynasty. Seven mounds in all were investigated, and there are twenty marked on the plan. We do not even know for certain if the mound that held the treasure was the latest of the series, as it presumably would be were it the grave of Redwald. The problem is complicated further by a series of humbler burials, about thirty in all; twelve of these were in the neighbourhood of Mound 5, and roughly contemporary with it, while there was a further group of eighteen similar burials on the eastern periphery of the cemetery (Carver and Copp 1990b:9). These additional graves were carefully dug, but contained virtually no grave-goods, and a number of the occupants had met with a violent end. Some had wrists and ankles bound, while others had been beheaded; one was in a peculiar position, as if running or leaping, and seemed to be holding a primitive plough (Figure 3). The bodies were unfortunately not well preserved, and have only been

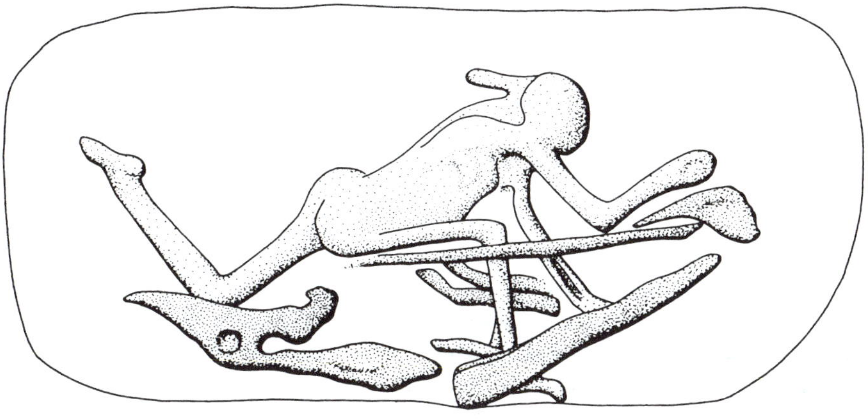

Figure 3 'Ploughman' figure from Sutton Hoo cemetery (after Carver).

recorded through a new technique that reveals the outline left in the grave (Carver and Royle 1988:20; Carver and Copp 1990a:7). It now seems possible that the graves associated with Mound 5, some of which had traces of animal remains in the vicinity, might be sacrificial burials; evidence of this kind is difficult to interpret, however, since such victims of violence might be the result of a massacre or of execution in later times, buried in an abandoned pre-Christian cemetery (Davidson 1992a). There are clearly some animal remains at Sutton Hoo, but no sign of the lines of animals, mainly horses and dogs, found in the great Scandinavian ship-graves.

Further excavation will throw more light on these problems, but no doubt will also create new ones as our knowledge increases. We are most fortunate to have the opportunity to gain detailed information about so important a site as Sutton Hoo, recently excavated and re-examined with great thoroughness according to a systematic plan in a way that should add greatly to our understanding of the pre-Christian religion in East Anglia (Carver 1992).

THE HALL AT YEAVERING

A site of a different kind which also belongs to the period of transition before the establishment of the Christian church in Anglo-Saxon England is that of Yeavering in Northumberland (Figure 4). This was excavated by Hope-Taylor, and is the subject of a detailed report (Hope-Taylor 1977). Above the road and the river Derwent, in which the first Christians were baptized, is a high rounded hill known as Yeavering Bell. This had served the Celtic people of the area as a place of assembly and perhaps a holy place. The enclosure there was not a defensive earthwork; it could have been used for holding cattle or for a market, but there was also a tumulus and a stone circle with cremation burials scattered in and around it, as well as a cemetery which had been ploughed over, probably in Roman times. When the Anglo-Saxons gained control of Bernicia, this area seems to have been established as a royal centre, visited by the king from time to time. There were two halls, one of which may have been used as a temple, or at least as a place where people gathered for sacrificial feasts which formed an essential part of the old religion. There were traces also of a curious structure like a wooden amphitheatre, thought to mark the place of assembly, and these impressive additions are probably due to Edwin, who became king of Northumbria about 625. His dramatic rise to the kingship and his relationship with Redwald of East Anglia are told in some detail by Bede in his *Ecclesiastical History* (II, 12 ff.). He was baptized by Paulinus in 927.

The building known as D2 on the excavation plan, the supposed temple, had a huge post outside at the northern corner, while there were three posts inside at the south end. Inside the east door was a huge pile of ox-bones and a heap of ox-skulls. The hall was rectangular in plan, with inner walls of wattle and daub strengthened outside by timber; beside it stood a second smaller building which could have served as the place where the food was cooked. If the skulls repre-

Figure 4 Reconstruction of centre at Yeavering in the seventh century (after Hope-Taylor). The possible temple is the building nearest to the amphitheatre (top).

sented the animals killed, it is clear that there was a large number of victims, and the hall could have been used for the sacrificial feasts held at certain points in the year, over which the king would preside if he were present. The hall measured 11 × 5.5 m and would have held a considerable number of people. Later the post-holes inside had been filled up with stones and the building apparently abandoned. A Christian church with a new cemetery was finally added to the site.

This is the only case up to now of a building containing some evidence for ceremonial religious feasts, with the possible exception of Hofstaðir in Iceland (O. Olsen 1966:182ff.). Bede (*Ecclesiastical History* 1, 30) records a letter from Pope Gregory, advocating that such places be retained and used for Christian feasts at appropriate festivals; Christians, he suggested, should continue to put up temporary shelters outside while the festival was in progress, presumably because many people came in from the surrounding countryside, and in fact some flimsy hut-structures were found outside the hall at Yeavering. This site seems to have replaced the earlier holy place of the Bernicians. Various animal remains apart from the ox-bones may have had cult significance. The name of Edwin's town was Gefrin, meaning 'Hill of Goats', and a goat's skull was found in what may have been a dedicatory burial of a man with a staff, although whether he was a Saxon or a Celt is not known (Hope-Taylor 1977:245–6), while in one grave there was a body in one half of the area and a single ox-tooth in the other (102). The site at Yeavering is an example of how archaeological discovery can fill gaps when we have some knowledge of the historic past, and shows also how fruitful systematic excavation of a site may prove even though no treasure or even elaborate buildings are discovered there.

THE STRETTWEG WAGON

Clearly it is possible to learn something of a lost religion from the evidence from burials and sites used for ceremonial purposes. A further source of evidence comes from single objects that appear to have ritual significance, some left in the earth as offerings or hidden there to save them from pillage or desecration, and others included in graves, found on cult sites or abandoned in bogs. An example from a very early period comes from a cremation grave of about the seventh century BC, found along with a number of metal vessels at Strettweg in Austria (Megaw 1970:59). Unfortunately, as in many similar cases, the find was made (in 1851) in the period before effective archaeological techniques had been developed. The so-called wagon is a bronze platform on wheels, 240 mm (nearly 14 inches) in length, with a number of standing figures on it, arranged in a systematic group. In the centre, towering over the others, is a female figure with ear-rings, wearing a belt; she carries a shallow bowl on her head, supported by a small protective pad, such as women still use in countries where they are accustomed to carry burdens in this way. This figure resembles in style a Greek warrior in bronze from Olympia, and Sandars (1968:215) suggested that it had been made by a Greek craftsman working to native orders or by someone trained in a Greek workshop. Before and behind this female figure there is a pair of mounted warriors, facing away from her, and between the pair of horsemen stand a woman and an ithyphallic man brandishing an axe. At the front of each group is a fine antlered stag, with a youthful figure on either side of it, with a hand on one of its horns. All except the central figure are naked.

There are many possible explanations of this impressive little group, but without comparative material from the period or literary analogies we are left groping in the dark. It might be a representation of some ceremony in honour of the stag, or of the central figure, which certainly suggests a goddess, depicted as larger than human. It has been suggested that the stags are mythical creatures associated with the sun, which has been related to these animals in early medieval times. The Huns, for instance, retained a legend of the stag with a sun on its forehead, while there are later Christian legends of St Hubert and St Eustace meeting a stag bearing the cross on its horns, which might be a development of the same tradition. The fact that the model was placed beside ashes of the dead might indicate that it had some link for the mourners with the afterlife, possibly indicating a welcome by the goddess. But in our present lack of knowledge of religious practices at this early time, we can only note it as an example of possible mythological imagery associated with wild creatures of the forest world.

THE GUNDESTRUP CAULDRON

Perhaps the most celebrated find of a ceremonial vessel is the bowl or cauldron found in 1891 by a man cutting peat in an area of bogland in Vesthimmerland in North Jutland. It had been beaten out of a single sheet of silver, and decorated with a series of plates inside and out. A round medallion was fitted in the centre, and there were five inner and seven outer panels, on which traces of gilding remained and which were all richly ornamented, soldered on to it (Figure 5a and b). Before the bowl was deposited, however, these plates had been torn off with considerable force and placed inside it. Although a careful search was made, certain parts such as portions of the rim were never found; it is possible that some of the lost pieces had been of gold. It is generally assumed that the bowl was left as a votive sacrifice, like other famous finds of the early Iron Age in Denmark, although Taylor (1992:66) suggests that the recorded evidence of the discovery indicates that it had been left on dry ground in rough grass, presumably with the intention of recovering it.

The outside plates consist of busts of four male and three female figures, who presumably represent deities (see Figure 5a). The seven plates (a–g, using letters introduced by Klindt-Jensen in 1950) do not completely cover the cauldron, and some have thought that an eighth is missing. Their order is uncertain, but that of the inner plates is agreed to have been B, A, C, E, D (moving clockwise). The supposed deities had eyes set with red or blue glass, and they are accompanied by various small figures and attributes. The inner plates are more varied in subject and treatment (see Figure 5b). Plate A shows a male figure seated cross-legged, with antlers rising from his head, accompanied by a stag and a boar, with more fantastic animals round the outside. This is probably the best-known scene from Celtic art, appearing in countless publications. Plate B has the figure of a goddess, closely resembling one of those on the outside plates (Plate e); below her are two small wheels, which might represent a chariot or wagon, and she is accompanied by two elephants, depicted like horses with trunks, two griffins and what seems to be a lion. Plate C also has a central deity, in this case a male, who closely resembles one of the small outside busts accompanying the goddess on plate e. Beside him is a large figure in a horned helmet, either kneeling or leaping, holding part of a wheel, while there are also griffins, lions and a serpent. Plate D shows three animals thought to be bulls, accompanied by three men with swords who seem about to slay them. Plate E, another famous scene, shows one large

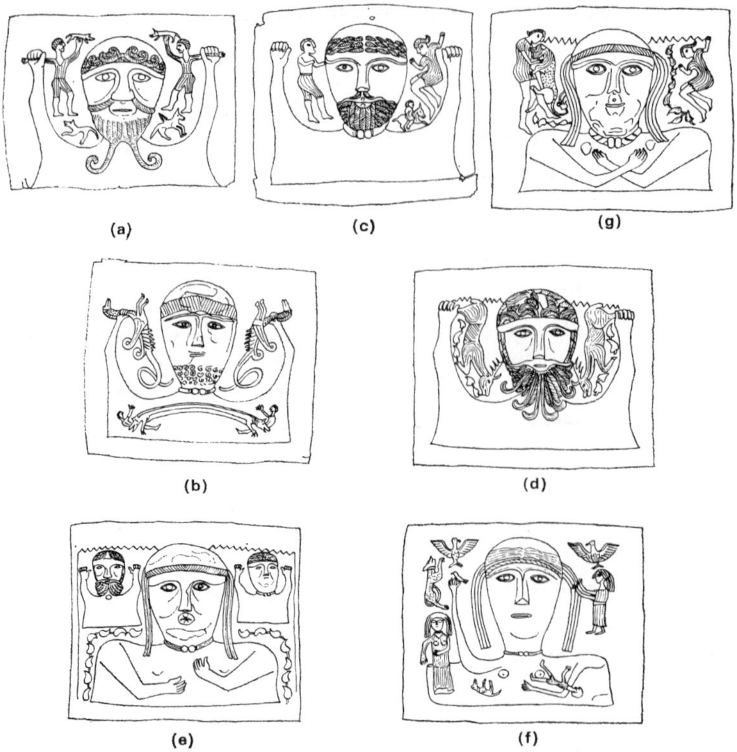

(a)

upright figure and two lines of smaller warriors, those at the top on horseback and those below on foot, accompanied by three men playing the Celtic war-trumpet known as the carnyx, which ends in a boar's head. The dominating figure is holding up a small man, and either plunging him into a kind of tub or lifting him out of it, and he has a leaping dog at his side. The medallion at the base has a scene in a different style, showing a huge majestic bull apparently sinking to the ground while it is attacked by a man with dogs. One dog appears to have been killed, but the attacker seems about to deliver the final blow.

When a replica of the cauldron was shown in London in 1970 as part of an exhibition of Early Celtic Art, it greatly impressed those who only knew it from illustrations by its size and splendour. It is 69 cm in diameter and 42 cm high, and is clearly a treasure-house of myth and religious symbolism. There has been long and complex argument as to where and at what date it was made, and we can only guess at its purpose and at the reasons for the choice of deities and ritual scenes, which are now thought to have been the work of as many as five different craftsmen (Larsen 1987). Megaw (1970:131) said of the cauldron: 'Probably no other surviving relic of prehistoric European craftsmanship – with the exception of Stonehenge – has occasioned so much publication and dispute.' At first many

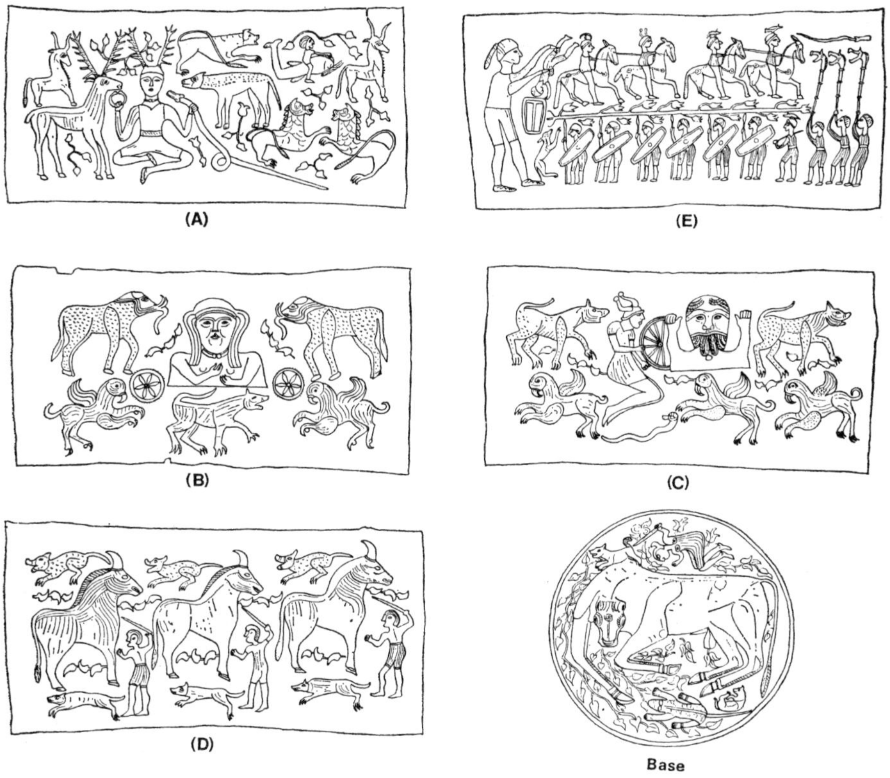

(b)

Figure 5 The Gundestrup Cauldron. (a) Outlines of outer plates and (b) outlines of inner plates. Klindt-Jensen's lettering is followed in both cases but rearranged (after Powell).

believed it had been made in Denmark, but later there were claims that it had come from Gaul or from the Danubian provinces near the Black Sea, as well as more remote areas such as Persia or India. Indian influence has again been recently stressed by Taylor (1992), who believes the cauldron to have been made in Thrace. Suggested dating has varied from the fourth century BC to the sixth century AD. The most popular dating however is the first century BC, which was originally suggested by Sophus Muller in 1891.

A detailed study by Olmsted published in 1979, based on styles of art, craftsmanship and iconography, has come out firmly in support of this dating, and he would suggest the period 80–50 BC and claim north-western Gaul as the place of origin. Such an object could have been taken across the Rhine from some religious centre in Gaul, perhaps as loot allowed as part-payment to German cavalry employed by Julius Caesar on his campaigns, and in this way could have reached Denmark. Part of the difficulty in reaching conclusions about the cauldron is the variety of styles in the plates, and the use of animal motifs familiar in the Mediterranean, Near East and Scythian regions of Europe. It has even been suggested that additional plates from some casket or shrine have been fitted on to the bowl at some stage (Megaw 1970:131). The treatment of the great bull on the base has been recognized as oriental rather than Celtic (Powell 1971:203), and it is now claimed that it was originally a horse's bridle decoration, soldered over a hole in the cauldron (Larsen 1987). The griffins and lions and elephants must also be due to non-Celtic influences. However, there are also a number of features unquestionably Celtic in character, such as the carnyx, the torcs worn by the deities, the serpent with ram's horns, and the more realistic animals such as stag and boar. Olmsted has produced a number of parallels from Gaul to the various motifs and styles of art used on the cauldron.

The purpose of the cauldron must have been a ritual one. It is hardly suitable for holding liquids, whether wine, ale, blood or water, because of the elaborate internal decoration (Sandars 1968:253). It seems probable that it belonged to some shrine, and the busts on the outside and on some of the inner plates indicate that it was made in honour of certain deities. In these representations on the outside of the cauldron we have no action, only existence in a timeless setting with men and animals alike in the grasp of divine powers (Sandars 1968:256). One male deity holds a man in each hand, while each man in turn holds a boar; another grasps two stags, and a third two sea-creatures. Below this last there is a fantastic animal with a head at either end, and the most plausible explanation of this is that it represents one of the metal 'fire-dogs' used to hold logs, found in Celtic areas (Powell 1971:202); this is confirmed by the tiny seated figures by each head holding cups as if drinking at the hearth. The three goddesses are shown with varying arm-gestures. One raises hers as if in welcome, and has two small male busts, one on either side; she seems almost identical with the goddess with wheels on plate B. The second (g) has crossed arms, and on one side of her is a youth struggling with a lion (the popular Heracles motif) and on the other a wild dancing figure. The third (f) holds a bird in one hand, while her other is across her breast, where there is a human figure apparently falling and an animal on its back: these might be helpless victims of her power or intended to be under her protection. She has two women attendants, one plaiting her hair and the other upright on her shoulder.

Various attempts have been made to identify these deities, none of them wholly convincing. The study by Olmsted is the most ambitious one, giving strong arguments for an origin in north-western Gaul and going on to claim close links between the religion of the Celts in the early Iron Age in Gaul and Ireland, and to argue that a study of deities in Irish medieval sources should therefore lead to a better understanding of those on the cauldron. The bull is clearly of importance, because of the two bull-slaying scenes, and Olmsted has endeavoured to link the plates with episodes and characters in the Old Irish epic, the *Táin Bó Cúailnge*, in which the hero Setanta, better known by his nickname of Cú Chulainn, plays a major part in the struggle over the possession of a marvellous bull, the Donn Cúailnge, which Medb, Queen of Connacht, was determined to obtain from Ulster whatever the cost. According to one version outside the main manuscripts, the bull was finally killed by warriors (Olmsted 1979:205), and Olmsted suggests that this killing, and also the conflict between this bull and the other famous bull, the Finnbennach, explain scenes on the cauldron. Two small bulls confronting one another on Plate A could be a representation of the fight, while various creatures on the same plate could represent the animal shapes taken by the two swineherds who finally became bulls in the Irish epic (Olmsted 1979:144 ff.). He also links the tall figure by the wheel on plate C with the hero Cú Chulainn fighting Medb's lover Fergus with a broken chariot (Olmsted 1979:154). He follows an earlier scholar, Jubainville, in suggesting that Cú Chulainn was originally the god Esus, well known in Gaul, who appears with a bull on certain monuments.

It is generally accepted that Medb herself, with her long record of royal husbands and lovers, her fury in battle, and her links with territorial possession, is based on memories of an earlier goddess (p. 109). Olmsted associates her with the bust on plate B representing a goddess in a chariot, pointing out that in the *Táin* Medb's chariot is driven clockwise round the army to bring good fortune. The serpent on the same plate he links with the Morrígan, who took the shape of an eel to hamper Cú Chulainn in battle. The plate with the marching and riding warriors can, of course, be fitted into any tale of battle, and the figure holding a man over a vessel Olmsted identifies with the god Teutates, to whom men were sacrificed by drowning, taking Teutates as another name for Esus. He sees Lug and Esus as two linked gods in Celtic tradition, and the cross-legged god with antlers as Mercury/Lug, father of Cú Chulainn in the Irish epic.

Thus by many references to passages from the *Táin* and other early Irish texts, as well as to various figures of deities on monuments in Gaul, Olmsted has claimed to elucidate the various plates on the cauldron, arguing that they have been carefully put together to illustrate a major mythological theme, of which we possess a late version in the *Táin*. Here we have an attempt to make sense of a series of mythological pictures by selecting various details and finding parallels in a literary framework of a much later date. Surviving manuscripts of the *Táin* are all later than the eleventh century, although the material is known to be a good deal earlier than this. We can see here both the rich possibilities and the problems of iconographical interpretation with the aid of later literary sources from the Christian period. So much clearly depends on selection if the whole is to be made to fit together. In this case one weak point is the doubt as to whether the figure on plate C really holds a broken wheel, with which he is attacking the bearded 'god'. Others have seen it as the symbol of a turning wheel, and it seems to be held in the hand of the central figure. There is no really valid reason for identifying the goddess on plate B with Medb; even if she is meant to be riding in a chariot or wagon, this symbol of the travelling goddess is so widespread in both Celtic and Germanic tradition that it might lead to quite different interpretations (p. 198). The two male figures at her side (e) might be worshippers, or could fit into various symbolic patterns beside that of her husband and lover, Ailill and Fergus, as suggested by Olmsted. There is nothing about the similar goddess on plate g to strengthen the interpretation, and the idea that the Heracles figure with the lion and the dancing man represent Cú Chulainn being trained in warfare during his visit to Scáthach is unconvincing. The insistence that the tall man in the warrior scene must be putting a man into a tub and could not possibly be lifting him out of it seems unreasonable, nor does the object in the picture really resemble the Marlborough bucket and so appear to be a funeral vessel. The solution given in this last case is simply one of a series of guesses such as have been put forward over the years to explain this tantalizing ritual scene. Again, if the main legend depends on the fight between two bulls and the slaying of the survivor, why are there three animals on plate D? Bull sacrifice is known to have played an important part in early Celtic religion, and there are many other possible reasons for the presence of the bulls outside the plot of the *Táin*.

However, anyone who battles with the vexed question of the interpretation of scenes on the cauldron will have to take the arguments used and the evidence presented by Olmsted into consideration. Attempts of this kind are essential if any progress is to be made, and certain parts of the mythological framework may be valid even if weaknesses are found in details of the argument. The horned deity who sits cross-legged, with a torc round his neck and another in his hand, while his other hand grasps a serpent, is clearly a figure of major importance. He is evidently closely linked with the stag beside him, whose antlers match his own, and with the boar on the other side, and these two seem unquestionably to be of native Celtic origin in contrast to more fantastic animals elsewhere on the cauldron. Olmsted is unwilling to accept this horned deity as a god called Cernunnos, and seems justified in this. The basis of such claims is one incomplete inscription on a piece of an altar found at Notre Dame in Paris, which reads *.ERNUNNO*; it shows a deity with short horns, not antlers as on the cauldron. The interpretation *Cernunnos* ('Horned One') is not accepted by all (Le Roux 1953), and might be a title. Horns as a sign of power are a very widespread symbol, and it cannot be assumed that all horned figures represent one particular deity. Both the torc, symbol of prosperity, and the serpent can be found in Gaul as attributes of Mercury, and Mercury is the Roman equivalent of the god Lug, known to be important in Gaul (p. 46). The serene and enigmatic appearance of this figure certainly conveys an impression of divine power, while the link with the animals of the wild, the stag and the boar, is in keeping with Celtic imagery of the divine world. The possibility of eastern influences in this panel, however, has been strongly stressed by Taylor (1992), who accounts for them by the assumption that the cauldron was the work of silversmiths working in Thrace.

Faced with such a rich series of what appear to be divine figures, male and female, together with ritual scenes, we realize the wealth of religious imagery from the past to which we possess no satisfactory key. When examined at any point in detail, the evidence is found to be rich and promising, but we are speedily led away from the simple outlines of a past religion as depicted in popular mythologies, and are left groping for the way. This is especially the case when we are dealing, as here, with a ceremonial object found in isolation, by accident, connected with no recognizable site, and hard to date, and when the pictorial art, as in this case, shows obvious signs of foreign influences. In spite of the enormous amount of published literature on the cauldron and its acknowledged importance, we still have little understanding of its use in religious ritual, or why it came to be finally abandoned in a Danish peat-bog; but we are left with a conviction of rich mythological symbolism, and with the impression of a series of deities once of great importance in Celtic religion.

THE MEMORIAL STONES OF GOTLAND

Many centuries after the probable date of the Gundestrup Cauldron we have another rich field of pictorial imagery in monuments raised to honour the dead on the little island of Gotland in the Baltic, an important place on the route to eastern Europe from Sweden in the Viking Age. The Gotlanders became rich because of the many travellers and merchants and fighting bands who made a stop on the island when leaving or returning to Scandinavia, and many of their own folk must have left on Viking expeditions never to return. There is a whole army of stones raised to commemorate the Gotland dead, some enormous memorials about 10 m high, others smaller but elaborately decorated. They must have been a striking sight when new, for traces of colouring have been found on them and details of the pictures may have been filled in in bright shades, where now only the silhouettes are left to us. The biggest stones with many panels of pictures must have originally resembled great paintings or rich inlaid metalwork (Lindqvist 1941:23). Some stones are still standing in the countryside, while many have been found beneath the floors of medieval churches, and are in the museum at Visby.

They continued to be put up throughout the Viking Age until about the eleventh century, the majority before the coming of Christianity, although a few late ones bear Christian symbols. Thus they offer a unique opportunity to learn something of ideas about the Otherworld and the fate of the dead, and it is possible to compare the imagery used on the stones with that of some of the earliest poetry that survives in Iceland. The first stones were put up in the Migration Period, and were probably inspired by memorial stones of the Roman Empire in southern Europe. A number have a great whirling disc as centre-piece, accompanied by two smaller discs which may be imitated from symbols of the sun and moon on Roman tombstones, together with variations such as spirals and rosettes and small figures of men and fantastic animals (Figure 6). It seems possible that such stones reflected ideas about the cosmos, since on one stone there is the outline of a central tree, corresponding to the image of the world in mythological poetry (Davidson 1975:175 ff.). At the beginning of the Viking Age, about the eighth century, elaborate pictures of ships were introduced, usually in the lowest panel of the stones, and other panels were added showing

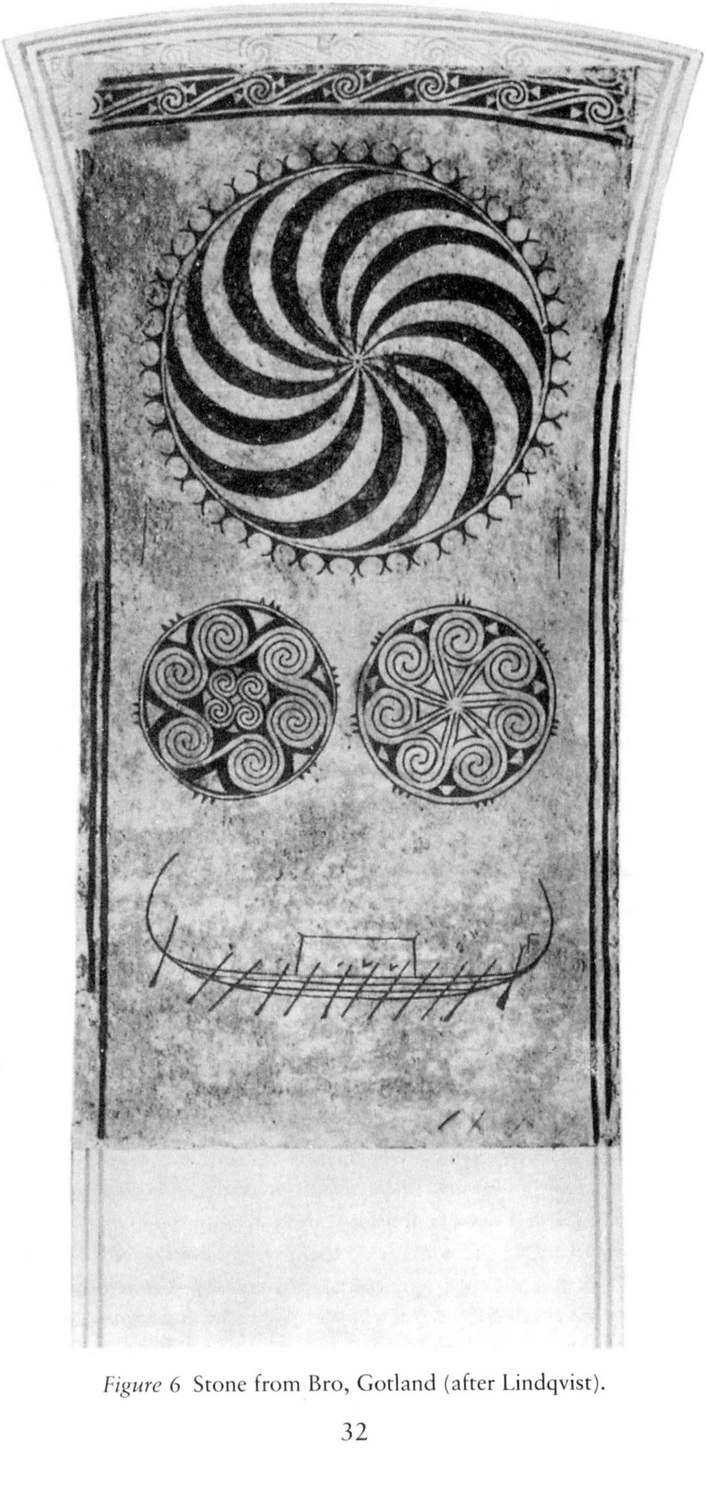

Figure 6 Stone from Bro, Gotland (after Lindqvist).

scenes of action. The ships are of considerable interest in view of the increasing popularity of ship-funeral at this period in Scandinavia, but as with the ships in the graves, we cannot be sure whether they represent a voyage to the Otherworld or whether the man to whom the stone was raised as a memorial was lost at sea and perhaps owned his own ship. Both factors may have made the ship symbol a popular one. The other picture most frequently found on stones of the Viking Age is that of a rider on a horse welcomed by a woman who offers him a drinking-horn (Davidson 1976:300 ff.). There are as many as twelve examples of this in Lindqvist's recorded list of stones (1941) and other possible cases where stones have been damaged; the woman with the horn has also been found elsewhere, for instance on a stone dating from the Viking Age at Sockburn-on-Tees in Yorkshire (Lang 1972) and also as an amulet in a grave at Birka in Sweden, while her companion, the riding man, was found as an amulet in another grave (Davidson 1967:201, nos 62, 63). The welcoming scene is usually depicted on the top panel of the stone (Figure 7), and is clearly of importance; sometimes it appears above the ship, and sometimes a number of other panels are added, some depicting scenes from heroic tradition, particularly those concerned with various heroes of Odin.

From western Scandinavia we find a similar motif in early poems, two of which, *Eiríksmál* and *Hákonarmál*, were composed in the tenth century by court poets in honour of two Norwegian kings, Eirik Bloodaxe and Hakon the Good. In these the dead king is described as entering the hall of Odin after his last battle, to join the heroes feasting with the god; when he arrives at Valhalla, he is welcomed by valkyries, one of whom greets each newcomer with a horn of ale, and is then taken in to meet Odin. In view of this tradition, borne out by poetic imagery in other sources, certain details in the welcoming scene on the stones become significant. There is what appears to be a stylized hall, which bears some resemblance to a burial mound; a flying figure with a spear might be identified as a valkyrie above the battlefield, while a dog that appears beside the warrior could be the dog mentioned in mythological poems as guarding the road to the land of the dead. Here where we have some literary evidence to draw upon, the various motifs on the stones fit together to make some sense, and we may be more confident in our interpretation.

There is no doubt that the idea of a hero welcomed by a woman with a horn was a familiar symbol in the pre-Christian Viking Age, although we cannot be certain whether the rider depicted on the stones is a dead warrior or possibly Odin himself. Two stones show him on a horse with eight legs, indicating that this is Sleipnir, the eight-legged horse of Odin which could bear him between the worlds. I have suggested that the basis of the eight-legged steed is the bier, carried by four men to the grave (Davidson 1964:142), and Odin's steed may also be deliberately used here as a symbol of the journey of the dead hero to the Otherworld. The evidence of the Gotland stones shows how useful iconography can be when we have a number of examples of the same motif, and at the same time some knowledge of the date and historical background, so that it is

Figure 7 Stone from Alskog, Gotland (after Nylen).

profitable to compare the imagery with that used in literature; but we are left wondering how far the image of the dead man riding to Valhalla is to be viewed as a poetic one only, like the final crossing of Jordan in Negro spirituals. Was it an image used by poets and stone-carvers alike because it appealed to the imagination at that particular time, and was a means of expressing praise and appreciation of a king or leader, or are we to assume that at some period it was a generally held religious belief? To such questions archaeological evidence alone is unlikely to give us an answer.

THE CONTRIBUTION OF ARCHAEOLOGY

Archaeology offers one clear advantage in a quest for a lost religion: it can take us back beyond the limits of written sources. In the case of the religions of northern Europe, most of our literary evidence comes well after the acceptance of Christianity, and sometimes centuries have passed since the old faith was abandoned. Graves and holy places and iconographical material, on the other hand, take us directly back into the time when the religion of the gods still had meaning. Archaeology may also help to establish reliable dating for a custom or expression of belief, especially when objects such as coins, weapons, pottery or brooches are included in the find, since these can be fitted into an existing series of types already dated from previous work. In addition, there are now scientific methods of checking dating, such as carbon-dating, pollen analysis and dendrochronology, which have become increasingly reliable in recent years. Third, archaeology may provide us at any time with a new find that makes us revise previous assumptions when we are faced with exciting, though perhaps disturbing, fresh material. New methods of examining archaeological evidence, like the reconstruction of decayed bodies in some of the minor graves at Sutton Hoo (p. 22), may add considerably to our knowledge. Earlier archaeologists concentrated on artistic treasures or interesting artefacts that might be obtained from a site, but this has now given place to a wider curiosity concerning methods of workmanship, ways of disposing of the dead, and information about living conditions of the time. The practical problems presented by burial or cult places and the religious practices of the past are gradually being outlined in surer strokes.

On the other hand, we cannot expect the evidence of archaeology to lead us to an understanding of the thought-processes of those who performed the ritual or disposed of the dead with complex rites. There is much in ceremonial that leaves no trace for the most careful archaeologist to find, and we may well jump to precipitate conclusions concerning human sacrifice or barbaric rites from incomplete evidence. Oversimplification is always a danger, as is also the linking of widely separated pieces of evidence because of the desire to fit them into a favourite theory. There is also the danger of taking short-cuts in the desire to identify some mysterious figure in wood or stone with a particular god or hero with whom we happen to be familiar. Two rudely carved but impressive figures from a cult place on the moor at Braak in Schleswig, for instance, one male and one female, were hailed on their discovery as early Celtic or Germanic deities, or the founders of the race in German tradition. More recent tests by pollen analysis have dated them to the Viking Age, and it is possible that they were set up by Slavs in that area (Jankuhn 1957:50). While post-holes on a cult site can give us some idea of the size of the posts for which they were intended, they can tell us nothing of the purpose or appearance of the posts once set in them. The amount that can be conjectured and confidently published on the strength of a few post-holes is illustrated by the many models presented as reconstructions of the pre-Christian temple at Uppsala (p. 87). Moreover, the bewildering variety of funeral customs in the pre-Christian period that becomes apparent when we have a considerable amount of archaeological evidence from one area makes it very difficult to draw any firm conclusions as to beliefs about the dead. A good illustration of this is the evidence from cemeteries and isolated graves in Roman Britain (Hutton 1991:234 ff.).

Certainly archaeology can bring us closer with startling vividness to religious images from the pre-Christian past; we may look directly into a face that once represented a deity that men and women worshipped, or see how objects in a burial chamber were left after the last rites were performed. No prose description can have quite the same impact, and vivid, eye-witness accounts that are also objective are extremely rare. We are able also to see the splendid treasures that once graced a shrine or a grave when these can be restored to reveal their dignity and power, even though they are separated for ever from their ritual setting, and the words spoken over them lost to us. One of the most valuable contributions of archaeology to our knowledge of past religions is its power to confirm or throw new light on accounts of beliefs and customs in the written sources whose reliability has been doubted. When different sources of evidence are brought together, we may come closer to an understanding of ritual and imagery. There is little hope now of finding new literary material, but a major archaeological discovery may happen at any time. We have the example of what happened in 1982 on a 'rescue excavation' at Flag Fen in Peterborough, when the remains of a great wooden platform were discovered, with wooden buildings on it, much of the wood from the Bronze Age preserved in the waterlogged soil. This may prove to have been a great sacred centre, although it is as yet too early to say, and will certainly add considerably to our knowledge of the period (Pryor 1990). Archaeology is the most likely means of extending our knowledge of religious practices of the past, and can confidently be relied on to provide new problems and challenges as our knowledge increases.

2

Glimpses of the Gods

Then said Gangleri: Who are the gods, in whom folk should put their trust?
(Prose Edda: *Gylfaginning* 19)

The identity of gods and goddesses and various supernatural beings remains one of the outstanding problems in the study of archaeological or iconographical evidence. Many names of divine beings from the old religion were remembered in Christian times in both Scandinavian and Irish sources, but it is difficult to establish how many of these names are ancient ones unless we find them in early inscriptions or recognize them in place-names. We may be helped by iconographical sources, such as the memorial stones of Gotland discussed in the last chapter, which provide evidence for the cult of Odin in the Viking Age in eastern Scandinavia, and support imagery from skaldic poetry concerned with the deaths of kings and heroes. Odin himself, however, remains an elusive figure, as he proved himself to be in tales of his visits to the mortal world, and even if his eight-legged horse appears on the stones, we cannot be sure that the rider is Odin himself (p. 33). The same is true of various riding warriors from the Migration Period, depicted in stone or metalwork, which have been identified with the god (Kuhn 1938) (Figure 8). The rider shown on one of the helmets from a grave at Vendel in Sweden, dating from the period before the Viking Age, with an eagle and raven flying above him, and a spear in his hand, seems likely to be a representation of Odin (Davidson 1965:24) (Figure 9), but even here the position is complicated by possible influences from pictures of warrior saints from southern Europe. There is no simple road to establish the identity of supernatural figures in early art, but it may be helpful to consider some of the attempts that have been made.

EARLY AMULETS

A possible source of information about the beings of the divine world is the amazingly rich series of small hanging ornaments in gold and silver, which began as imitations of Roman medallions, but swiftly developed on original lines based on native tradition. These were produced in Scandinavia from the fifth to the

Figure 8 Metal ornament showing horseman with spear, Bräunlingen, Kr. Donaueschingen. Drawing by Eileen Aldworth.

Figure 9 Odin (?) with eagle and raven on helmet plate, from Vendel, Sweden (after Simpson).

early seventh century, with a few made in the sixth century in Kent for rich Scandinavians who settled there (Hawkes and Pollard 1981). They are known as 'bracteates', from the Latin name *aureae bracteae* given to them in Denmark in the seventeenth century. About 300 examples are recorded, the majority about the size of an old penny, although some are larger and have been set in elaborate frames. The fact that so many survive testifies to the value set on them, and they seem to have been used as amulets. They have been found in graves of both men and women, though more frequently in women's graves, and also in hoards of gold or silver, while isolated examples have been recovered from the earth. These last may have been deliberately buried to make the soil fertile, while the presence of one or two in a hoard might be due to the belief that they gave protection to buried wealth. They were presumably worn round the neck to give luck and protection to their owners.

There are four main types of bracteate; Group A has developed from medallions showing the head of an Emperor (Figure 10); Group B shows one, two or three standing figures, and is based on the Roman motif of Victory crowning a hero (Figure 11); while Group C originates from the figure of an Emperor on horseback (Figure 12). There is also a type D decorated with abstract animal ornament in the Germanic style, not dependent on classical models.

Figure 10 Bracteate from Sievern, type A (after Hauck).

Figure 11 Bracteate from Denmark, site unknown, type B.

Figure 12 Bracteate from Holmsland, Ringkøbing, Denmark, type C (after Hauck).

In 1952 Mackeprang published a list of known bracteates with illustrations, and worked out the system of classification. More recently, Hauck has produced a major study of bracteates in 1970 and a Corpus in four volumes, listing all known examples, in 1985. He gives enlarged photographs and drawings which enable the details to be studied, and has sought to link the figures and symbols on them with the cults of the Germanic gods. His work makes clear the complex art and vigour of these strange little ornaments, far removed in spirit from Roman or Byzantine models. A number have runic inscriptions, unfortunately not easy to decipher, which appear to be magical formulae to enhance the power of the bracteates. Hauck takes the symbol of breath issuing from the mouth of the single head on the A bracteates as a symbol of creative power coming from a god, while the bird which is often found with the head, presumably copied from the Roman eagle, he associates with Wodan's raven. The ending of the Emperor's helmet or diadem in a bird's head is taken as a further indication of the character of the god and his ability to take on bird-shape, while he also links the horse on the bracteates with the Germanic cult of Wodan (Hauck 1970:396 ff.). Some of the B group of bracteates he interprets as representing the slaying of Balder, and those showing a figure with his hand between the jaws of a wolf-like creature (Figure 13) as an early illustration of Tyr's binding of the wolf resulting in the loss of his hand (p. 74). One small group of bracteates shows a female figure holding what appear to be weaving implements (Figure 14), who may represent a Germanic goddess (Enright 1990), and this is an important piece of evidence in view of later literary descriptions of supernatural female beings (p. 115). All these are possibilities worth noting, but we do not yet seem able to identify any of the figures on the bracteates consistently with later deities worshipped in Scandinavia. As Enright (1990:154) states in his discussion of the weaving figure, recent work on the bracteates can add to our understanding of early religion, but 'they

Figure 13 Bracteate from Trollhättan, Sweden, thought to show Tyr and wolf (after Hauck).

Figure 14 Bracteate showing weaving goddess, from south-west Germany (after Enright).

demand a highly specialized and intense type of scrutiny before their often enigmatic messages can be deciphered and understood'.

A similar use of what might be seen as symbols of power, perhaps associated with the luck of one particular family, can be found on Germanic and Anglo-Saxon brooches with elaborate designs in relief, and also in scenes and figures used in the decoration of helmets, scabbards, sword pommels and shields. In one series of Anglo-Saxon brooches, parallels to which are found in Germany, Vierck identified a face with staring eyes, sometimes shown with a triangle below the mouth enclosing the disjointed parts of an animal figure (Figure 15), as representing the creative god of the Germans (Vierck 1967). Helmets made in Sweden

Figure 15 Anglo-Saxon brooch from Warwick (after Vierck).

and England in the sixth and early seventh century may have ornamental plates partly based on classical models, like those on the helmet from Sutton Hoo showing a warrior riding over a prostrate enemy (Figure 16). Again, however, native tradition may influence the original design, as in the addition of a tiny dancing man on the Sutton Hoo plate, who is guiding the spear of the warrior (Davidson 1965). On Swedish and Alamannic helmet plates of the same period warriors are shown together with bears and wolves, and are sometimes depicted in dancing attitudes (Figure 17); these have been claimed as representations of the god Wodan, closely associated with warriors and the dead (Paulsen 1967:142). Such representations may bring us nearer to an understanding of the cult of the warrior god, but we still cannot be sure whether he was instantly recognizable to his worshippers in such pictures, or whether some of the figures may represent dedicated warriors who followed the god rather than the deity himself.

There are some tiny pictures in metal of another type which might be seen as amulets, which have not been imitated from sophisticated southern models. They consist of minute pieces of gold foil, not much bigger than a finger-nail, which are found in sets in the foundations of certain buildings. As many as 19 were laid in the post-holes that once held the supports of a possible pre-Christian temple under the medieval church of Mære in Trondheim (Lidén 1969), while 26 were discovered at Helgö in Sweden, in what appears to have been a sacred centre, probably used for feasts (Holmqvist 1975). The usual scene depicted on them is of a man and woman facing one another, sometimes embracing and sometimes separated by a leafy branch, and the generally accepted explanation is that they represent the Vanir fertility deities, who could bring blessing to the land, to flocks and herds and to human families (Figure 18). It is perhaps significant that the pieces from Helgö show great variety in the treatment and dress of the tiny figures, only two being identical, which suggests that they may have been deposited there on different occasions. M. Olsen (1909) long ago interpreted the poem *Skírnismál*, in which the fertility god Freyr woos the fair maid Gerd,

Figure 16 Design on helmet plate (reconstructed) from the Sutton Hoo helmet (after Evans).

Figure 17 Metal plate from Alamannic grave showing dancing warrior (after Paulsen).

Figure 18 Embracing figures on tiny piece of gold foil, Helgö, Sweden. Drawing by Eileen Aldworth.

daughter of a giant in the underworld, as a myth of the divine marriage, in which the coming-together of these divine powers connected with the sky and the earth meant new life in spring and a season of plenty, and many have taken this as the significance of the tiny golden figures. It is possible that they were used for weddings to bring good fortune and fertility to bride and groom (Grieg 1954), as well as for such occasions as the building of a new house or setting up of a place of assembly, but their exact use remains an unsolved problem.

In these various cases, divine figures or symbols representing the gods seem to be used in a general rather than a particular fashion. The purpose behind such representations was presumably to give power or bring luck, so that wearing them as an ornament, adding them as a decoration to weapons or defensive armour, or placing them in the earth might result in blessing and protect against harm. Such symbols or pictures on weapons could be linked with Odin or earlier gods controlling the field of battle, although Thor, the sky god, and Freyr, god of fertility, could also help their followers in warfare, so that their symbols too might be used in this way. Amulets placed in the earth seem likely to represent the power of the fertility deities; on the other hand, Odin had powers over buried treasure while Thor guarded boundaries, so they both might have had connections with the earth. Clearly recognizable representations of individual gods and goddesses cannot, it seems, be found on amulets.

Nor have early coins hitherto proved helpful in this direction. Images on Celtic coins, such as those of Apollo, were presumably copied from the Romans, while the majority of Scandinavian coins were made for Christian kings, and designs again tended to be copied from southern neighbours. Hutton, however, selects one coin of the early first century AD as seeming to show the face of a Celtic deity (Hutton 1991:164). It came from Petersfield in Hampshire and is now in the National Museum of Wales, and shows a male head with antlers and a wheel set on what seems to be a crown. Once more, however, identification is difficult. We need to turn to other types of iconographical evidence where more details are given and names may also be provided.

STONES FROM THE ROMAN PROVINCES

There is one rich field for the identification of divine figures of which, as yet, full use has not been made. The Roman occupation of England, France, Germany and the Netherlands resulted in an enormous number of inscribed stones dedicated to various gods and goddesses, including statues, altars and votive plaques. Some have an inscription only, while others have pictures of the deities, according to Roman fashion, in anthropomorphic form. Any museum in a Roman town or military centre is likely to include a number of such stones, some presented in conventional Roman style, some clumsy copies of such works, and others powerful and barbaric, with little attempt at naturalistic treatment. Such stones may be dedicated to deities from distant parts of the Roman world, such as Astarte, commemorated on a stone at Corstopitum on the Roman Wall, when they were erected by men of various nationalities serving in the Roman army. Many others, however, represent local deities, and have been placed by farmers or landowners on their estates, or perhaps erected by small communities. Those who introduced them were evidently desirous to follow the new fashions in art and to honour their favourite deities in the Roman manner.

Both Celtic and Germanic deities are usually identified with one of the main Roman gods, such as Apollo, Jupiter or Mars, but their own titles may be included in the inscription. On such stones lost gods occasionally manifest themselves, and we can learn something more of their characters from the titles given to them. Unfortunately, it is not always obvious which native deities have been honoured in this way. The Roman gods could be defined with some precision, and each was deemed to preside over certain aspects of life, but the Celtic and Germanic deities were far from being specialists, and the same Roman god is not always chosen to represent one of them. It seems that numerous local deities might possess powers to heal, help in battle, rule the sky and the winds, and give the land fertility. Many Celtic names occur once only, and Sjoestedt pointed out that there were as many as 59 different ones associated with Mars, so that what is obviously one Roman deity could be used to represent a great many local gods

(Sjoestedt 1982:27). There are, for instance, a number of stones in Cumbria dedicated to Mars Belatucadros, meaning 'Fair Shining One', or 'Fair Slayer' (Ross 1967:181). In this case pictures are lacking, although it is possible that this local god was represented by carvings of warrior figures without inscriptions found in the area (Hutton 1991:224). Another name of a deity found in both Britain and Gaul is Maponus, meaning 'son' or 'youth', represented as Apollo on an altar from Hexham (Richmond 1943). He may be remembered as Mabon in the Welsh *Mabinogion*, a mighty hunter who pursued the great boar in the tale of Culhwch and Olwen, while his mother Modron seems to correspond to the Celtic Matrona, the divine Mother, who gave her name to the river Marne in France. Here, then, we may have traces of a mother and son linked with hunting and the countryside.

There seems to be a clear link between the Roman Mercury and Lug, one of the outstanding Celtic gods of the Roman period, who gave his name to one of the four festivals of the Celtic year, Lugnasa on 1st August, and was worshipped in every part of the Celtic world, Gaul and Britain, Spain and Ireland (Tovar 1982). Apollo, like Mars, however, is linked with many different names and titles. One name found in conjunction with him is Belenus, probably from *bel* ('shining'), recalling another Celtic festival, Beltene. Another name is Grannus, again thought to mean something like 'shining' or 'burning'. However, neither of these gods appears in the literature, and we cannot conclude that they were simply sun gods, since inscriptions in which they occur indicate other characteristics beside those of warmth and brightness.

Problems raised by almost forgotten Celtic divinities are well illustrated by the enigmatic figure of the horned deity on the Gundestrup Cauldron, often referred to as Cernunnos (p. 30). Opinions differ widely as to whether various other horned figures in Celtic art can be identified with one particular god. In some cases, knobs on the heads of male divinities claimed as horns, for instance, have been explained away as rough representations of the winged hat of the Roman Mercury. Some early horned figures associated with serpents have been linked with the figure on the Gundestrup Cauldron, and attempts have been made to identify him with the Lord of the Animals in early Irish literature; but the extent to which such a deity was ever worshipped by Celtic tribes still remains an open question.

There were fewer attempts to find classical counterparts for the Celtic goddesses, although Brigantia and Brigid are sometimes identified with the Roman goddess Minerva, who had powers of healing, encouraged crafts, and was associated with thermal waters (Ross 1967:360 ff.). The Celtic name of a goddess is often retained in the inscriptions. Thus we have Rosmerta, often shown along with Mercury, who presumably represents some local deity; he may carry a purse while she has a basket of fruit, indicating that they are bringers of fruitfulness and prosperity and connected with the land. Rosmerta's name has been interpreted as 'Good Purveyor' (Green 1986:97), and she is sometimes depicted stirring a tub or bucket which Webster (1986:61) finds hard to explain, but which surely might

Figure 19 Rosmerta with her churn (?), from Corbridge, Northumberland (after Ross).

represent a churn (Figure 19). Another important goddess was Epona, mentioned in many inscriptions and represented on stones in Britain and on the continent, including nearly 300 in Gaul alone. She is consistently associated with horses, and may be shown riding, usually side-saddle, accompanied by a mare or foal or by two or more horses which she feeds with corn (Johns 1971:39). She is also associated with dogs, birds and healing springs, and is linked with the Mother Goddesses who brought fertility and protection for their worshippers, and were concerned with the well-being of the land, the care of animals, including domestic ones, and the destinies of young children. Epona seems to have been called on by those interested in horse-breeding and the use of horses on farms, while some classical writers refer to her presiding over stables (Linduff 1979), and there are dedications to her put up by soldiers in Roman cavalry regiments. As Linduff points out, many auxiliaries from Gaul fought on horseback, providing their own horses, and kept up their native traditions and beliefs. It seems likely that Epona goes back into the Celtic past, since horses had long been of great importance to the Celts, but that in Roman times she was adapted to a new way of life, and attracted a wider range of worshippers. It has been suggested that she was linked with the goddess Macha in Irish tradition, and with the Welsh Rhiannon (Ross 1967:224 ff.), but if memories of her are preserved in later literature, it is under some name other than Epona.

The German gods depicted in the Roman style are a little easier to identify. It is possible roughly to equate Jupiter with the Germanic thunder god Donar (later known as Thunor and Thor), and Mercury with the Germanic Wodan (OE Woden and ON Óðinn), while Mars was sometimes identified with the god **Tîwaz* (remembered as Tīw or Tīg by the Anglo-Saxons and by the Scandinavians as *Týr*). We cannot, however, assume that such identifications can always be relied upon; the thunder god with his club, for instance, may sometimes be represented by Hercules. The Roman Mercury and the later Odin have a number of traits in common. Both wore cloaks and wide-brimmed hats, although Odin was thought of usually as an old man and Mercury usually (though not invariably) as a divine youth. Both were regarded as guides to the underworld, helped their followers to gain treasure, and featured as cunning thieves, so that they both may be viewed as trickster figures. Titles such as *Mercurius Mercator* and *Negotiator* in inscriptions recall one of Odin's names, *Farmatýr*, 'God of Cargoes', a side of the god that tends to be forgotten because of the emphasis laid on him as god of battle. The association of Odin with the battlefield and his great spear which caused strife among men may have been taken over from Tîwaz, who had become a shadowy figure by the late Viking Age. The Germanic Wodan is thought by some to have been primarily a ruler of the land of the dead, whose cult came into Scandinavia comparatively late.

Titles given on the stones often serve as helpful clues to the characters of the deities. Two dedications at Housesteads on the Roman Wall refer to Mars Thincsus, and these presumably refer to the god's association with the *thing* or 'Assembly' where law cases were held and new laws decided. Thor presided over the Althing in Iceland, but Tîwaz may have been the guardian of law at an earlier period. It must be recognized that the Germanic gods inevitably changed in character as tribes moved from one area to another, and communities developed new needs and organizations. In Iceland, for instance, there was no royal dynasty to depend on Odin's favour for continued rule and no regular army was needed where young men could be trained in the lore of the warrior god. Thus traditions concerning Odin are largely based on those remembered from Norway or Denmark, and the strongest emphasis in Icelandic poetry is on Odin's power to inspire poets.

Germanic female deities fall into two main classes. First, there are the war goddesses or battle spirits, like the Alaisiagae, mentioned together with Mars on three stones at Housesteads, whose names – Bede, Finnilene, Baudihillie and Friagabi – are similar to some of those given to the valkyries in Norse literary tradition: the last two are interpreted as 'Ruler of Battle' and 'Giver of Freedom' (Bosanquet 1922). This seems to indicate female spirits who helped to determine the course of battle and saved warriors from the panic that led to defeat and death, and who were associated with the Germanic war god long before the Viking Age (Davidson 1988:69). A second group of female spirits are those who come under the heading of the Mothers (Matres, Matronae), the 'Giving Ones', who are also found in Celtic tradition. Names like Garmangabi, 'Giving' or 'Generous' One, on a stone from Lanchester near Durham may be compared with later goddess names such as Gefion and Gefn, emphasizing their power to bring gifts. The cults of such goddesses must have brought in the women of the community, but they certainly had their male worshippers also, as in Roman Britain stones in their honour were in many cases set up by men serving in the army (Barnard 1985). Some of the dedications are to 'foreign' (*ollotatae*) or 'overseas' (*tramarinae*) Mothers as well as to local ones, perhaps because those making them wished for continued help and luck from the supernatural beings associated with districts where they had previously lived or served (Barnard 1985:243). This emphasizes the link between such goddesses and particular regions, and indicates general recognition that those of other peoples belonged to the same category as the familiar beings on home ground.

Nehalennia appears to have been an important Germanic goddess of this type, although we have no indications of the particular tribe to which she originally belonged. She had two temples on the island of Walcheren at the mouth of the Rhine, which were overwhelmed by the sea, but a large number of altars and inscribed stones associated with her cult have been recovered from the sand. Many were set up by merchants and travellers in thankfulness for a safe crossing, and she is often shown beside the prow of a ship. She also appears, however, with baskets of fruit, horns of plenty, loaves (some very like the products of local bakeries in recent times) and with a small dog sitting beside her (Figure 20). Such attributes indicate that she was a fertility goddess, who may also have possessed powers of healing and been associated with the realm of the dead (Hondius-Crone 1955; Stuart *et al.* 1971).

Figure 20 Drawing of goddess Nehalennia by Cannegieter, as shown on an altar from her shrine at Domburg, The Netherlands (after Hondius-Crone).

Much more might be done in further study of this large body of evidence for cults and native traditions of the Roman period. One scholar who made considerable use of it was de Vries (1957–8), but the tendency to keep Celtic and Germanic studies apart, together with the fact that the carved stones have remained largely within the province of the classicists, has halted progress, particularly on the Germanic side. The absence of any comprehensive handbook of such stones was lamented by Buchholz (1975). Much of the material was collected in museums many years ago, but there has been a steady increase in finds from excavations or chance discoveries on Roman sites; one example among many is the discovery in 1957 of a number of carved stones deliberately broken and thrown into a well at Lower Slaughter in Gloucestershire, thought to have been deposited there in the late fourth or fifth century by disapproving Christians (Toynbee 1976:89 ff.). Certainly, study of this type of evidence from any part of the Roman provinces soon makes clear the complexity of local cults and worship of individual Celtic and Germanic deities and prevents any simplistic approach.

MYTHS AND MONUMENTS

Representations of divine beings and scenes from pre-Christian myths have been found on crosses and grave stones of the early Christian period in Scandinavia, northern England and the Isle of Man. It seems to have been the practice to introduce Christian teaching by comparison with earlier myths, and one opportunity for doing this was on crosses and memorial stones in honour of the dead. A striking example is that of Thorwald's Cross from Andreas in the Isle of Man, dated to the eleventh century, which shows Odin being devoured by the wolf in the last great battle (Figure 21). The god can be identified by the raven on his shoulder, by his spear, turned downwards as a sign of defeat, and by a characteristic knot often associated with him, as on some of the Gotland stones. The intention seems to be to contrast the destruction of the pagan god at Ragnarok with the resurrection of Christ and his victory over evil, as the Odin figure is placed below one of the arms of the cross. Other subjects associated with Ragnarok are found on the cross still standing in the churchyard at Gosforth in Cumbria. One panel appears to show the bound Loki, with his wife beside him catching poison in a bowl as it drops from snakes hanging above the hapless prisoner, exactly as described by Snorri in *Gylfaginning* 49, some centuries later. The resemblance here seems too close for mere coincidence, and attempts to argue that the scene is based on some obscure Christian allegory are not convincing.

It may be assumed that such mythological scenes were once carved earlier in wood to decorate the halls of rich men and to enrich the shrines of the gods, since there are allusions to such carvings in early Icelandic poems (p. 103). Several poems describe the exploit of the god Thor when he fished for the World Serpent: one early poem on this subject by Bragi is presented as a description of a

Figure 21 Odin devoured by the wolf, Andreas Cross, Isle of Man (after Simpson).

carving in a hall, while another by Thjodolf of Hvin describes a picture on a shield. The tale of Thor's fishing is also told in direct narrative style in the Edda poem *Hymiskviða*, and finally retold in prose by Snorri in the Prose Edda in the thirteenth century. Here then we have a well-substantiated pagan myth preserved in early literature, clearly felt to be important.

There are four surviving carvings of Thor's fishing. In each case he is in a boat, and in three out of the four he has a companion with him, assumed to be the giant who accompanied him in the Edda poem and cut the line in terror when he saw the monster. The only stone showing Thor alone is from Altuna in Sweden, dated to the early eleventh century, on which the ox-head that Thor was said to use for bait and the struggling serpent are visible (Figure 22). There is no indication that this stone was a Christian monument. Another stone from Hørdum in Denmark is in bad condition and hard to date, but the fishing-line and part of the serpent can be made out, while both here and on the Altuna Stone Thor has his foot through the bottom of the boat, as in Snorri's account. A third stone from Gosforth in Cumbria, dated to the tenth century, has been built into the inside wall of the church, but may originally have been a panel from a Christian cross (Figure 23). Thor is seen in the boat holding up his hammer, and the ox-head and several fish are visible, but not the serpent; this might, however, have been shown on a lower panel. Earlier than any of these stones is one from Ardre in Gotland, probably from the early eighth century, which has several little scenes on it: one has been interpreted as Thor obtaining the ox, and another shows him with a companion in a boat.

The literary sources and the carvings have been discussed in detail by P.M. Sørensen (1986), who claims that this particular myth must have continued in a

Figure 22 The serpent takes Thor's bait, on stone from Altuna, Sweden.

reasonably stable form for over 500 years. Snorri in his account seems to have kept faithfully to the version in the early poems. We do not know whether the hooking of the serpent originally formed part of the story of creation, fitting into the familiar pattern of a god overcoming a monster so that order might replace chaos, or whether it was one of the happenings foreshadowing Ragnarok, when Thor was finally slain by the serpent although he overcame it. Snorri refers to two different traditions: one was that Thor slew the serpent when he pulled it up from the depths, and the other that it fell back into the sea when the giant cut the line, so that the end of the world was postponed for a little longer. Thor's struggle to lift the giant's cat from the floor in another of Snorri's tales (p. 82) is evidently based on the latter version.

Sørensen points out that both artists and early poets have emphasized the confrontation between serpent and god, each staring into the eyes of the other. The giant, he thinks, may have been introduced into the myth in the Viking Age, symbolizing Thor's journey from the cultivated farming world to which he belonged to the wild country of the giants where monsters abounded. He

Figure 23 Thor and the giant fishing, on stone in Gosforth church, Cumbria.

reminds us how myths are likely to change over a long period of time, and also how limited pictorial material must be: 'The picture is a primitive medium compared to the written word, and it is in reality not intelligible if we do not know the story which it illustrates' (1986:258). However, one great advantage of such evidence is that it may reveal the essential point of the myth, and also give a date at which a myth was known, perhaps much earlier than any surviving written source.

Some of the more elaborate of the Thor's hammer amulets, popular in the tenth century and perhaps made in imitation of Christian crosses, could have been inspired by the contest between god and serpent (Figure 24). Two examples from Östergötland and Scania show a bearded face with round staring eyes representing the god, and a twisted shape which could represent the serpent (Davidson 1967: pl. 67). Once we are familiar with a myth, as here, it is possible to recognize symbolism based on it. It has been suggested that the use of the fishing scene on a Christian monument might have been inspired by a learned Christian allegory of God the Father fishing for the devil and using the crucified Christ as bait, but it is doubtful whether this was ever used in art at a date as early as the first

Figure 24 Thor's hammer amulet in silver, from Kabbarg, Scania, Sweden (after Simpson).

Thor carvings. Nor does it seem likely that such an obscure motif would be used on monuments intended for public edification. However, the work of Roe on early Christian crosses in Ireland has shown how somewhat fantastic scenes once taken as non-Christian can be shown to belong to a firm Biblical tradition or to have been inspired by Christian legend (Roe 1945). Another example is that of the impressive carved stone found at Repton in Derbyshire in 1979, showing a rider on one side and on the other a serpentine creature with a human face, apparently devouring two men. The conclusion reached in a detailed study (Biddle and Kjolbye-Biddle 1985) is that this should be dated to the eighth century in Mercia, and that it forms part of an early Christian cross. To reach a conclusion in such cases is difficult unless we have a number of examples of a particular motif for comparison, as in the case of Thor's fishing. When the theme has also been treated in later literature, evidence of the carvings can clearly be of great value for the study of northern mythology.

NAMING AFTER THE GODS

It is clearly difficult to identify divine beings shown in metalwork or stone carvings unless these are accompanied by a helpful inscription. Certain attributes like the hammer of Thor may help to identify a god, or we may be able to recognize a scene from an account in literary sources, as in the picture of the bound Loki on the Gosforth Cross. Fortunately, however, there are other ways of tracing the names of deities, and one is by a study of the landscape and of the names given to local features that go back to early times. Such names have to be traced back in early records, and it is important to realize that the study of place-names is a discipline in which short-cuts may prove misleading. Some names that seem to link up with the pre-Christian past may be due to antiquarian speculation, as

O. Olsen (1966:92 ff.) pointed out in discussing the use of the term *hof* in Scandinavian place-names. This word is often translated 'temple' but seems sometimes to have been used for secular enclosures and buildings. In Norway he found 22 farms where the name of a god had been linked with the syllable *hof*, and 85 simply called *Hof*, and thought it possible that in these cases a farm had been used as a place to hold feasts in honour of the gods. In Iceland about 100 farms with the name *Hof* were recorded in 1910, but of these only 5 were recorded in the early eighteenth century; so that many may have been added in reports on local antiquities made by clergy a century or so later (O. Olsen 1966:172 ff.). A few of these may be genuine temple sites, the most probable being a farm in north-eastern Iceland called Hofstaðir, which has a different lay-out from the normal hall and traces of a field-kitchen outside, so that it could have been used to prepare food for a large number of people. But great caution is needed, since even if *hof* names can be traced back to medieval times, they may merely indicate chapels built by Christians, so that there is little reliable evidence on which to draw.

Another name denoting some kind of holy place is ON *hǫrgr* (OE *hearg*), which may originally have denoted a place of sacrifice out of doors, but was later applied to buildings (Turville-Petre 1964:239–40). One English example of its use is Harrow, where there is an impressive hilltop site appropriate for a holy place. In Scandinavia such elements can be combined in place-names with the name of a god, but not in England, so if they mark places there where sanctuaries once stood, they were presumably for the worship of the gods in general. In Denmark the word *hylde* is found in place-names, and is thought to mean a shrine of wood or possibly a wooden platform on which the gods were placed, as in Onsild, earlier 'Othenshylle' (Hald 1965:251). Another word thought to be used for a holy place is OE *weoh/wig* (cf. ON *vé*, Danish *wi*, Swedish *vi*), but it is hard to trace this in later place-names – one possible example is Weyhill in Hampshire (Gelling 1973:110 ff.).

There are, however, many names that seem to be associated with a particular god or goddess. These may be linked with some noteworthy feature of the landscape. A Celtic example from Kerry in Ireland is that of two rounded hills resembling breasts, known as the Paps of Anu (*Dá Chich nAnann*). In the literature Anu is called 'Mother of the Gods', and a ninth-century glossary comments 'Good is the food which she gave' (Ó hÓgáin 1990:151); the naming of hills after her shows that traditionally she was identified with the earth itself, even if a particular example may not go back to a time when she was worshipped as a deity. The god Lug (p. 46) plays some part in Irish literature, but the chief evidence for his cult in pre-Roman times comes from place-names. Lyon in France was formerly Lugudunum, derived from his name, and other towns such as Laon, Loudon and Leiden were also called after him, as well as Carlisle in England, whose Roman name was Luguvallium. There are many places called after him in Ireland, including hills, earthworks and lakes, one of which is Lough Lugborta at Uisnech, where according to local legend he was drowned (MacNeill 1982:7).

MacNeill has shown how the Irish festival of Lugnasa is associated with various customs and traditions, and these help to build up a picture of the god.

In Anglo-Saxon England a considerable number of place-names have been claimed as proof of the worship of pre-Christian deities, some still in use for towns and villages and others former names for fields or farms. However, Gelling (1973) has shown that a number previously accepted by Stenton, Ekwall and others have proved unacceptable when earlier spellings were examined in greater detail. She accepts a few Woden names as evidence for the worship of the god, such as Woodnesborough in Kent, meaning Woden's Hill or Tumulus, which is confirmed by the survival of a large mound beside the church up to the end of the eighteenth century (Davidson and Webster 1967:7). The name *Wodneslawe* near Biggleswade, a site now lost, has a similar meaning. Names accepted by Gelling as associated with Thunor, the Anglo-Saxon thunder god, are Thunderley and Thundersley in Essex, names meaning Grove of Thunor, and perhaps used of a holy place in a forest clearing or a sacred grove. The close link between the thunder god and the great oaks of the forest in Germanic territory was pointed out by H.M. Chadwick as long ago as 1900. It was formerly thought that Thurstable in Essex was a good example of a name derived from Thor, and that the last part, from *stapol*, a post or pillar, confirmed Thor's association with the pillars of the hall in Norse tradition (Turville-Petre 1962). This is a warning example of over-rash conclusions where place-names are concerned. Bronnenkant (1982–3) has now shown that it is far more probable that the name 'Thurstable' was taken from that of a Danish settler, and that the pillar could have been some kind of boundary-mark without religious significance.

Names based on Tīw or Tīg are harder to find, but one good example is Tysoe in Warwickshire, which is of interest because it is close to the Vale of the Red Horse, where the figure of a horse was formerly cut in the turf (Davidson 1982:55), and might conceivably have had some connection with the earlier god. The fertility deities, and especially the goddess Frīg (the Germanic Frîja) after whom Friday was named, must have been important to the Anglo-Saxons, but places named after them are rarely found, perhaps because such names would tend to be suppressed by missionaries at the time of the conversion. However, it is worth noting that the name *frigedene* in a recently discovered charter of AD 963 means 'Valley of Frīg', and indicates that the modern Fridon in Derbyshire was named after her (Brooks *et al.* 1984:150–1). The puzzling distribution of pagan names may be because those that survive were outside the immediate area controlled by the local ruler and the first Christian priests, who would object to names of pagan significance (Gelling 1961:20). Absence of place-names of this kind in certain areas of the country does not necessarily mean that the cults of the gods were unknown there.

In Scandinavian countries there are place-names associated with the main gods, Odin, Thor and Tyr, together with Freyr and Njord, the fertility deities, and lesser-known gods who may have been of importance before the Viking Age, such as Ull. Once more, the distribution raises problems. Odin names are rare in some areas and totally lacking in Iceland. Various suggestions have been made to account for this, such as the arrival of his cult late into the north, or the sinister nature of the god, leading to avoidance of his name. However, in Denmark some Odin names have survived, in particular three examples linked with *vi*, denoting a shrine or holy place, of which Odense is the outstanding example. No other god's name in Denmark is linked with *vi*, and Hald suggests that this marks Odin's importance as the warrior god worshipped by kings and aristocrats in the last period before Christianity (Hald 1965:252). Two of the *vi* names are near Lejre, and may have been on the royal estate there. The lack of Odin names in Iceland, where there was no royal dynasty, is consistent with this. One isolated example of an Odin name in northern England is *Othenesberg* (Hill of Odin), recorded in a document of 1119 for the hill now known as Roseberry Topping in the North Riding of Yorkshire. This conical hill is a striking landmark; it is not a burial mound or artificial hill like some of those in England named after the Anglo-Saxon Woden, such as Wodnesbeorg for a long barrow in Wiltshire. However, it is possible that the naming after Odin in Yorkshire was the result of late legends about the god rather than of a cult place dedicated to him in pre-Christian times by early Viking settlers. Both Woden and Odin apparently continued to be associated with high places and graves after the coming of Christianity.

Another feature hard to explain is the presence of Ti names in Denmark, where his name is next in popularity to that of Thor, although it is rare in Norway or Sweden. In Denmark as in England many place-names have now been rejected as evidence for the existence of pre-Christian cults (Hald 1969:50ff.). Undoubtedly the most popular god was Thor, to judge by the number of places called after him throughout Scandinavia, while his name forms part of many personal names of both men and women. Nevertheless, the popularity of Thor may lead us astray. An English example of this is Thurstaston in the Wirral, an area settled by Scandinavians in the Viking Age. Here a huge stone on a stretch of heathland is locally known as Thor's Stone, and children and readers of popular guidebooks are likely to be told that Thurstaston was named after the god Thor and that human victims were formerly sacrificed on the stone, a theory apparently due to a confident pronouncement by Sir James Picton, the Liverpool antiquarian (N. Ellison 1955:78). However, the name comes from Thorstein, presumably one of the Scandinavian settlers, and the last syllable is from *tun*, indicating not a stone but the enclosure for a house. The stone itself is a piece of soft red sandstone left behind by quarrymen when they removed the harder stone round it.

Examples of later folk-traditions influencing place-names can sometimes be helpful, however, and such names are often found in Ireland. In Munster, for instance, there are tales from the end of the last century of a supernatural woman called Áine, said to inhabit a certain mound, a little hill called Cnoc Áine. On St John's Eve, the midsummer festival celebrated by bonfires, bunches of burning hay and straw were carried round it and then taken to the fields to bring a blessing to the cattle. It is said that one year a group of girls lingered on the hill, until finally Áine herself appeared and politely asked them to leave, since 'they wanted to have the hill to themselves'. To explain what she meant, she let them look through a ring, and they saw the hill crowded with a host of fairy beings previously invisible (Fitzgerald 1879–80:189ff.). In such tales we have an echo of traditions linked with the land itself, inhabited by supernatural beings who could bring good fortune if treated with respect, even if, as in this case, the link with a particular hill or spring may not go back to pre-Christian times. Although the names of goddesses have left less imprint on place-names than those of male deities, we can find compensation for this in the large number of local legends in Scotland and Ireland, as well as Norway and Sweden, associated with hills, preserving the memory of Otherworld female beings. If used with a full knowledge of their limitations, place-names may offer essential clues to the existence of pre-Christian cults.

Another place to search for the names of past gods is in personal names recorded in written sources or inscriptions. We know little of the god Ull, occasionally mentioned in the literature, whose name is found in a few place-names in Norway and Sweden in two forms, *Ullr* and *Ullinn*. The name (o)*wlþuþewaR* was inscribed in runes on a scabbard chape found at Thorsbjerg in Denmark, dated about AD 300. This has been interpreted as Servant of Ull, which would indicate knowledge of the god at an early date. Ull's name is related to the Gothic word for glory, *wulþus*, and it has been thought that he was an early sky god. However, he is also said in early Icelandic poetry to be the god of skis, which suggests links with northern Scandinavia, and there is little trace of his cult in Denmark. The name 'Servant of Ull' is not in itself a definite proof that the man who bore it was a worshipper of the god, and indeed it is hard to be sure what naming after a god implies. While there were some places named after Odin, he was rarely remembered in personal names, unless some name like Hrafn (Raven) was used as a substitute, because of the association of the raven with the god. The name Othinkarl has indeed been found on four Danish runestones as well as in a Norwegian inscription and again in a Swedish document, and it has been suggested that the use of 'karl' here might signify 'Odin's man'. On the other hand, two bishops of the late tenth and early eleventh century bore this name, possibly because both belonged to aristocratic families in which a link with Odin was an established tradition (Hald 1971:38), and if such a name denoted a dedicated follower of the god, it seems unlikely that it would have been retained by Church dignitaries soon after the conversion. Thor names also present problems. Out of about a thousand names recorded in *Landnámabók*, of Icelandic settlers and their families, about one-quarter have Thor as an element, showing that such names were extremely popular in the Viking Age. Thor names are not, however, found in earlier heroic sources, and are rare in Germanic territory on the continent, supporting the theory that the cult of the god was mainly a northern one.

New fashions in names do not, however, always come from new cults. Such evidence as we have linking Thor names with the worship of the god comes from fairly late sources, such as *Eyrbyggja Saga*, where a youth called Grim is said to be renamed Thorgrim and to become a priest of Thor, and Thorolf of Mostur who set up a temple to Thor is said originally to have been named Hrolf. One explanation suggested for the lack of early Thor names is that those with the prefix *ás* (from *áss*, god), such as Asmund and Aslak, might indicate the influence of Thor, frequently called Ása-Thor in the literature. There is an example of a man called Asbjorn in *Landnámabók* (M, 8; H, 302:346) dedicating his land to Thor and calling it *Thorsmørk*, but this is hardly sufficient to prove the theory correct. Only one name with such a prefix (*Ansu-*) is found in runic inscriptions and no examples are known from early place-names, so Hald concludes that Thor names were a fairly late development in Scandinavia (1971:50). On the other hand, the name Thorir is found reasonably early, and it has been suggested that in its earlier form (*Wihar*) it might mean Priest of Thor. Clearly, it is difficult to establish anything about cults of the gods on place-names alone, but in conjunction with other evidence they may provide valuable information.

DIVINE NAMES AND TITLES

One further way to discover the nature of the northern deities is to study the names by which they were known. Unfortunately, there is often considerable disagreement as to how a name should be interpreted. The important but elusive Celtic god Lug bears a name generally taken to mean 'shining' or 'brilliant', and we are told in the literature that his face shone. Many earlier scholars assumed, therefore, that he was a sun god. However, another school of thought derived his name from the word for raven, since coins and medallions of the Roman period showed the youthful genius of the city of Lyon, presumed to be Lug, accompanied by ravens. A Greek writer also stated that *lugus* in the language of the Gauls meant raven, possibly because it resembled the Greek word for 'black' (Ross 1967:249 ff.); again the evidence is insufficient to be convincing. One of the stock epithets applied to Lug, *lambdada* (of the Long Arm), is ambiguous, possibly referring to his famous spear or to his wide powers as a ruler. The identification of Lug with Mercury (p. 79) hardly fits in with the conception of a sun god, although the bringing of light and warmth could have been one of Lug's many functions. He was also called the Many-Skilled, indicating diverse powers. Sometimes it seems as if he was regarded as a triad of deities, for there are references to his two brothers of the same name, and in inscriptions his name is sometimes in the plural form (Sjoestedt 1982:57). Thus, while his name contributes something to our understanding of his character, it leaves many problems unsolved.

Another of the main Irish gods, the Dagda, has a name meaning the Good God, a title rather than a personal name. It signifies a being of many powers once again, 'generous in giving' rather than 'good' in any moral sense; he was famed for his hospitality in the tales, and other titles he bore were 'Father of All', and 'Mighty One of Great Knowledge'. In view of this, it is a little surprising to find him represented as an undignified, pot-bellied individual, armed with a primitive club and clad in a short tunic and hood like a worker on the land. However, he was clearly a dynamic figure, with abundance of energy and a huge appetite. This formidable character who mates with giantesses seems, like the Scandinavian Thor whom in some ways he resembles, to embody the disturbing power of the ancient gods, still remembered in tales told in Christian times.

The complications surrounding the names of divine beings are illustrated by those of Odin. In one poem of the Poetic Edda, *Grímnismál*, a list of 47 names is given, and others may be found elsewhere to make a total of about 170 (Falk 1924). Some of these names are comprehensible in the light of surviving tales and legends, such as 'God of the Hanged', since hanging was the traditional method by which victims, human and animal, were said to be sacrificed to the god. Some of his names are related to his power on the battlefield, such as 'Father of Victory' and 'Raven God', since slaughter in war provided food for the ravens preying on corpses. Other names are in keeping with his reputation as a wanderer through the world in disguise, such as *Vegtamr* (Roadwise), or *Grimnir* (Masked One); Karl and Greybeard recall his appearance as an old man in a cloak. The name Odin is derived from the adjective *óðr*, meaning 'raging' or 'intoxicated', and the German forms Wodan/Wutan come from **woþu*, meaning 'madness' or 'fury'. Adam of Bremen's comment on the god's name was *id est furor*. As in the case of Ull, the name of the god is found in two forms, *Óðinn* and *Óðr*.

A god may be referred to by a title rather than a name, and a powerful deity is likely to have many titles, which may be used in inscriptions as well as literary sources, and are sometimes mistaken for names of separate deities. In Icelandic skaldic verse we find descriptive phrases for the deities in the form of kennings, which rely on a knowledge of myths. In his Prose Edda Snorri has much to say about the composition of skaldic verse, and when he describes gods or goddesses he often turns to kennings used in such verses for his information. In a kenning, the name of a person, place or object is not given directly, but replaced by a statement of its relationship to some person or thing. A skaldic poet would not call a spade a spade, but might refer to it as 'sword of the soil', or 'ladle of earth', or even 'ladle of Thor's mother', whose name was Jord, 'Earth'. Thus kennings might be as complex as modern crossword-puzzle clues. A king or leader could be alluded to as 'hater of the fire-bed of the serpent', as was Harald Hardradi in a poem by Thjodolf Arnorsson quoted in *Heimskringla* (*Haralds Saga Sigurðarsonar* 5, verse 81). 'The bed' and 'the fire of the serpent' are two familiar kennings for gold, because gold shines like a fire, and serpent-dragons were said to lie on golden treasure in burial mounds, while 'the hater of gold' means a leader who does not keep wealth for himself but shares it among his followers, so that the phrase could denote a generous leader. At their best, kennings can be surprising and creative, providing rich imagery to add depth to a poem; at their worst, they are boring conceits and exercises in ingenuity. Their importance for the study of Norse mythology is that they may throw light on lost or incomplete myths or mythical beings. The kenning quoted above is based on heroic legend; the famous serpent guarding treasure was Fafnir, slain by the hero Sigurd the Volsung to gain an enormous treasure. Thus without using a dull simile, and employing very few words, the poet compares Harald in his youth to a courageous prince of the past by recalling this well-known story. There might also be a touch of humour here, since Harald was known to be greedy for gold and to show great skill in amassing it.

Women described in kennings are usually represented as goddesses, valkyries or norns, and a study of such kennings is one way of learning more about such beings. In a tenth-century poem, Kormak, a pre-Christian poet, described the girl he loved as the Gunna of the sun of the sea (Turville-Petre 1976:47–8). Gunna is a valkyrie name, from a word meaning 'battle', which may be used in personal names such as Thorgunna, although we are told nothing about Gunna herself in mythological sources. 'The sun of the sea' is another kenning for gold, which is also called 'fire', 'gleam' or 'light of the sea' or 'of rivers'. This might be based on a memory of lost treasure-ships, or of gold thrown into the water as an offering. The meaning of the kenning 'goddess of gold' is a woman, since women wear gold as ornaments. Kormak often uses sea-images in his love poetry, which is far from being artificial verse-making and ranks among the best examples of skaldic poetry that have survived. In this particular poem he declares that the girl he loves is worth more than all the world's wealth, and while the image of ever-moving light on the sea is used to express his own wanderings, she is said to be held in his constant heart, and in a further kenning is described as 'tree of riches'.

In this case we have the name of a goddess, presumably of a minor kind, and such kennings often record such names, and occasionally tell us something of the attributes of a goddess. Skadi, for instance, is said to have been the wife of the god Njord, one of the fertility deities associated with seas and lakes, who was of some importance in the Viking Age. However, she was forced to part from him because she belonged to the mountains and he to the sea-shore, and they could never dwell happily together. Skadi is called 'divinity of skis' in two early skaldic poems. Snorri says of her: 'She goes about much on skis and with a bow and arrow and shoots wild creatures' (*Gylfaginning* 22). The mysterious god Ull, thought to be important before the Viking Age, is also said to be a god of skis, and said to use a bow and to hunt. On the basis of this it has been suggested that the two are a pair of deities connected with the north and with winter, and some have gone further and claimed that Skadi was originally a male deity, as her name is a possible masculine form, or even tried to identify her with Ull. She is one of the few goddesses, however, about whom we are told a fair amount in the literature, and the reference to her holy places (*véum ok vǫngum*) in *Lokasenna* 51 indicates that she was of some importance. It seems possible that her cult flourished in Halogaland, since she shows characteristics of the Saami, who were renowned for skiing, shooting with the bow and hunting; her separation from Njord might point to a split between her cult and that of the Vanir in this region, where Scandinavians and Saami were in close contact (Davidson 1990). Her name, unfortunately, gives little help; it might be related to the noun *skaði*, meaning 'harm', or to Gothic *skadus*/OE *sceadu*, 'shadow'. In this case, the early kennings indicate certain characteristics of this goddess which might have gone unnoticed.

The main Scandinavian deities are often described in kennings. Snorri in *Skáldskaparmál* 1 states that one god may be named in terms of another: 'when we say the Tyr of victory or the Tyr of the hanged, or the Tyr of cargoes, these are terms for Odin'. The connection of Odin with victory in battle and with hanged victims is well attested, but the name 'God of Cargoes' is more surprising; however, Snorri in *Ynglinga Saga* 6 claims that Odin found treasure in the earth for his followers and brought them wealth, and this is another characteristic shared with the Roman Mercury (p. 79). A point worth noting in Snorri's statement quoted above is that Tyr could have his name used as an equivalent for 'god' in a kenning; this seems to indicate that he had some special significance in early tradition, although by the late Viking Age he plays little part in the myths. Tyr's name is also used for a warrior in kennings: in a humorous poem said to be composed in Vinland in *Eiríks Saga rauða* 9, in which the poet refers to himself as a warrior, he uses the kenning: 'the Tyr who demands the hat of Bild'. Bild is one of Odin's names, and his hat is a helmet, so the poet is a fighting man ready for conflict. If Tyr were in early times associated with battle and identified with Mars (p. 47) this might help to explain the part he plays in kennings.

Some kennings simply state the relationship of two or more deities, as when Thor is called 'Son of Odin'. Since this link is found in early kennings, the idea of Odin as his father cannot be a late invention by Snorri. Other kennings refer to Jord (Earth) as Thor's mother, indicating a link between sky god and earth goddess. When Thor is called the father of Modi and Magni, whose names mean 'strength' and 'anger', it seems that we simply have personified qualities of the god, and the same is true of his daughter Thrud (strength), while he is also said to dwell at Thrudheim. Other Thor kennings, such as 'Possessor of Mjollnir', his famous hammer-axe, can be understood from the recorded myths, as may also such kennings as 'Defender of Asgard' and 'Defender of Midgard', since he protected the world of the gods and the inhabited earth, as well as those that describe him as the slayer of various giants.

The kennings certainly create problems, but it is essential to study them if any serious attempt to understand the myths and the nature of the various northern deities is to be made. Fortunately, systematic lists of kennings according to subject have been made available by Meissner (1921), which makes it possible to trace those used of supernatural beings, and to discover which were used by the early poets. Since many of the kennings come from the pre-Christian period, they can, like early works of art, give us a direct link with the Scandinavian world-picture before the coming of Christianity.

When we survey the different kinds of evidence that can extend our knowledge of the gods and their significance in daily life, it soon becomes apparent that we are losing our guide-lines and straying away from the neat, rational picture of deities that tends to be given in popular mythologies. This is generally based on the myths that have come down to us, but only after simplifying these and avoiding their obscurities and contradictions. It is essential to realize how tangled the web of beliefs and traditions concerning the gods must in fact have been, and this has been apparent in attempts to come to terms with the divine world pictured on the carved stones or remembered in poetic imagery. Certainly without the background of the northern myths themselves it would be hard to fit the surviving evidence into any sort of coherent pattern, and it is to these therefore that we must now turn.

3

The Gods in the Myths

> The Germans do not think it in keeping with the divine majesty to confine gods within walls or to portray them in the likeness of any human countenance. Their holy places are woods and groves, and they apply the names of deities to that hidden presence which is seen only by the eye of reverence.
>
> (Tacitus, *Germania* 9: trans. Mattingly)

SOURCES OF THE MYTHS

What Tacitus noted of the Germans of the first century AD has a convincing ring, and is borne out by the crude yet impressive wooden figures surviving from both Germanic and Celtic territory. Such figures served as symbols for the divine powers without any attempt to represent them as either handsome or monstrous beings; they existed as vague symbols of those 'hidden presences'. Animal or bird symbols might also represent the power and presence of divinities. Although anthropomorphic figures of gods were known in the northern Bronze Age, it was not until the Romans were established in Gaul and Britain that the new fashion of depicting deities in the form of men and women gradually became popular among the native population (p. 45). Stories of the gods, however, must have been told from very early times, and as these developed the deities were likely to take on more human shapes and characteristics, while retaining majestic or demonic powers. Thus Thor is described as a huge red-bearded man with flaming eyes and a quick temper, and the Dagda is a robust, pot-bellied figure in shabby clothes but of enormous virility and strength. Irish goddesses who give birth to divine offspring in rivers are represented as daughters of Irish kings, while the divine Freyja is something between a lusty giantess and a fair maiden whose white arms light up the darkness of the underworld. They are not sentimentalized and do not become amiable figures, although they may be gift-bearers and bring great benefits to mankind; on the contrary, they remain ruthless, unpredictable and prone to take offence, so that it is dangerous to encounter them.

This picture of the deities is not due to hostile Christian influence; it is characteristic of the earliest surviving material, although Christian writers may stress the less admirable features of the pagan gods, and represent them as corrupt or stupid. Humour in tales of the deities seems to have existed from the beginning, and is found in mythological tales from many areas of the world. In northern Europe, this may take the form of broad comedy, as in the poem *Thrymskviða* when Thor disguises himself as the fair Freyja and gets entry into the hall of the giants arrayed as a goddess bride under a veil. He shocks even these barbarous characters by the gusto with which he demolishes a large portion of the bridal feast, not contenting himself with the dainties prepared for the women, but devouring also roast oxen and salmon in huge quantities, while he out-drinks the stoutest of the wedding guests. Yet this is more than a crude caricature of the powerful thunder-god, for skilful reminders of his divine power and energy are given at every turn. So terrible are his fiery eyes seen through the bridal veil that the prospective bridegroom retreats the length of the hall in alarm when he attempts to steal a kiss, and once the god gets his hands on his hammer again – the object of the whole charade – he shatters the skulls of the giants round the table and leaves them dead. This is no comic Thor set up by an anti-pagan poet as a target for mockery, but the ancient thunder-god constantly threatened by the forces of chaos and using his great hammer-axe to defend gods and men from attack (p. 80).

The sources of the Norse myths are varied, and attempts to interpret incomplete or confused texts often frustrating. There are references to lost tales and occasional snatches of somewhat obscure narratives about the gods in early Icelandic skaldic verse of the pre-Christian period, and poems of the Poetic Edda which deal with mythological subjects. Eddic poems are not always narrative poems, since a number consist of questions and answers exchanged between two supernatural beings; such compositions must have been popular in the Viking Age among those skilled in lore about the gods and their world.

We have also tales of gods and goddesses in the prose literature, some clearly late, others likely to be based on earlier sources. A number of the myths have been collected and retold in the Prose Edda of Snorri Sturluson, and in many cases they come from poems still extant, so that we can compare the two versions, but there are others whose sources are lost. A few more stories are included in *Ynglinga Saga*, the first section of Snorri's *Heimskringla*. There are some further tales, mainly about Odin, in the early books of the Danish history of Saxo Grammaticus, which he had heard or read in the late twelfth century, and some of these are not found elsewhere, while others are earlier than surviving Icelandic versions of the same tales. Saxo, however, was a sophisticated Christian writer, who had received a modern education at one of the new universities, and cannot be wholly relied on to pass on an old tale in the form in which he received it. Snorri, on the other hand, wanted to retell the tales as they were found in early poetry, so that young poets could understand allusions to the myths. He is not likely to invent or alter material deliberately, although he may yield to the temptation to make slightly better sense of an obscure source. Each individual tale has its own problems and complex links with other sources; there may be signs of Christian or foreign influence, or links with myths outside Scandinavia. The tales need to be seen also as part of a larger cosmic background, often neglected in popular collections of the myths. We have no detailed, consistent account of this setting, and it has to be reconstructed from hints and references found here and there.

In early Irish literature the mythological material is more limited, but because of the wealth of stories recorded, there are many indications of traditions concerning gods and goddesses and their divine world. In some of the heroic tales they are represented as human figures from royal families ruling the separate kingdoms of Ireland in the early Middle Ages. The tales may contain poems, some of which are lyrical descriptions of the Otherworld, while others are speeches, sometimes by supernatural beings. There is also mythological material in local legends, and in the tales of journeys to supernatural realms where time and the ordinary conditions of human life are no longer applicable. The tales were recorded in the monasteries, and sometimes attempts were made to fit them into a biblical framework so that much of the original content is lost, and it may be hard to find any purpose behind some apparently pointless narrative. In a study of Christian influence in Irish sagas and other prose works of the early medieval period, McCone (1990) stresses the importance of the introduction of Christian tradition or the deliberate use of allegory in many of the tales. His emphasis on the unlikelihood of pre-Christian tradition surviving unchanged through centuries of Christian education is in general agreement with the present attitude towards the Icelandic sagas. Nevertheless, the survival of oral tradition in both cultures, together with a strong antiquarian interest in the past, makes it possible for some memories to survive, even though deliberately edited from a Christian viewpoint. Clearly, each separate text must be treated with great caution.

Traditions of early battles in which the gods take part have survived in a confused form in Ireland; we have the accounts of the two battles of Mag Tuired, in which Lug and the Dagda and other possible gods appear (p. 72). There are also pre-Christian traditions in the collection of tales about Finn, leader of a band of hunters and warriors in the forest; these became popular from about the twelfth century onwards and contain material that differs from that of the heroic tales told at court. In addition, there are collections of twelfth-century material about local places and past events, known as the *Dindsenchus*, which have been described as 'mythological geography' (Sjoestedt 1982:12). They seek to explain various place-names, while the *Lebor Gabala* (Book of Invasions) gives an account, half-way between antiquarian history and fantasy, of the various invasions of Ireland in the remote past. In the twelfth century various manuscript compilations were made in Wales, but this material is less rewarding from the mythological standpoint than the collections made in Ireland and Scandinavia at that period. Some mythological traditions can be recognized in the prose tales making up the *Mabinogion*, but these are no more than fragments recast in skilfully wrought tales, and the Arthurian romances similarly can only give us fugitive glimpses of possible lost material.

In any case, the myths seem to have developed separately in the various Celtic areas, so that painstaking attempts to fit them into a coherent religious pattern by taking isolated items of evidence and tracing similarity in names are not very rewarding. Further progress must depend on detailed and disciplined study of individual sources. It is proposed here to deal mainly with the main northern myths that appear likely to go back into the pre-Christian past. A favourite approach to these myths is to review the evidence for the main deities, the dates and nature of the various sources, and any philological clues that seem relevant. It is important also, however, to consider the character of a deity in a wider context, as we find it in the realms of early literature and art, and to assess the importance of the cult for rulers, warriors, travellers and farmers, and in the life of the community. In many cases we are left with the names of supernatural beings for which no evidence of a cult exists, so that we have to consider the problems of literary traditions about the deities on the one hand, and their influence on the lives of men and women on the other. The myths under consideration in this chapter come from literary tradition, but in many cases it is evident that visual imagery from early art has to be considered along with them.

THE DIVINE WORLD

Mythical geography is found in the Scandinavian tradition, as in the Irish, although here it is not a case of listing localities associated with the Otherworld, but rather of attempts to map the Otherworld itself. The mythological poems of the Edda of the question-and-answer type name many places out of this world where cosmic events have taken place or will take place at the end of time, as well as obscure characters who may be minor gods or giants or supernatural animals who have played some part in these events or will do so in the future. Thus it is asked where the last battle between gods and giants will be fought (*Vafþrúðnismál* 18) and the reply is that it will be on *Vígríðr* (Field of Battle), although in another poem (*Fáfnismál* 15) an island with a different name is given. In *Grímnismál* names of the dwellings of various gods are mentioned. Odin's hall, Valhalla (Hall of the Slain), is well known because it plays so large a part in images of warfare and death, but the significance of other halls, like Yewdale (*Ydalar*) where Ull is said to dwell, or Folkfield (*Folkvangr*) where Freyja allots seats to the dead, has been lost. The poems also have many allusions to rivers in the underworld, and in the lands of gods and giants. For instance, one river called Fearful (*Slíðr*) is mentioned in *Vǫluspá* (36), flowing through poison dales near where Loki lies in his bonds, bearing weapons in its current, and such a river seems also to have been known to Saxo Grammaticus (Davidson 1980:35). In Snorri's account in *Gylfaginning* of Hermod's ride to Hel to reach the dead Balder, we have an impressive account of a journey through vast spaces of gloom and darkness, which at one point is lit up by a bridge with a thatched roof of bright gold which spans the river *Giǫll* (Resounding), and is guarded by a maiden called Modgud, who directs him on his way to the realm of the dead.

Neither bridge, river nor maiden is mentioned elsewhere in early literature, although Giǫll Bridge (*Gjallarbrú*) is remembered in the Norwegian ballad *Draumkvaede* which deals with a vision of the Otherworld and the road to be taken by the dead (Liestøl 1946:36).

Such a wealth of obscure names indicates that there was a whole body of lore connected with the worlds of gods and giants, and it is interesting to speculate as to how it came to be built up. There is little evidence for an established priesthood of the gods in Scandinavia, but there are references to wise men at the courts of kings who gave counsel, interpreted dreams, and foretold the future, and they may have contributed to the background of the myths. It is also possible that poets made an intellectual game of inventing such names. De Vries (1933:97) draws attention to a question near the end of *Hymiskviða* (38), the poem describing Thor's fishing for the Serpent: 'Who out of those who relate tales of the gods (*goðmǫlugar*) can tell it better?' He suggests that this term, not found elsewhere, refers to a professional class responsible for relating myths, and giving, so to speak, the approved version.

A possible parallel to the Scandinavian examples may be found in the accounts of visits to fabulous lands in Irish literature, known as *echtrai* or *immrama* (Dumville 1976). The former may be roughly defined as accounts of journeys by human beings to a supernatural realm, either by a voyage across the sea or by entry into a fairy mound (Mac Mathuna 1985:255). The *immram* is a voyage to an island, largely ecclesiastical in inspiration, although parts may be derived from secular literature, but it is not always possible to make a clear-cut distinction between the two (McCone 1990:79). The *immrama* may be regarded as frame-tales, for once the framework of a visit to an island of marvels became popular, it was easy to find new ways to fill it. The original idea of a supernatural realm, from which Otherworld beings came to visit kings and heroes and sometimes to take them back with them, must be pre-Christian, but in many of the tales that have come down to us there are signs of Christian imagery and learned speculation. The ingenuity of poets and story-tellers did not end with the coming of Christianity, and it is not always easy to distinguish between the old lore and the new. The existence of this perplexing mass of details must not be forgotten; it is all too easy to select a few that seem to make sense and to ignore all the rest.

Certain features concerning the world of the gods, however, seem reasonably well established. One is the importance of its centre, represented in local sacred places by a tree or a pillar, a mound or a great stone. The central tree of the gods had more than one name, but in the poetry of the Edda it is most often given as Yggdrasil, thought to mean Horse of Ygg, a name for Odin; if this is the correct interpretation it may refer to Odin hanging on the tree, as described in *Hávamál*. In the Irish *Dindsenchus* there is mention of huge trees that in the past marked sacred places, and that were linked with the choice and fate of legendary kings (Watson 1981). In Asgard itself, Yggdrasil marked the place of assembly for the gods, where decisions were made affecting them and mankind. The fruit of the tree was linked with human births, and was also a source of healing. Yggdrasil was said to grow and to be destroyed continually, as living creatures of the mythological world, hart, goat and squirrel, gnawed at it; this suggests that it symbolized the ever-changing existence of a kingdom or tribe, or indeed of human life on earth. Not only was it the centre of the kingdom of the gods, but also of a series of worlds making up the cosmos. Nine worlds are mentioned more than once, but never clearly specified. A possible list can be built up from one of the Edda poems, *Alvíssmál*, in which different terms for parts of the natural world such as sun, wind, clouds and sea, are said to be used by different classes of beings. I have suggested elsewhere (Davidson 1975:83) that the nine worlds might be those of Asgard and Vanaheim for the two races of gods, Midgard for mankind, Jotunheim for the giants, Alfheim for the elves, the world of dwarves in the earth, Hel for the dead, and, in the last two cases, possibly the world of the heroes in Valhalla and that of the most powerful gods who are named in the poem as the Holy or Mighty Ones. No doubt the identity of the nine varied from time to time as the emphasis changed or new imagery was introduced.

The representation of Yggdrasil as the centre of the nine worlds brings in a fresh complication, that of the conception of a tree rising through a number of worlds which is found in northern Eurasia and forms part of the shamanic lore shared by many peoples of this region. This seems to be a very ancient conception, perhaps based on the Pole Star, the centre of the heavens, and the image of the central tree in Scandinavia may have been influenced by it (Hultkranz 1990). Among Siberian shamans, a central tree may be used as a ladder to ascend the heavens (Eliade 1951:244 ff.). In Norse tradition, however, it is not clear whether the various worlds are one above the other or grouped round the tree. There are allusions to worlds under the roots of the tree, while the realm of the gods may be pictured in the sky, with a rainbow bridge connecting it with other worlds. Those who have tried to produce a convincing diagram of the Scandinavian cosmos from what we are told in the sources have only added to the confusion. The conception of an eagle at the top of the tree and of the World Serpent curled round its roots echoes various cosmologies in Asia which may have influenced Scandinavia from the north. On the other hand, we know that the Germanic peoples in central Europe worshipped their gods in forest clearings, and that the sky god in particular was associated with the oak (H.M. Chadwick 1900), so that a central tree was a natural symbol for them also.

A characteristic of the Otherworld tree in Irish tradition is that it bears blossoms and fruit of gold and silver, making music when shaken and healing sickness and despair. It is usually pictured as an apple tree, although the great trees of the past are sometimes described as bearing mixed fruit of apples, acorns and nuts. In a number of the tales describing journeys to the Otherworld, branches are brought by visitants to earth which bear gold or silver fruit, from which some of the fabulous trees of the past were said to have grown (Watson 1981). The land where such wonderful fruit trees grew was known as the Land of Youth or the Land of Promise, the Plain of Delight or other alluring names

(Dumville 1976:79 ff.). It was a place of happiness and beauty where sickness and decay were unknown, inhabited by lovely women who welcomed heroes from earth; it remained outside human time, so that what seemed a brief stay there might afterwards prove to have lasted for centuries.

Traces of a bright Otherworld with golden trees are discernible in Norse literature also; it is suggested, for instance, by some names for the dwellings of the gods (Davidson 1988:187), while golden apples were among the treasures of Asgard, preventing the gods from growing old (p. 73). The bright realm is sometimes contrasted with a dark and noisome place of death, haunted by serpents. This is perhaps an image of the grave; and the two opposed pictures may owe something to Christian teaching concerning heaven and hell, although again some elements here may go back to pre-Christian tradition. There is no consistent picture in Norse literary tradition of the fate of the dead, although the road to the Otherworld appears to have left vivid memories in the literature.

The magnificent poem *Vǫluspá*, usually dated to about AD 1000, is one of our main sources of knowledge for the creation and destruction of the worlds of gods and men, and also of Norse cosmography at the end of the pre-Christian period, as it was for Snorri. The unknown poet appears to be familiar with Christian traditions, although not necessarily of the Christian faith. Certainly he (or she) was surveying the lore of the gods at a time when the doom of the old religion seemed certain, and the familiar world-picture of past generations was rapidly being replaced by that offered by Christian teachers and missionaries.

In this poem the powerful gods Odin and Thor and a host of lesser deities are represented as dwelling together in Asgard, a stronghold surrounded by a wall and approached by a bridge guarded by Heimdall, watchman of the gods. The list of halls given in *Grímnismál* indicates a cluster of buildings roofed with gold, among which is Odin's hall, Valhalla. This has come to occupy a major place in any account of Norse religion, because of the emphasis on the many great kings and heroes who died in battle and went to join Odin, enjoying unending battle and feasting until the end of time. The arrival of a hero at Valhalla was a popular motif used on memorial stones erected in Gotland about the eighth century (p. 33). Valhalla was never the dwelling-place of the universal dead, but intended for outstanding heroes to support Odin in the final battle against giants and monsters, giving him a powerful reason for summoning them to his hall and bringing their careers on earth to a close. Somewhere not far from Asgard was Jotunheim, where dwelt the frost-giants who were the enemies of the gods, eager to rob them of their treasures, carry off the fair Freyja and the sun and moon, and destroy Asgard and the inhabited earth. It is less clear where the Vanir dwelt, since the chief gods, Freyr and Njord with a number of others, are represented along with the Æsir in Asgard, but it seems probable that it was in the underworld. There is certainly a link between the Vanir and the land-spirits who dwelt in mounds and hills and in water, supernatural beings who befriended some of the early settlers in Iceland (p. 119), and probably also between the Vanir and the Elves, who lived on in folk tradition as lesser beings. Most of the goddesses who became the wives of the gods came from the underworld, and were said to be the daughters of giants. The greatest of the goddesses was Freyja, sister of Freyr and daughter of Njord; she is a goddess of many names, and may originally have been the same as Frigg, the wife of Odin, since elsewhere in Germanic tradition we hear only of one goddess, Frija, who was the wife of the sky god (p. 108).

Once more it must be stressed that we are dealing with shifting and often confused traditions. In the Edda poem *Skírnismál*, for instance, Freyr or his messenger travels down into the underworld, a long and daunting journey, to seek out the fair maiden Gerd, the daughter of a fearsome giant. The journey takes him over high mountains, dark valleys and turbulent rivers, like the road to the Land of the Dead (Ellis 1943:178 ff.). The purpose of this wooing has been taken as the marriage of sky god with earth goddess, and Gerd is threatened with utter sterility and negation if she rejects Freyr's love. The unknown editor of the manuscript book of poems in which *Skírnismál* is found has linked this theme with Asgard in his introduction by making Freyr seat himself on the seat of Odin, from which he can look out over all the worlds, so that he catches sight of Gerd in the underworld and is overcome with desire for her. This may be seen as an example of how separate themes have been linked together in the twelfth and thirteenth centuries in an endeavour, like that of Snorri in his Prose Edda, to create a rational whole out of disconnected fragments. The earlier poets and story-tellers would have been unlikely to demand such accuracy and consistency as is required by the modern academic mind.

Thus we are left with glimpses of a rich and complex world of gods and other supernatural beings, with entries and exits linking it to the everyday world known to us. It has been coloured by the imagination of poets and the teaching of wise men and women concerning the supernatural world, and continued to furnish inspiration to many poets and story-tellers over the centuries. Some scholars, like the Swedish Rydborg in the last century, have persevered in the hope that a convincing structure could be built up from the scattered clues, accepting all as of equal value; but this is a hopeless quest, based on the erroneous assumption that a set mythology once existed that was logical and tidy in every detail, and remained so over a long period. All that can be claimed is that certain conceptions concerning the Otherworld were generally accepted, and that the most powerful myths were enacted against this vivid but confused background.

MYTHS OF THE DIVINE COMMUNITY

One myth found in both Germanic and Celtic traditions is that of a war in the beginning between two companies of deities, possibly those of the sky opposed to those of earth and sea. In Scandinavian tradition the two opposing sides were those of the Æsir and the Vanir, while in Irish tradition the Túatha Dé first defeated the Fir Bolg and then the Fomorians, the latter led by a former king of the gods deposed for his meanness and tyranny. The first battle was a victory for the gods and ended in a truce, with Ireland divided between them. The second battle, described in greater detail, was one in which the Fomorians displayed powerful magical skills and the gods had to meet them with both force and spells. At this point Lug, the Many-Skilled, became their leader, and they achieved victory, because those slain on their own side were brought back to life by immersing them in the Well of Regeneration, and Lug himself slew their chief opponent, Balor of the Evil Eye, with a stone from his sling. These are described as the two battles of Mag Tuired, which some think was derived from an earlier account of one battle (Gray 1980–1:196). Points of importance are the truce that ended the first battle, the various institutions established among the people as a result, and the emphasis on the four treasures of the gods, which were the stone of Fal, the spear of Lug, the sword of Núadu and the cauldron of the Dagda. In her study of the myth, Gray (1980–1:184) emphasized that here we are concerned with the establishment of society and its periodic regeneration.

In Scandinavian tradition as we have it in the poem *Vǫluspá* and the account in *Ynglinga Saga* 4, there is little information about battles (though Snorri clearly implies there was more than one), but we are told that this was the first war in the world, beginning when Odin hurled his spear. It ended in an agreement by which both sides exchanged hostages, so that Freyr and Njord came to dwell with the Æsir. One important result was the creation of the divine mead of inspiration. It began when the gods all spat into a bowl as a sign of unity, and from the divine spittle created a wise giant, Kvasir, who could answer all questions. However, he was killed by two malicious dwarves, who let his blood flow into three vats and mixed it with honey to make mead. This was the drink bringing inspiration and wisdom, but they were forced to give it up to a giant named Suttung, whose parents they had killed, when he threatened to drown them. Thus in poetry the treasured drink might be described as 'blood of Kvasir', or 'ship of the dwarves' (since it saved them from a watery death). Suttung shut up the mead within a mountain, but Odin found a way to reach it, boring a hole in the rock and crawling in in serpent form. He then persuaded the giant's daughter to let him take three drinks of the mead after three nights of love-making, and having swallowed it he flew back to Asgard in eagle-form and spewed it out into vessels that the gods had made ready to receive it. This part of the tale is depicted on one of the Gotland stones from Lärbro, in Stora Hammars (Lindqvist 1941:I, fig. 85; II, 83 ff.), so that it was known as early as the eighth century (Figure 25). The idea of a divine drink is found in other mythologies, and the tradition of the sacred soma in Iranian sources is particularly interesting to compare with the Norse myth as related by Snorri in *Skáldskaparmál* and referred to in the poem *Hávamál* (Davidson 1978b:107).

Another myth concerning the gods as a group is that of the building of their stronghold. This also is one of the myths of the beginning, and is told in *Gylfaginning* 41. Snorri declares it a story worth telling, but we do not know his source. When the gods were setting up Asgard, a craftsman offered to build a wall round it, as a defence against the giants, and to complete his work in a year and a half, by the first day of summer, or forfeit any payment. If he succeeded, he

Figure 25 Odin returns with magic mead, on memorial stone from Lärbro, St Hammars, Gotland (after Nylen).

was promised Freyja for his wife and the sun and moon besides. The gods thought that he could never finish in so short a time, since he was to have no other builders to help him, but he was assisted by his powerful and sagacious horse, which moved the stones without difficulty and did twice as much as his master. Three days before the time was up, he had almost reached the gateway and ended the wall, and the gods were appalled. As on other occasions, they were saved by the cunning of Loki, who took on the form of a mare and lured away the giant's stallion. The work was left incomplete, the smith flew into a mighty rage, and was slain by Thor's hammer, as he recognized him as a hostile giant. One result of this was a splendid stronghold for the gods, and another a colt produced by Loki in his mare-form; this grew into the wonderful eight-legged horse of Odin.

Another tale of a contest between gods and giants is that of the theft of the golden apples that enabled the gods to retain perpetual youth. Here we are fortunate in having a skaldic poem of the ninth or early tenth century, *Haustlǫng*, considerably earlier than the account in Snorri's *Skáldskaparmál* (Holtsmark 1949; Kiil 1959), giving us part of the story. As Snorri tells it, the three gods, Odin, Loki and Hoenir were on a journey together and became hungry. They took an ox from a herd nearby and set about roasting it, but the meat failed to cook. Then they saw a huge eagle on the tree above who offered to cook the meat if he might have his share. They agreed to this, but when the eagle carried off the greater part of the carcase, Loki struck it with a stick, whereupon the bird flew up into the air with the stick attached to him and Loki clinging desperately on to it. The giant Thjazi, as the eagle proved to be, refused to release Loki until he promised to bring to him the goddess Idun (possibly Freyja under another name) and her apples of youth. Loki enticed Idun out of Asgard so that the eagle could bear her away. Before long the gods developed wrinkles and grey hair, and when they discovered Loki's guilt they threatened him with death if he did not bring the goddess back. He borrowed Freyja's feather-coat and flew as a falcon to Jotunheim, changed Idun into a nut, and carried her back to Asgard. There the gods had prepared a heap of shavings to which they set fire as Thjazi came in pursuit of Loki in his eagle-form; his wings were singed, and he fell, to be killed in what Snorri declared to be a most famous slaying. There are few differences between Snorri's account and the early poem, which professes to describe pictures on a shield; it may be noted that Snorri makes specific reference to apples, while the poem refers only to the secret of youth known to Idun, and also that there is mention in the poem of flaming darts used to slay Thjazi, presumably the lightning of Thor. Snorri cannot, however, be accused of having changed or remodelled the tale to any great extent.

The gods again appear as a group in the myth of the binding of the wolf Fenrir. As Snorri tells it in *Gylfaginning* 24, the most dangerous of Loki's sinister offspring was a wolf cub, which was raised in Asgard, and which grew so huge and ferocious that only Tyr was bold enough to feed him. The gods tried to bind him, but every chain broke as soon as he exerted his mighty strength. Finally, Odin had a special chain forged from secret, invisible things, such as the roots of a mountain and the breath of a fish; this appeared to be a silken cord, but no force could break it. The wolf refused to have it round his neck unless one of the gods put a hand between his jaws as a pledge that the cord was as harmless as it looked. Tyr was the only one prepared to risk his hand, and he lost it when the wolf found the chain could not be broken, while the other gods laughed. Thus the wolf was bound, but Odin knew that he would break loose at Ragnarok, and that it was Fenrir who was fated to destroy him, as shown on a cross in the Isle of Man of about AD 1000 (p. 50). Tyr with his hand in the jaws of a wolf has been claimed to be recognizable on a group of bracteates of about the sixth century (p. 40).

Again, the gods are represented as a company in the account of Balder's funeral. The source for Snorri's description of this in *Gylfaginning* is not known, and it is possible that he is describing a picture here, or making use of some early poem which described one. Snorri retells the Balder story at some length, representing him as the divine son of Odin, loved by his mother Frigg, who did all she could to protect him. In the poem *Baldrs Draumar* ('Balder's Dreams') Balder had a series of ominous dreams, and Odin rode down into the underworld to discover what fate had been decreed for him. Snorri makes his death a result of the machinations of Loki and caused by a shaft of mistletoe, the only plant that had given no pledge to Frigg never to harm her son. Balder's death acts as a prelude to Ragnarok, the time when the ruling gods were destroyed and the earth, engulfed in flame, sank beneath the sea.

When the gods and goddesses assembled at Balder's funeral, they watched while he was placed on a funeral pyre on his ship, which was then sent out to sea. It is a vivid account, followed by two strange tales. First, a character called Hermod rode down to the realm of the dead to see if Balder could be brought back from death; Snorri calls him a son of Odin, but he rode Sleipnir and may originally have been Odin himself. Hel, the ruler of the land of the dead, declared that Balder could only return if everything on earth wept for him, but again Loki prevented this, appearing as a giantess in a cave who refused to join the others in their weeping. Then comes the account of the punishment the gods imposed on Loki, binding him under three great stones and leaving him with venomous snakes dropping poison from above. His wife helped him by catching most of the poison in a bowl, and this is apparently the scene carved on the Gosforth Cross in Cumbria in the Viking Age (p. 50).

The coming of Ragnarok is again something that concerns all the gods, since giant adversaries ride across the rainbow bridge and enter Asgard, and others come by sea with Loki, escaped from his bonds. In what may have been a separate tradition, the wolf, serpent and Loki himself all escape from the places where the gods have secured them and join in the attack. The poem *Vǫluspá* tells of a series of duels in which Odin, Thor, Tyr, Freyr and Heimdall fall, although their opponents also perish. In the scenario of the fall of the gods, however, it is Odin who remains in the centre of the picture.

Although Balder's name occasionally occurs in place-names, there is no clear evidence that he was ever worshipped as a god, and the origin of the Balder legend is one of the most tantalizing problems in Scandinavian mythology. According to Saxo, he was one of the warriors of Odin, and therefore like other famous champions known as his son, and he was killed by a rival warrior, Hother. Balder received aid from a group of supernatural women who seem to be valkyries, and was clearly under Odin's protection. Instead of the plant mistletoe, there was one special sword which could cause his death; Hother obtained it from the underworld and dealt Balder a fatal wound. The idea of a young god smitten down and lamented by all nature might come from some tradition associated with the fertility deities, or brought in from abroad, but the question remains unresolved. It is a good example of a tradition brilliantly retold by Snorri in the thirteenth century which has been accepted without question in most books on northern mythology and in Frazer's *Golden Bough*. There is general agreement, however, that Balder's death marks a final setback to the power of Odin, and leads on inevitably to Ragnarok and the fall of the gods.

The conception of a company of gods living together in Asgard appears well established in the religion of the Viking Age. The gods were honoured in a group at religious feasts, and several were mentioned together in oath formulas, while they could be appealed to as a group in cases of treachery and oath-breaking. In *Vǫluspá* there is a convincing picture of them establishing order and sitting as a council to deliberate and make judgements. Plural terms are used for the gods in the poetry: such as *Regin*, emphasizing their power to rule; and *Hǫpt* and *Bǫnd*, words referring to their power to bind. It may be noted that in the first century AD Tacitus refers to the Germans consulting or appealing to the gods as a group. There is no myth of a single creator god; in *Vǫluspá* three of them are said to co-operate in the creation of man.

The Irish sources also give a strong impression of a company of divine beings, the *Tuátha Dé Danann* (people or tribes of the goddess Dana). These inhabit a number of mounds or islands, or dwell under the sea, just as the various Scandinavian deities have separate dwellings but form a company united against the giants. There seems no possibility that the conception of the gods as a group developed late in the work of writers like Snorri. Indeed, the picture of a settled divine community, even if disturbed by quarrels and rivalries from time to time, is paralleled in many other mythologies throughout the world. There is also evidence for Scandinavians setting up a number of wooden figures to represent their gods, to whom they made offerings (p.94), and references to more than one image in pre-Christian shrines. As far back as we are able to go, there is evidence for organized worship of a group of deities, although separate gods might have their individual cults.

MYTHS OF ODIN

Odin appears in the northern myths in three main aspects, as ruler of the land of the dead, god of battle, and god of inspiration, magic and wisdom; his long list of names emphasizes these varied characteristics and powers. In the myths as we have them, he is Allfather, leader of the gods, some of whom are called his sons, the eldest being Thor, according to *Gylfaginning*. In Snorri's preface to the Prose Edda, however, he makes Odin a distant descendant of Thor, here represented as a prince from Troy who moved into the northern world. Once the urge to compile genealogies comes over a writer of the twelfth or thirteenth century, it seems that he moves on learned lines of his own and departs from oral tradition.

The myths representing Odin as the god of death are linked with his power to rule the battlefield and to award victory to whichever side he chooses. In his desire to bring great champions to Valhalla, he either comes to summon them himself or sends the valkyries, his female attendants, to escort them to the Otherworld when their time on earth is over. He shows great favour to many kings and heroes, such as Sigmund the Volsung, whose story is told in the late *Vǫlsunga Saga*, partly based on earlier heroic poems. In his youth Sigmund obtained a splendid sword from the god, when Odin as an old man in a cloak entered the hall of King Volsung and plunged it into the tree-trunk supporting the roof. None could draw it out except the young Sigmund, and from that time he was Odin's favoured warrior, until finally the same old man met him on the battlefield and shattered the sword with his spear.

Another king supported by Odin was Harald Wartooth of Denmark, who according to the Danish historian Saxo (VIII, 263) was instructed in battle strategy by the god and granted many victories; finally, however, at the battle of Bråvalla Odin took the place of his charioteer, and in spite of the old king's pleas flung him down and slew him with his own sword as he fell. Other tales of Odin's gifts and relentless withdrawal of luck in the end can be found in the literature, and he is more than once accused of faithlessness and treachery. In the tenth-century poem *Hákonarmál*, Odin is asked why he allows noble kings to fall in battle, and his reply is significant: 'The grey wolf watches the abodes of the gods.' Under the constant threat of Ragnarok, when the wolf will devour him, Odin must gather the finest champions to defend Asgard from the expected attack.

Tales of Odin's doings on earth are linked with his image as a divine supporter of kings, and this is partly responsible for the large part that he plays in the mythological literature, much of which must have been popular in royal halls. Valhalla was reserved for princely champions and warriors of outstanding renown, while the dead in general passed to the realm of Hel, personified as a giantess and said to be Loki's daughter. Odin knew the way down to the realm of death, and sometimes travelled there to learn what the future was to be, as in the poem *Baldrs Draumar*. Sometimes, like the Greek Hermes, he is the guide who conducts the dead to the Otherworld. In *Vǫlsunga Saga* he carries away the dead son of Sigmund in his boat, and in one poem, *Hárbarðsljóð*, he is represented as a ferryman.

There is no doubt that Odin in the myths displays certain shamanic characteristics, since the main function of the shaman is to journey in spirit to the Otherworld, consult the gods or the dead, and bring back the soul of someone threatened with death. It is usually on Sleipnir, his eight-legged horse, that Odin travels from one world to another, although when on earth he is usually said to walk in the guise of an old man with one eye, his face hidden by a hood or a broad-brimmed hat. The eight-legged horse is portrayed on Gotland stones of about the eighth century (p. 33). Like the shaman again, Odin could journey in animal- or bird-form, while his body lay in a trance (*Ynglinga Saga* 7), and in some early poems he travels as an eagle; again like the shaman, he receives news of happenings far away, brought to him by his two ravens. In the poetry their names are given as Thought and Memory (*Grímnismál* 20), a partial rationalization, but perhaps based on earlier tradition, since a pair of birds is found on bracteates well before the Viking Age. The image of Odin hanging on a tree and enduring torment in order to win mastery of the runes, as given in *Hávamál* (138), is also consistent with the initiation of a shaman through torture, death and resurrection before he can achieve his full powers.

Odin was seen as the god of ecstasy and inspiration. He could inspire warriors in battle to a state of berserk rage in which they feared nothing and felt no pain (Davidson 1988:79 ff.), and could also give command over words to poets and orators. The meaning of his names Wodan/Odin was 'fury', or 'madness', and this is in accordance with this side of his character. The emphasis on the mead of inspiration is strong in skaldic poetry; poets like Egil Skallagrimsson claimed to have drunk from it, and often refer to poetry as the gift of Odin, using a wealth of kennings. The story of the recovery of the mead from the giants, referred to earlier, seems likely to be an ancient one. Part of the gift of inspiration offered by Odin is that of wisdom and magic. He has knowledge of the future, gained through the power to visit other worlds, and this is much stressed in the mythological poems. In *Vafþrúðnismál*, in spite of the warnings of Frigg, he visits another ancient giant in pursuit of wisdom, although he risks death if he loses the question-and-answer game. As a practitioner of magic, Odin is supreme. Many spells associated with him in *Hávamál* are for use in battle, and he was famed for his power to free men from bonds, either material or psychological, and to bind his enemies. This destructive influence over the mind was the opposite of the gift of ecstasy which gave freedom from fear. The object of his sacrifice on the World Tree was to gain knowledge of runes, which were employed in divination ceremonies, and probably reddened with sacrificial blood (Davidson 1988:148, 153). There is a second tradition of how he gained knowledge by sacrifice, by giving one of his eyes to the guardian of the spring beneath the root of the World Tree in return for a drink of the water that could reveal hidden secrets. This guardian was the mysterious giant Mimir, who according to Snorri had his head cut off by the Vanir to whom he was sent as a hostage (*Ynglinga Saga* 4). The head was returned to Odin, who preserved it and consulted it in times of crisis. Some have assumed this to be a borrowing from Ireland, but the link between a speaking head and a well has interesting parallels in English folk tradition (Simpson 1962). In *Hávamál* Odin is represented as a mighty seer, and his knowledge of the future is another of his gifts to men, though not always a welcome one. This foreknowledge of the god, acquired through dangerous journeys and personal torment, was linked with the destinies of kings and kingdoms, an important element in the religion of the gods.

Odin must be seen mainly as a deity of aristocratic warriors, and his cult, like that of Mithraism, was well suited to fighting men. On the whole, he appears hostile to women, although the Odin tales contain a number of intrepid women of noble birth who are prepared, like Brynhild, to end their lives and join the dead heroes in another world. However, the picture of women given in *Hávamál* stresses their fickle nature and dangerous influence on any who trust them. Starkad, a typical hero of Odin, whose story is told most fully in Saxo's history, held women in utter contempt. Odin's own unsuccessful wooing of Billing's daughter (not known elsewhere) is presented in *Hávamál* as comedy. Arriving at her invitation to enjoy a night with her, Odin found armed guards awaiting him, and when he came back later a dog was tied to the bed. The wooing of Rind, however, was a different matter, and came about, not because he was overcome with desire for her, but because he knew he must have a son by her to avenge the killing of Balder. Saxo tells this story (III, 78), indicating that there were other versions, and, according to him, all Odin's efforts to woo the princess failed, until he disguised himself as a woman doctor and persuaded her father to leave Rind in his charge. Later a son, Vali, was born to her who grew up to kill Hother, Balder's slayer. An early poem of the tenth century refers to Odin working magic on Rind, and in the poem *Baldrs Draumar* the vengeance of Vali on Hother is prophesied, so that this story may be an early myth. In his dealings with the daughters of giants, Odin shows himself a deceiver and trickster, using them for his own ends, not an ardent lover, like Freyr, or a dangerous enemy, like Thor.

The Celtic god who most closely resembles Odin is Lug, who was a major deity among the early Celts on the continent and in Britain (p. 59). Not many tales about him survive, but in the account of the Second Battle of Mag Tuired we are told how he came by the title of 'the Many-Skilled.' He arrived at the court of Tara, and when asked what he could do, made a series of offers, saying that he was skilled as a craftsman, a smith, a champion, a harper, a poet, a wizard, a doctor, a cup-bearer and a worker in metals. There were already men possessing such skills in Tara, but since no one possessed them all as he did, he was welcomed in, to become the new ruler of the gods. He killed Balor, their most dangerous opponent, and brought them victory (p. 72). Another tale tells how Lug was visited by a king from Tara, who saw him reigning as a king in the underworld, attended by a fair lady who represented the sovereignty of Ireland (MacCana 1955–8). Lug was said to be the divine father of the great hero Cú Chulainn, whom he protected in battle and healed when wounded. Both Lug and Odin were identified with Mercury by the Romans; both were protectors of kings and warriors, and might father heroes; both were gods of varied skills, carried great spears, and had marvellous steeds to bear them over land and sea. They were associated with ravens and crows, and each had a pair of ravens to bring tidings, while they could also fly in eagle-form. Both had cult places on hills, and are represented as ruling over the dead. There are, however, considerable differences between them. Lug is usually represented as a youthful figure, like the young Mercury, and heals wounded warriors, which is not very characteristic of Odin, although his protégé Starkad survives terrible wounds. In fact, the resemblances between them are not of the kind to suggest borrowings at a late date; they are more likely to be memories of a powerful god who developed differently among the Celts and the Germans.

Few myths concerning the earlier Germanic Wodan or the Woden of the Anglo-Saxons have survived, but there is one related by Paul the Deacon, in his eighth-century *History*, probably taken from an earlier work, the *Orbo Gentis Langobardum*. In this, Wodan's wife Frija wanted her husband to give the people of the Winniles, whom she favoured, a new name and grant them victory in battle. She told the whole tribe to come out at sunrise, bringing their women with them with their hair hanging over their faces, and turned Wodan's bed round so that he would see them as he woke and no longer be facing the Vandals whom he had previously favoured. His first words were: 'Who are these longbeards?' and Frija then told him that now he had given them a name he must grant the gift of victory to go with it. The idea of the god and his wife supporting rival claimants is found again in the prose introduction to *Grímnismál*. Wodan is the Langobardic myth seems to be regarded as a sky god, associated with the rising sun, and the idea of Odin looking down on earth is found again in the tradition of his seat, from which he can view all worlds at once. This suggests that his powers for the Germanic peoples were by no means restricted to the dark underworld and the realm of the dead.

MYTHS OF THOR

Whereas myths about Odin are concerned largely with the acquisition of wisdom and the fates of rulers and kingdoms, ending with the fall of his own realm of Asgard, those associated with Thor are of a different kind. They emphasize his power over the natural world, and his many contests with supernatural adversaries in his position as protector of the gods and of mankind. In some of the earliest skaldic verse, going back to the ninth century, he is described as advancing with fire and thunderous clamour, rending rocks and destroying his opponents. He is associated with storms and wind, but above all with thunder and lightning. There seems no doubt that his great axe-hammer, one of the treasures of the gods and greatly coveted by the giants, represents the power of lightning to fell trees and shatter rocks. The poem *Thrymskviða* deals with the attempts of the giants to acquire it; we are not told how the theft came about, but it might have been due to the treachery of Loki, when forced in some desperate situation to agree to the giant's demands, as happens in other tales. Once the hammer was lost, there was no possibility of Asgard surviving for long, and if Freyja were taken from the gods, the loss would be a fatal one.

Thor in various myths is said to be absent from Asgard, busy killing giants, and he evidently made many journeys into Jotunheim, some of which feature in the surviving tales. His journey to the realm of Geirrod was remembered from an early period, as there is a long poem, *Thórsdrápa*, about it by Eilif Godrunarson which goes back to about the year 1000 (*Skáldskaparmál* 18). In Snorri's account, Loki was captured by the giant when he was flying in his hawk-shape, and Geirrod starved him until he agreed to bring Thor to his realm without his hammer or his belt of strength. However, the god was warned of his danger by a friendly giantess, who lent him another belt, her own iron gloves, and a magic staff. With Loki clinging to his belt, Thor crossed a mighty river, and they were nearly swept away. Then he saw that the flooding was caused by one of the giant daughters of Geirrod, standing astride the river and urinating into it. He struck her down with a boulder, and then caught hold of a rowan tree (henceforward called by poets 'Salvation of Thor') and climbed out into the giant's kingdom. He was given a goat-shed for lodging, with one seat, and when he sat on this it began to move upwards towards the roof, until he forced it down with his magic staff. Thus he broke the backs of the two remaining daughters of Geirrod, who had intended to kill him. Then Thor entered the giant's hall to take part in games of skill. Geirrod hurled a red-hot iron-bolt at him, but he caught it in his iron gloves and flung it back, piercing the pillar behind which the giant tried to shelter and running him through.

This myth has a number of interesting features. The giantess causing the river to swell is also found in Irish tradition, for the Morrígan, a sinister battle goddess, increases the flow of a river in this way, and there are other relevant examples (Bower 1975). It certainly emphasizes the link between the huge giantesses and the natural world, and is an example of the monstrous, barbaric element found in a number of myths. In this case, however, it is not clear where Snorri found his story. He certainly knew *Thórsdrápa*, but also gives a quotation from another poem in direct narrative style, referring to the increase of Thor's divine strength, which suggests a lost source. Perhaps from this also comes Thor's robust comment as he flings a rock at the giantess: 'A spring must be dammed at the source!' Unfortunately the language of *Thórsdrápa* is obscure, with complex multiple kennings, so that it is hard to be sure exactly what is implied. It is clear that Loki deceived Thor into making the journey, while much emphasis is laid on the crossing of the tumultuous river, and on the increase in Thor's divine might. The flood is connected with the giantess, but in what way is not made clear. There is a reference to water as 'the blood of the sun's dwelling' (that is, rain falling from clouds) and the river is called 'the water of the women of the giant'. In the poem Thor has his servant Thjalfi with him as well as Loki, and there is apparently a fight with giants before the god reaches the hall. This is a good illustration of the problems confronting anyone who attempts to continue the search for a particular myth beyond Snorri.

The episode where Thor overcomes the giant in the hall is included in the poem, and this could be developed in different ways by later writers, as Simpson shows in her study of the fourteenth-century *Thorsteins Saga* (1966:13 ff.). The theme was also treated by Saxo Grammaticus, at about the beginning of the thirteenth century, in his account of Thorkill the Far-Travelled in Book VIII, who discovers the battered bodies of Geirrod and his daughters among the rocks. He refers to Thor driving a flaming ingot through the giant which smashed the mountain to pieces, while his thunderbolts destroyed the giantesses. There seems no indication apart from Snorri that Thor travelled without his hammer on this occasion, but he was evidently lured into a trap of some kind. It seems that there was a tradition that Geirrod was an underworld smith, since on one occasion in a poem he is called the giant 'of the big bellows' (*Flateyjarbók* III:417).

Another tale told by Snorri but not found in the skaldic poets, is Thor's journey to the kingdom of Utgard-Loki. Part of this as told in *Gylfaginning* 43 ff. may be Snorri's own invention, since the account of the contest in the giant's hall is witty and sophisticated, with use of allegory and personification not normally found in Norse myths, but this does not mean that the framework of the tale was not based on an early source. Thor was accompanied here by Loki and Thjalfi, the latter said to be the son of a farmer at whose house he stayed on the way. That night Thor sacrificed his goats for dinner and cooked them in his cauldron; after the meal he collected the bones on the skins, and restored them to life by raising his hammer over them. Unfortunately the farmer, disregarding Thor's warnings, had cracked a leg-bone, so that one goat was lame. He was terrified by Thor's rage at his disobedience, but in the end the god relented, only taking Thjalfi and his sister (who plays no further part in the tale) with him as his servants. They travelled through a huge forest, where they met an enormous giant called Skrymir ('Big Fellow'), whose glove was so huge that Thor and his party took it for a hall. The giant journeyed with them and humiliated Thor by leaving him with a bag of provisions which he was unable to open, and keeping them awake at night by his snoring. Even when Thor struck him with his hammer, he remained apparently unaffected. Utgard-Loki's stronghold was so huge that Thor was able to crawl in under the gate, and more humiliation awaited him inside. Thjalfi, a swift runner, was utterly outstripped by his opponent, while Loki was defeated in an eating contest. Thor himself failed to drain a huge horn in three draughts, to overcome an old woman in a wrestling match, or even to lift the giant's grey cat from the floor. Not until they were outside the gate next morning was it revealed how deceiving magic had been practised against them. The blow from Thor's hammer had fallen on a mountain and left a huge cavity in it; the bag he could not undo was fastened with bands of iron; Thjalfi had raced against Thought, swifter than any runner; while Loki's opponent was Fire, which devoured dish and meat together. Thor himself had been given a horn with its tip in the sea, and his great efforts to empty it had brought down the level of the ocean, while he had wrestled with Old Age, against which the strongest fights in vain. The cat was in reality the World Serpent, and all were terrified when he got one of its feet off the ground, lest he should pull the monster out of the depths.

We have no idea what original myth may lie behind this brilliantly told tale. N.K. Chadwick (1964) has shown that there are parallels to the adventures in the forest in Russian medieval poetry about the giant hero Svyatogor, who plays a part resembling that of Skrymir, while the hero Ilya finds himself in a position resembling that of Thor. The term 'Utgard' can be used for 'regions beyond', and might in this case refer to the mountains of the Caucasus, where there were early traditions of a bound giant, still remembered locally in the nineteenth century; like Loki, this giant was to break free from his bonds at the end of the world. Tales about him might have been brought into Scandinavia by Vikings visiting the Caucasus region in the tenth century (Davidson 1976:314 ff.). The problems involved in this single well-known tale indicate the limitation of our knowledge.

Another tale of Thor matched against a giant is that of his duel with Hrungnir, again found in a tenth-century poem, *Haustlǫng*, and retold by Snorri. In the account in *Skáldskaparmál* (17), Thor was away from Asgard when Odin was challenged by the giant Hrungnir to race his horse Sleipnir against that of the giant. Odin won easily, but Hrungnir galloped into Asgard, where he was invited to drink with the gods, and became boastful and abusive, threatening to sink their stronghold into the sea and carry off the goddesses. When Thor arrived with his hammer, Hrungnir claimed immunity as a guest and challenged Thor to a duel. For no very clear reason, the giants made a huge man out of clay with a mare's heart, called Mistcalf, to stand beside Hrungnir with his heart of stone, stone shield, and whetstone for a weapon. Thjalfi told him to stand on his shield in case Thor came up from below, but the god appeared with thunder and lightning and hurled his hammer. Hrungnir threw his whetstone, and the weapons met in mid-air so that the whetstone was shattered, one piece lodging in Thor's head, while the hammer smashed Hrungnir's skull, and Thjalfi broke up the clay giant. The seeress Groa failed to remove the stone from Thor's head and there it remained.

Much of the skaldic poem is taken up by description of the god's preparations for battle and his approach in the terror of the storm. Hrungnir is said to fall before the hammer, with no reference to a clay giant; such an irrelevant figure might conceivably be based on some kind of ritual performed to illustrate the myth. The whetstone is mentioned, and there might be a link between the piece lodged in Thor's head and the so-called gods' nails (*reginnaglar*) set in the high seat pillars of hall or shrine, which were apparently associated with Thor (*Eyrbyggja Saga* 4). The duel with Hrungnir seems to have been one of Thor's most celebrated exploits. In *Lokasenna* his hammer is called 'Bane of Hrungnir', and other kennings that refer to this battle indicate that it was part of a widespread myth, although as retold by Snorri it gives the impression that he does not understand what is recorded about it by the poets.

The most popular of the myths about Thor in the Viking Age, however, appears to have been the tale of his fishing for the World Serpent. The surviving carvings of this in various parts of the Viking world, together with accounts from early skaldic poems, show a continuous tradition for at least four centuries (p. 51). This myth may originally have been one concerning the events at the beginning, when the gods secured various monsters who threatened their security. In some of the surviving accounts, however, it seems to indicate a moment of crisis, when Thor almost raised the serpent from the deep but it sank down again, leaving the world safe for a while; the account of the struggle to lift the grey cat in the hall of Utgard-Loki sounds like a humorous echo of this.

There must have been other supernatural adversaries of Thor afterwards forgotten. A verse in his praise by Thorbjorn Dísarskáld lists two giants and six giantesses as his victims, while another poet Vetrlidi refers to the killing of two other giants and a giantess as well as the crushing of Gjalp, one of Geirrod's daughters. Unfortunately, our knowledge of the giant world is all too limited. Thor's enemies are usually called frost-giants, living in the mountains, and frost-giants were said to be among the first beings created, many of which perished in the blood of Ymir, the first being from whose body the world was created. There were also giants of the underworld, ancient beings full of wisdom and knowledge of the past which went beyond that of the gods. The tales preserve remnants only of what must have been a great body of giant lore. Sometimes the Vanir, the deities of fertility, are represented as fair giants of earth and water, and giants are often fathers of the goddesses.

The god in Irish tradition who has most in common with Thor is the Dagda, the 'Good God'. Like Thor he is enormously strong, and renowned for his huge appetite. This is shown in the tale of the Second Battle of Mag Tuired, when his enemies the Fomorians prepared a meal of porridge for him containing 80 gallons of milk and equal amounts of meal and fat, together with carcases of goats, sheep and swine. This they poured into a hole in the ground, and challenged him to eat it all. He devoured it with the help of an enormous ladle, and even managed to mate with the daughter of the Fomorian leader afterwards. Like Thor, who in *Hymiskviða* is seeking cauldrons for the gods' feast, he was associated with such vessels, possessing a famous cauldron that held enough to satisfy every guest, and he had a huge club as his weapon with which he could both slay and recall the dead to life, as Thor did with his hammer. Both these weapons seem to have been associated with the marking of boundaries. Thor and the Dagda were down-to-earth, undignified figures, walking rather than riding, although Thor had his wagon drawn by goats. Yet just as Thor was associated with law and was patron of the Assembly, so the Dagda is called 'Lord of Perfect Knowledge'. Again there is little indication of borrowing here, yet the two gods have much in common in their tremendous power and virility and closeness to the land, and their somewhat primitive weapons, while they are convincingly represented as possessors of divine energy.

MYTHS OF LOKI

Among the complexities of giant lore must be counted the double nature of Loki, sometimes a small, nimble figure, clinging to Thor's belt or carried by an eagle, and sometimes a mighty bound giant who will break loose along with wolf and serpent on the last day and lead other giants in an attack on Asgard. There is uncertainty as to whether he was ever counted as a god, yet he was a friend of both Odin and Thor and went on adventures with them, while he made illicit love to the goddesses and was a resident of Asgard, knowing its most intimate secrets, according to the cynical poem *Lokasenna*. He was usually responsible for the theft of divine treasures by the giants, but also the only one who found a way to get them back again. Thus he helped to recover Thor's stolen hammer, stage-managing the scene where Thor was disguised as Freyja (p. 65); he deprived the giant builder of his horse, and rescued Idun and her apples. He was also largely responsible for the making of the gods' finest treasures, as recounted in *Skáldskaparmál*. When he cut off the golden hair of Thor's wife, Sif, Thor showed such fury that Loki had to find dwarf craftsmen to make her new hair of pure gold. They then went on to make a magic ship for Freyr which could go against wind and tide, and a wonderful spear for Odin. After this Loki assembled a rival team of craftsmen, wagering his head that these could not produce finer treasures. However, they set to work and made a golden boar for Freyr and Freyja, the gold ring Draupnir for Odin from which more rings dropped every ninth night, and finally Thor's hammer, declared the most valuable treasure of all. Thus Loki finally lost his wager, but in the end kept his head, although the dwarves sewed up his lips for a while. According to this tale the very existence of the gods, depending as it did on the invincible hammer, was due to Loki, although characteristically he did his best to spoil it in the making.

Other myths about Loki show him to be a master of shape-changing. He could become a mare, and even produce a colt, so that Sleipnir, the eight-legged horse of Odin, was among the treasures of the gods; he could fly in hawk-form, and after Balder's death became a salmon in a vain attempt to escape the fury of the gods. The early poem *Haustlǫng* implies that Loki and Heimdall fought in the form of seals in the sea. Many of the sources telling of Loki's tricks are late (de Vries 1933), and entertaining trickster tales of this kind are likely to be invented by story-tellers long after active belief in the gods came to an end. His character of divine thief, however, may well go back to early times. There have been many attempts to analyse Loki's part in the myths, and he has been interpreted as a fire demon, a water demon, a figure closely linked with the Christian devil, or with the spider (*locke* in Swedish) in folk tradition (Rooth 1961). The general character of Loki in the myths, however, is that of the trickster who appears in a number of mythologies. Such figures are ambivalent, doing both good and harm to their companion deities; they act to some extent as culture heroes, since their adventures, which often bring comic mishaps upon themselves, may result in great and lasting benefits for the gods and for mankind. By their relationship to the great gods, they act as catalysts, releasing creative activity.

There is a parallel to Loki in Irish tradition in the form of Bricriu, nicknamed 'Poison-Tongue', who is represented as a satiric poet at the court of Conchobar (Ó hÓgain 1990:58). He, like Loki, was a builder, for while Loki built a special house facing in four directions when attempting to escape from the gods, Bricriu in the tale of 'Bricriu's Feast' built a wonderful hall in which he held a banquet for the champions of Ulster and their wives (Ganz 1981:221 ff.). He threatened to create endless strife if they did not accept his invitation, and when they came he skilfully set one against another, just as Loki in *Lokasenna* arrived uninvited at the feast of the gods and flung inflammatory words and insults at both gods and goddesses; but his scheming, like Loki's, led to his downfall and he suffered in the end more than his victims. Loki's involvement in the Balder tale has caused much argument, and some have thought it a late addition to the myth. Even more mysterious is his appearance as a sinister giant, associated with death, and finally bound under rocks until the coming of Ragnarok, while he is also said to have fathered three evil monsters, the wolf, the serpent and Hel, ruler of the realm of death. He has sometimes been seen as the shadow-side of Odin, a second creator whose plans are essentially evil. It may also be noted that he plays an essential part in early sources in luring both gods and goddesses out of Asgard into the realm of the giants, and such expeditions end with the triumph of the gods over their enemies. Detailed studies of Loki, such as those by de Vries (1933), Dumézil (1948) and Rooth (1961), with discussion of various theories, show how difficult it is to establish the early background of these stories of the gods, or to discover what they meant to those who listened to them or narrated them. The Loki tales, amusing, lively and deservedly popular, are among the most difficult to assess.

OTHER DEITIES IN THE MYTHS

Other gods appear only briefly in the myths. Freyr in *Skírnismál* is the wooer of Gerd (p. 71). Tyr is the central actor in the story of the binding of the wolf; it has been claimed that he was an early sky god whose powers later passed to Thor and Odin. Njord, Heimdall, Hoenir, Aegir and Bragi figure briefly, but knowledge of them is limited. The goddesses were clearly important in northern religion, yet only Frigg and Freyja play any main part in the tales, while there are brief appearances by Skadi, daughter of Thjazi the giant, Gefion, who ploughed the island of Sjaelland out of Sweden, and Idun who guarded the golden apples; it is possible that these last two are to be identified with Freyja under different names. The subject of the goddesses, however, will be discussed in a later chapter (p. 108). The main myths of the gods referred to here show what problems of interpretation face us if we scrutinize them in detail. Clearly the poets have done much to build up a large body of religious literature, and it is possible, as Phillpotts (1929), Holtsmark (1949) and more recently Haugen (1983) have suggested, that some of the poems were acted at assemblies or religious festivals; the wooing of Gerd in *Skírnismál* and the account of the stealing of Idun have been suggested as possibilities. There are a number of poems in praise of Thor, but none on Odin or other gods has survived, although the wisdom of Odin is extolled in some of the poems that make up *Hávamál*. However, before we attempt to draw conclusions from this kind of evidence, it is necessary to survey the material that has to do with the cults of the gods, in order to discover the part they played in the communities to which their worshippers belonged.

4

The Cults of the Northern Gods

> It was the ancient custom when sacrifice was made, that all landowners should come to the place where the sacrifice was to be, bringing with them the provisions needed for as long as the feast should last. All people should have ale at the offering.
>
> (*Heimskringla, Hákonar Saga goða* 14)

Evidence that needs to be kept separate from the recorded myths concerning the gods is that which has to do with the religious practices of the pre-Christian northern world, concerning the worship of the gods and cult rituals in which the rulers, individual worshippers or the people in general took part. Various written sources tell us something of such religious practices in the Viking Age, with occasional glimpses further back in time, and such evidence must be joined with that obtained from archaeology, artefacts and iconography to fill some of the gaps in our knowledge of the past. Since much of the literary evidence was recorded in Christian monasteries, we face the usual difficulties of possible misunderstandings and prejudice; we have to remember also that those genuinely interested in the religion of the old gods could have been influenced by what they had read of heathen deities in the Old Testament or in writers like Virgil. For instance, there is little archaeological evidence for elaborate temples in pre-Christian Scandinavia, and some literary descriptions may have, therefore, to be discounted as unlikely to be based on genuine tradition. What are we to make of Adam of Bremen's description of the temple at Uppsala, written in the eleventh century? (O. Olsen 1966:116 ff.). His account of the figures of the gods there is of great interest, but a note added to the text (scholium 139) tells us:

> A golden chain goes round the temple. It hangs over the gable of the building and sends its glitter far off to those who approach it, because the shrine stands on level ground with mountains all about it like an amphitheatre.
>
> (Jones 1968:327)

Various attempts have been made to explain this chain. Was it taken from the biblical account of Solomon's temple (II Chronicles 3:16; I Kings 7:17)? Or is the description based simply on gilded carving in wood running along the roof? In the Edda poems there are references to halls of the gods roofed with gold, and these might have been suggested by the gilded roofs of palaces in Constantinople, which greatly impressed Scandinavian visitors (Davidson 1976:271); it is conceivable that such memories influenced the description of the Uppsala temple. Another possibility, suggested by Lindqvist (1923), was that the writer had seen a shrine for a reliquary with this type of decoration in the church of St Erik in Westgotland. As for the reference to mountains (*montes*), these presumably were the great burial mounds that still stand near the medieval church at Gamle Uppsala, since there are no high hills around it.

Such are the complications that can arise from a single descriptive passage, and in this case archaeology cannot offer much help. As Olsen pointed out, the traces of an earlier building were limited to a few post-holes under the medieval church. From these Lindqvist built up the model exhibited in Swedish museums, but there were other different reconstructions. Lindqvist was influenced by a detailed description of the temple of the Wends destroyed by the Danes in the twelfth century, as described by Saxo Grammaticus in Book XVI. Of shrines and temples erected in the pre-Christian period in north-western Europe, we in fact know very little (p. 139). What further evidence, then, can be found regarding public worship in the pre-Christian period?

COMMUNAL WORSHIP

Among the Celtic peoples, the druids are known to have been a well-organized group, who acted as priests and possessed considerable power and influence. The Germans and Scandinavians appear to have been without any such highly trained professionals, with the consequence that it was the king or chieftain who usually made contact with the gods on behalf of the people at the sacrificial feasts held at certain fixed points of the year. No doubt the time of such feasts varied in different periods and in different regions, but there were certain times when co-operation with the gods was felt to be especially necessary. The most important of these was that marking the new year, celebrated at the end of October, at the beginning of winter. This feast lasted over a number of days, and was known as the Winter Nights in Scandinavia, corresponding to the feast of Samain among the Celts. Like all periods of transition, it was a dangerous time, when there was communication with the dead as well as with the gods, and meetings with supernatural beings might take place. Celts and Germans used the half-year as the basic unit in time-reckoning, beginning with winter, and the other important point in the year was the opening of summer at the end of April. Hallowe'en and the first of May have remained important for folk customs in the British Isles over the centuries. There was also a festival at midwinter, originally in January, but tending to be identified with the Christmas festival in Christian times, and another at midsummer; the Eve of St John the Baptist on 23 June is still celebrated with bonfires in Scandinavia.

Snorri Sturluson in *Ynglinga Saga* 8 refers to three main sacrificial feasts in Scandinavia: one at the beginning of winter when men sacrificed for plenty, one at midwinter for the growth of crops, and one in summer for victory. In Ireland there were two further feasts, on 1st February and 1st August, the former probably connected with the rearing of young animals and the latter with the first-fruits of harvest. Snorri's reference to sacrifice for victory is important to remind us, however, that offerings to the gods were intended to bring not only a blessing on crops and herds and the health of the land, but also good fortune in battle. The feast at the beginning of summer was important for the opening of the fishing season, and also for the setting-out of Viking expeditions and for campaigns against other kingdoms, while at the same time traders might be starting on long hazardous journeys in search of wealth.

The essential element on such occasions was the feast, in which all took part, and this was a commensal meal shared with the gods. The brewing of the ale or mead was of particular importance, and this was hallowed to the gods before the feasting began. Sometimes drinking-horns were passed round the hall, like the great aurochs horns included in the Sutton Hoo treasure (p. 20), while smaller horns have been found in many graves, recognizable from their metal fittings. In the fifth century in Denmark, feasters may have made use of the splendid silver horns decorated with gold plates found at Gallehus (Figure 26), unfortunately stolen and melted down in the early nineteenth century; the little scenes shown

Figure 26 Panels from the golden horn from Gallehus (afer Oxenstiern).

on them, including a possible horse sacrifice, could be associated with such festivals (Oxenstierna 1956). From Celtic areas there are many wonderful flagons and drinking-vessels of superb workmanship, some going back to early periods, as well as cauldrons for holding liquid and great vessels like the one from Vix (p. 14).

The obligation to drink to the gods at such feasts may have influenced the Christian custom of drinking to Christ, the Virgin and various saints at the medieval guild-feasts in Scandinavia (Grønbech 1931:II, 146 ff.). In *Hákonar Saga goða* 14 Snorri represents Jarl Sigurd drinking first to Odin for power and victory, second to Njord and Freyr for peace and good seasons, and finally to the memory of dead ancestors. As there was no king in Iceland, the *goði*, the leading man for each district, presided and drank to the gods, probably holding the feast in his own hall. The gods were honoured in a body at the feast, although the brewing of the drink was especially associated with Odin, and the animal sacrificed might be the symbol of a particular god, as the boar was linked with Freyr. Two tales from early continental sources indicate the importance of the hallowing of the drink. In the seventh-century *Life* of St Columbanus (ed. Krusch, 1905:213), the saint came across a group of Alamanni in Switzerland, clustered round a large vessel called a *cupa*, holding about 20 measures of beer, which they told him they were offering to Wodan. The saint rather unkindly blew upon the vessel, whereupon it shattered with a loud crash and the beer was lost. St Vedrastus performed a similar feat when accompanying the Frankish king Chlothar to a feast in the early days of Christianity, where the festival ale had been divided into two portions, and one left unhallowed for Christians to drink. Vedrastus made the sign of the cross over the hallowed ale, and the vessel holding it burst asunder; we are told that this made a great impression on non-Christians, and many were converted (*Monumenta Germaniae Historica, Scriptores Rerum Merovingicarum* 1896:III, 410).

The other essential for the feast was an animal to be sacrificed. The meat might be cooked in a cauldron or roasted over the fire, and the three animals singled out in the literature as sacrifices are the boar, the bull and the stallion, all three fighting animals, appropriate offerings for warrior peoples. We find them used for feasts in the Otherworld in both Norse and Irish literature. In *Gylfaginning* 37 a boar is cooked each evening for Odin's warriors to feast upon, yet is whole again the night after. The Celtic god Manannan had a supply of pigs that could be devoured over and over again (O'Rahilly 1946:122), while the Dagda in the Second Battle of Mag Tuired possessed pigs 'perpetually alive' so that the supply never gave out, together with a wonderful cauldron whose contents never failed to satisfy all who came to the feast. Similarly, Thor could raise his goats to life after they had been killed and eaten (p. 81) and in a number of Irish legends St Patrick could restore a bull to life (MacNeill 1982:393). It is possible that the widespread custom of placing food and drink and the vessels and dishes for a meal in many graves of the pre-Christian period may have been inspired by the symbolism of the Otherworld feast, and also by the idea of the feast as a means of communication between the worlds.

For the main sacrificial feasts, one outstanding animal seems to have been selected as a suitable offering to the gods. The name given to the boar sacrifice in Norway was *sónargǫltr*, which appears to mean 'pig of the herd', presumably the leader or prize boar. Accounts of famous boar-hunts in Welsh and Irish tradition may have had some ritual significance. The killing of the aurochs, the great wild bull that roamed round northern Europe, was said by Julius Caesar (*Gallic War* VI, 28) to have been a test of manhood among German youths, who had to trap it in a pit and then go down and kill it single-handed. In the case of the horse sacrifice, one way of selecting victims may have been by horse-races or horse-fights, of which we read in saga literature. There is archaeological evidence for feasts held on the shores of a lake at Skedemosse on the Baltic Island of Öland, where offerings of various kinds were thrown into the lake together with the bones of the slaughtered animals. The name of this site is thought to come from *skeið*, meaning either 'a fight between stallions' or 'a horse-race', and such contests could have taken place on the long ridge near the lake, to decide which animals should be killed in the autumn (Hagberg 1967:70 ff.). The ritual importance of the horse fight is confirmed by a carving of two men urging on their animals against one another on a stone from Häggeby in Sweden (Figure 27); it is dated from the Vendel period and roughly contemporary with the finds at Skedemosse.

Snorri gives an account of a horse sacrifice, the source of which is not known, in *Hákonar Saga goða* 17. It was held in Hladir and the king came for the sacrifice at the beginning of winter, and was expected to preside over it, although, having been brought up as a Christian in England, he was reluctant to do so. The horse-meat was cooked in a cauldron, and the king tried to satisfy the people by

Figure 27 Stone from Häggeby, Sweden, showing horse fight.

opening his mouth over it as the steam rose, but this only caused resentment. At the next feast he consented to eat some of the liver: what seems to be essential was to consume blood from the offering. After the conversion, Icelanders mocked at the pagan Swedes for licking their sacrificial bowls (Strömbäck 1975:79), apparently in their eagerness to consume the last vestiges of the blood of the sacrifice.

Memories of the horse sacrifice might still have existed in Snorri's time, but when we find an account of a sacrificial ritual recorded by Giraldus Cambrensis in the twelfth century as taking place in Ireland, it is difficult to know what reliance to put on it. He had heard, he stated in his *Topographia Hiberniae* (3.25) (thus suggesting an oral rather than a written source), that one tribe in Ireland celebrated the inauguration of a king by a shocking ceremony, whereby the chosen king acted the part of a stallion mating with a white mare in the presence of all the people. The animal was then killed and the meat cooked in a cauldron, after which the king bathed in the broth and also drank from it, as well as eating some of the flesh. This account has aroused interest because of resemblances to the Hindu rite of the *ásvamedha*, which is the subject of a hymn in the *Rigveda* with a detailed liturgical commentary. This took place at the consecration of a king, and again a white horse, this time a stallion that had never been ridden, was sacrificed, after a year of running free. The chief queen lay down beside the dead stallion, and both were covered by a cloth. A choir of priests and women then described the sexual union between them in explicit terms. Finally, the horse was roasted and offered to the god Prajapati; the animal appears to represent the universe (Campbell 1962:190 ff.). The traditional horse sacrifice can be traced back before the first millenium BC. It is hard, however, to accept that any such ceremony could have taken place at so late a date in Christian Ireland, although there may have been memories of it in local tradition. Again, the sacrifice is associated with a new king, and a bull sacrifice, the *tairbfeis*, was also connected with this in one of the Irish sagas, *Togail bruidne Da Derga* (Destruction of Da Derga's Hostel, Ganz 1981:65), when a man with second sight is said to eat some of the flesh and drink the blood of a sacrificed bull, and then dream of the future king. Strange rituals might have persisted in the selection of a king after the regular feasts to the gods had long been forgotten.

Possible memories of such feasts may also have survived in tales of 'Hostels', presided over by a supernatural host; these might possibly be memories of feasts in the Otherworld, as in Scandinavian tradition (Löffler 1983:114 ff.). Another significant tradition is the arrangement for the carving and distribution of the boar at feasts, which is found in a number of tales. The most celebrated warriors could lay claim to the choicest cuts, and according to Posidonius this custom went back to very early times among the continental Celts (Tierney 1959–60:247). Men were prepared to fight to the death rather than be cheated of their rightful portions, and lists indicating the correct distribution according to rank have survived in the written sources.

An important feature of the sacrificial feast was that as well as being an opportunity for sharing a meal with the gods it was an occasion for divination, as was also the feast at the inauguration of a king. The sacrifice was a time for looking forward to the future, seeking omens for the prosperity of the kingdom with the promise of rich harvests and victorious campaigns. The Scandinavian boar sacrifice was said to be associated with enquiry into the future (*Ynglinga Saga* 18), while people might to some extent influence their own futures by making a solemn vow to achieve some great exploit, while laying a hand on the sacrificial boar. The idea that the annual feasts were opportunities for learning the future of the kingdom or of individuals in the coming year has left traces in the customs and games linked with Hallowe'en; but the main purpose was to renew the contract with the gods, so that the luck and prosperity of the land might continue. Besides the feasting, there would be sports, racing, wrestling and many other activities and contests, probably including story-telling and the recounting of myths about the gods. There is an account in the *Fornmanna Sǫgur* (VI, 99) of Harald Hardradi of Norway arranging for the telling of a saga to last out the Yule feast, and such entertainment continued to form part of Christian festivals.

Times of crisis, such as the death of a king, or the threat of enemy attack, were occasions demanding sacrifice. The period between the death of a ruler and the installation of his successor was like that of the new year, when the kingdom was held to be particularly vulnerable. Another time for a public appeal to the gods was the annual opening of the Assembly in Scandinavia, so that law cases could be heard and decisions taken affecting the community as a whole. The gods were said in *Vǫluspá* to set up their own assembly, and were represented as supporting those held on earth. To break up a hallowed court, as King Eirik Bloodaxe is represented as doing in *Egils Saga* 56, was felt to arouse divine anger. In this case the king cut the ropes that enclosed the court before judgement had been given, and declared Egil an outlaw, but Egil retaliated by carving runes and setting up a horse's head on a pole as a spell to bring down a curse on the king and his wife. Two verses are quoted at this point which may well be genuine early material (Almqvist 1965:90 ff.), and Egil mentions three of the gods, Odin, Freyr and Njord, and demands also that the land-spirits drive the king from his realm.

The gods might also be called upon in various forms of oath, since the breaking of a solemn contract aroused their anger, and would result in loss of luck and perhaps of life itself. In *Landnámabók* (H, 268) the words of the oath taken on the holy ring reddened with the blood of sacrifice are given, beginning: 'I make an oath on the ring, a law oath, so help me Freyr and Njord and the Almight God ...'. There have been various suggestions as to who the Almighty God might be, including Thor, Odin, and even Ull, who is associated with a ring in the poetry; Thor seems most likely because of his close link with law and order, but the expression might simply be due to Christian influence at the time when the words were set down. The inclusion of Freyr and Njord in such formulae was probably due to their close link with the land, since there seems to be an assumption that the land itself was sullied by the breaking of an oath.

The sacred ring, for which in Iceland the *goði* was responsible, is mentioned in a number of sagas, and in *Eyrbyggja Saga* 4 it is said to be kept in Thor's temple, and called the altar-ring. It is described as without any join and about 20 *eyrar* in weight, which would make it a heavy arm-ring, about 550 g. In some later texts a weight of only 2 *eyrar* is given, suggesting a finger-ring, but Magoun (1949) argued that an arm-ring was more likely, pointing out that in *Eyrbyggja Saga* 44 Snorri *goði* escaped a wound from a sword because he was wearing the ring on his arm. Confirmation of the taking of an oath on a ring is found in the Anglo-Saxon Chronicle under the year AD 876, when the Danes made peace with Alfred of Wessex and 'swore oaths to him on the holy ring'. The oath hallowed the words spoken, establishing them as the will of the gods. In *Víga-Glúms Saga* 25 the hero, a follower of Odin the deceiver, swore a misleading oath; the trick depended on uttering words that were not literally untrue but gave a false impression due to the emphasis of the speaker. His cunning, however, did not save Glum from the anger of Freyr, whom he offended by sheltering an outlaw in the god's holy place. Outlawry, the most frequent punishment for a serious offence in the Viking Age, placed the condemned man outside the community of both his neighbours and the gods, and this too was confirmed by a religious form of words. What we learn of the worship of the gods as a group indicates that they were called on in all important matters concerning the community. The prosperity of the land depended on the right relationship between ruler and deities, so that the contract between human and divine worlds remained unbroken. While there was no moral obligation, there had to be faithfulness to a pledged word, and each side had certain claims on the other. There seems to be no sense of guilt, gloomy overtones, or required penance, although in the appeal to the gods of battle the position might possibly be different. In the regular feasts in honour of the gods the atmosphere was apparently one of hospitality and enjoyment: everything that can be discovered about the celebrations at Skedemosse in the period before the Viking Age, for instance, suggests that a good time was had by all, and that the torch-lit feasting and throwing of offerings into the water must have been a memorable experience (Hagberg 1967).

No doubt there were also appeals to the gods of a more practical nature when occupied in the business of everyday, and we have one brief but valuable eye-witness account by an Arab writer and traveller, Ibn Fadlan, who visited the Bulgarian capital on the Volga and watched the doings of some tough merchant-adventurers known as the Rus, assumed to be Swedish Vikings who came down the river in their ships hoping for successful trading. The value of this account is that the writer was interested in the customs of foreign peoples, and had no particular reason to slant his description for purposes of propaganda. He tells us that at Bulgar in AD 921 these northerners set up a group of crude wooden figures, one upright piece of wood with a face like a man's surrounded by smaller figures, and placed a number of long stakes in the ground behind them. A trader on his arrival would make offerings of bread, meat, leeks, silk and beer to the main figure, entreating him to let him obtain a good price for his wares. If all came about as he hoped, he returned to sacrifice sheep and cattle, leaving some of the flesh beside the figures and setting up the heads of the slaughtered beasts on the stakes. If, however, things did not go well, he would turn to some of the smaller figures and ask their help, and Ibn Fadlan was told that these were the sons and daughters of the god (Smyser 1965:97). We cannot tell who the main figure represented; it could have been Odin, since these were fighting men dependent on their swords. Among Odin's powers as listed by Snorri in *Ynglinga Saga* was that of gaining wealth for his followers, and since he was the Allfather, other deities could be called his children. Here we have an example of sacrifice by individual members of a group, in one of the few passages that afford a glimpse of how men away from home acted towards their gods in the Viking Age.

CULTS OF THE BATTLE-GODS

There is no doubt that the warrior nations turned to their gods for support in battle, and we learn from the literary sources of various practices used to obtain help from the gods and also to glorify them in warfare. What appears to be an early religious practice among the Celts which impressed and shocked other peoples was that of collecting and preserving the heads of enemies slain in battle. There is evidence for this in early literary sources, backed by archaeological finds, particularly from the sanctuary of Entremont in southern France where skulls or severed heads were carved on pillars, and actual skulls found in the sanctuary and sacred way; this sanctuary dates back to the third century BC and was destroyed by the Romans in AD 124. Some of the pillars had a skull-shaped niche with a hook inside, on which it is thought actual skulls were suspended (Benoit 1975). Posidonius in the late second century BC declared that the Celts cut off the heads of those slain in battle and attached them to the necks of their horses, displaying them in triumph, while they also embalmed and carefully preserved the heads of their most distinguished enemies (Tierney 1959–60:250). Here we have something distinct from sacrifice: it might be viewed as a test of courage, like the overcoming of a fierce animal in the wilds, or as the parade of a trophy, or as the acquisition of an object bringing luck and power. However, the preserved heads at Entremont were evidently linked in some way with the worship of the gods. Great statues of seated figures in the sacred way held in one hand something resembling a thunderbolt, while the other hand rested on a severed head. Livy in the third century BC (X, 26.11) stated that skulls might be decorated and used as drinking-cups in temples, and it seems likely that the preserving and consultation of severed heads was part of the cult of the gods.

Certainly the practice was remembered vividly in the Irish sagas. Many heroes or their wives boast of heads brought back from battle, and when the great hero Cú Chulainn slew a number of foes he piled up their heads and displayed them together with the weapons and armour he had won. It seems that such practices took place in battle in the Roman period in Britain, for at Bredon Hill in Gloucestershire, where an Iron Age camp was captured by the Romans, about 50 headless skeletons were found, and some skulls appear to have been set up on a gate (Hencken 1938:21 ff.). The practice was not restricted to the Celts, since according to Herodotus it was well established among the Scythians in the fifth century BC, and he details in Book IV the gruesome methods used to preserve and decorate the skull of an enemy and to strip off the skin to fasten it to the bridle of the successful warrior's horse. It seems that the Germans also preserved heads, although on a lesser scale. After the terrible defeat of the Romans at the Teutoberg Wood, Tacitus relates how human heads had been nailed to trees (*Annals* 1, 61), while heads were said to be collected by the Alamanni (Reinach 1913:44).

One link with the cult of the gods might be found in the motif of the speaking head, which is found in Scandinavian and English folk tradition as well as Irish. In the Yellow Book of Lecan there is the vivid account of the fate of the Irish story-teller and singer, Donn Bo. After he was killed in a battle along with his king, Fergal of Ulster, the victorious king sent a man to the battlefield to bring back a head. He heard the voice of Donn Bo singing in honour of his lord, and took back the head of the minstrel to the hall, where it was placed on a pillar, and sang so sweetly that the hearers were moved to tears. The head of King Fergal was also taken to the hall of another king, who treated it with much honour, washing it and combing the hair and putting a velvet cloth around it, while he offered sheep and pigs before it at the feast before it was taken back for burial. It is said that the head blushed with pleasure, and 'opened its eyes to God to render thanks for the respect and great honour which had been shown to it' (Stokes 1903). Veneration of a head in a Christian context may also be seen in the honour paid to that of St Oswald and other early saints in Anglo-Saxon England. The consultation of a speaking head is linked with Odin in the tradition of his use of the head of Mimir (p. 78), said to be the guardian of the spring of knowledge, but Snorri's account in *Ynglinga Saga* 4 leaves much unexplained.

Both Celts and Germans were notorious for the cruel killing of captives taken in warfare; the literary evidence suggests that the main motive behind such killings was to discover whether they would obtain victory. Posidonius states that the Celts observed the last convulsions of the dying and interpreted the future from them, and according to Strabo the priestesses of the Cimbri cut the throats of their prisoners to judge from the flow of blood what the result of warfare would be (p. 16). Other prisoners were disembowelled, presumably with the same end in view. Another reason given for the sacrifice of captives in the written sources is as a thank-offering for victory, along with horses and booty of various kinds, because a vow to this effect had been made to the gods before battle. Tacitus refers to such a sacrifice by the victorious Hermundari in the first century AD (*Annals* XIII, 57), and to confirm such statements we have extensive finds of the weapons and armour of fighting men, together with horses and sometimes human remains, in the peat bogs of Denmark and northern Germany (Hagberg 1967:79f.).

We read too of the practice of drawing lots to decide which out of a number of prisoners should be sacrificed, so that the choice might be made by the gods rather than by men. One particularly convincing tale of this kind is that of the escape from death of a young officer of Julius Caesar, sent as an envoy to the German leader Ariovistus and treated as a prisoner of war (*Gallic War* I, 53). He would have been put to death by burning immediately had the lots not gone against it, so that he was held for a later occasion, but then the Romans attacked and he managed to escape and rejoin his own side. There are similar tales of some of the early missionaries escaping death. St Willibrord in Heligoland in the seventh century was made a prisoner with some of his companions after he had killed sacred cattle and baptized converts in a sacred spring, and lots were consulted three times a day for three days to decide which prisoners should be put to death; Willibrord escaped on each occasion, although one of the monks with him was killed (Talbot 1954:10). A letter of Sidonius in the fifth century (Dalton 1915: VIII, 6; II, 150) refers casually to the custom of Saxon pirates of offering every tenth man among their captives to the god of the sea, when setting off for home after a successful raid. Sidonius, while deploring this, finds some excuse for them because it was the fulfilment of a vow that they felt bound to carry out.

There are many references to human sacrifice in classical and other writers who describe the customs of Germans and Celts, and some archaeological evidence seems to confirm this. Nevertheless, the question is far from simple, and the part played by human sacrifice in the cults of the gods is not easy to define. It seems that prisoners of war were sacrificed, and that human sacrifices also took place at times of crisis. In 1922 von Amira claimed that the cruel methods of execution carried out in the Middle Ages such as hanging, burning, drowning, burying alive and so on, were based on earlier sacrificial rites among the Germanic peoples, the method chosen depending on the nature of the crime and the god to whom the sacrifice was made. In 1942 Ström pointed out the weaknesses in this theory, which had been generally accepted by scholars. He argued that there was no evidence for human sacrifices on such a scale, and that the usual punishments for crime were fines and outlawry; moreover, the gods were not held to deliver moral judgements and impose death for wrongdoing as claimed by von Amira. There has been debate also over the significance of the large number of bodies found in the peat-bogs of Denmark and northern Germany within the last century, some showing signs of a violent death and with multiple injuries. It is possible that some of these could be sacrificial victims, particularly if they are accompanied by animal bones and signs of burning (Struve 1967). Many, however, might be the result of murders or revenge killing, while if the injuries were inflicted after death they could be due to hatred or fear of the dead. The discoveries of recent burials of what might be sacrificial victims at Sutton Hoo have forced us to reconsider the significance of such archaeological evidence (Davidson 1992a).

Many references to human sacrifice are associated either with the practices of the druids, who acted as priests, teachers and judges among the Celtic peoples of Gaul and Britain, or with the cult of Odin in Scandinavia. In both cases there is a link with warfare, in which the druids and the followers of Odin took an active part. The conclusions of Le Roux and Guyonvarc'h (1982:78 ff.) is that while druids performed sacrifices as part of their priestly function, human sacrifice was extremely rare, and we must be aware of the possibility of exaggerations and errors on the part of classical and later writers. There is a general tendency both in the past and in our own time to assume that human sacrifice has taken place when there are other possible interpretations. The elaborate theories put forward concerning the death of the young man found in the peat at Lindow in Cheshire in 1984 is an example of how speculation may be presented as scientific proof in such a way as to mislead the unwary reader (Ross and Robins 1989).

THE CULT OF ODIN

It does not seem possible to see any of the northern gods as simply a god of battle, but the favourite deity of those devoted to the craft of fighting in the Viking Age was unquestionably Odin. Those killed in battle were dedicated to him, according to the literary sources, and the custom of flinging a spear over the enemy at the outset of a battle with such words as 'Odin take you all' is reasonably well attested. A spear is thrown in *Eyrbyggja Saga* 44 before an attack as 'an ancient custom to bring good luck', while an early Danish chronicle records one flung into the sea after Otto I had defeated Harald Bluetooth of Denmark (Paulsen 1967:120). In the poem *Vǫluspá* Odin is said to have hurled his spear as the first act to bring war upon the world, giving a possible mythological basis for the custom. According to Saxo, who knew many tales of Odin, the god promised immunity from wounds to Harald Wartooth of Denmark if he promised him all those whom he killed by the sword (VII, 247), and warrior leaders themselves are represented as regarding their own deaths in battle or by torment as a sacrifice to the god.

The spear symbol was evidently of importance for Odin's cult, and in *Ynglinga Saga* 9 Snorri states that Odin was marked with a spear when at the point of death and required that his followers should imitate him, an obvious contradiction to the tradition that he was killed by the wolf at Ragnarok. If there were such a popular custom among those of Odin's worshippers who died at home, this might explain the very large number of spears buried with fighting men in Germanic cemeteries, some obviously fitted with difficulty into the graves, because of their length. There are also a number of splendidly ornamented spears, some with runic inscriptions, found on the continent from Roman to Merovingian times, and presumably of ritual importance. The symbol of a spear for a battle god may be very old, and was possibly linked with Tyr before it passed to Odin. When Odin hung on the World Tree as a sacrifice to obtain wisdom, according to the often-quoted passage in *Hávamál*, he was said to be pierced by a spear, and this may have been one way by which captives were despatched as sacrifices.

The purpose of Odin's self-sacrifice in the poem was to gain knowledge of runes and power to use them, and when sacrifice was used in divination, runes seem to have played a major part (Davidson 1988:153 ff.). The casting of lots to decide which prisoners should die may also have been linked with runes, and according to the literature the runes had to be reddened with sacrificial blood to be effective. The blood of the slain animal, known as *hlaut*, was consumed at the sacrificial feast, while some was also said to be kept in a bowl in the temple, and sprinkled on the walls (*Eyrbyggja Saga* 4). The verb *rjóða* ('to redden') is frequently used in references to sacrifice in the poetry; in *Hyndluljóð* for instance, a worshipper of Freyja is said to redden a sacrificial place until its stones shone like glass. It seems that it was the blood of a slain creature that made a sacrifice effective and knowledge of the future possible.

The cult of Odin included the knowledge of battle spells. A number of these are listed in *Hávamál*, supposedly spoken by Odin himself, and again in *Sigrdrífumál*, where they are said to be taught to the hero Sigurd by a valkyrie. One of the most important was the spell to free Odin's followers from bonds, together with another to put bonds on the enemy. This is a reference to helplessness and panic in battle, paralysing a fighting man so that he was incapable of the right reaction to save himself from defeat and death. Weapons are useless if the resolution to use them deserts the warrior, and in *Hávamál* 148 Odin claims the power to bring this about:

> Should I have urgent need of shackles with which to fetter my adversaries, I can blunt the edges of hostile weapons, and neither blades nor staves can harm me.

A reckless confidence in battle was one of Odin's gifts, of great value to the professional warrior and the leader who depended on his sword for survival. Among the various types of ecstasy that the god could grant to his worshippers was the wild ecstasy of battle. The extreme form of this was shown by the berserks, utterly dedicated to the cult of Odin, who knew no fear when fighting and were impervious to the pain of wounds. The indications are that such men dressed in the skins of wolves or bears and belonged to special warrior societies, in which they remained for life, while young fighting men from leading families for the most part served in the army for a while before settling down on their estates (Davidson 1989a). Although in the sagas the berserk appears as a kind of ogre with supernatural powers to blunt weapons, such warriors evidently formed an essential part of the fighting force, much valued by the early Scandinavian kings; in the tenth-century poem *Hrafnsmál* we are told how they were prized by Harald Fairhair, as warriors 'in which a wise ruler sets his trust'. Professional warriors of this type must have existed much earlier, since Tacitus in *Germania* 31 refers to men among the Chatti utterly dedicated to warfare, continuing in active service until too old to fight any longer.

Such a warrior appears in the literature in the person of Starkad, of whom Saxo tells us a good deal and who also plays a part in some of the legendary sagas. He was a ruthless, implacable figure, showing utter scorn for comfort, fine clothes, good food and drink or women, harsh and bitter in speech, and refusing even in old age to give way to wounds or weakness. Starkad is represented as a follower of Odin from his youth; it was said that the god trained him and even caused him to commit crimes such as the slaying of his king, actions that broke the normal heroic code of loyalties. On one occasion he conducted the sacrifice of a king to Odin, persuading the victim that it was to be mock sacrifice: the king was hanged and stabbed according to the rites of the god, so that the army could obtain a favourable wind. These traditions of Odin as a god of warriors were presumably passed on to young men who were learning the art of warfare, and those specially trained in his service, and this has helped them to survive in the literature.

The cult appears to have had a real impact on Scandinavian youth, since we hear accounts from outside sources, such as the Greek history of Leo the Deacon in the tenth century, of how the Vikings in battle would take their own lives rather than yield to the enemy (Davidson 1972:24). Such an act meant that they gave themselves to the god as an offering, and to die in this way was represented as a privilege, giving entry to Valhalla to join the great heroes of the past. This may have been a popular conception rather than a clearly defined belief put forward by religious teachers, and has no doubt been romanticized by later poets and story-tellers, as in the death-song of Ragnar Lodbrok, one of Odin's heroes, with its flamboyant delight in a painful death: 'Gladly shall I drink ale in the high-seat with the Æsir. My life-days are ended. I laugh as I die' (*Krákumál*, verse 25). The effect of such lore on young fighting men cannot be doubted, however, and it must have been partly responsible for the vigorous impact of the Viking forces on Europe.

Odin's cult in the Viking Age was not limited to warfare; it was closely linked with the power of the king and his contact with the gods, for the god was viewed as the ancestor of kings as well as famous warriors, like the Irish Lug with whom he had much in common (p. 79). Neither Odin nor Lug can be viewed as a specialized god of battle; rather, both were deities of varied aspects, whose cults were peculiarly appropriate for warrior societies ruled by kings who were called on to wage warfare in order to survive. Odin's contacts with the world of the dead and journeys between the worlds may have been primarily associated with this, but since so many kings and their followers died on the battlefield, the link with warfare received constant emphasis in both literature and art. Similarly, Odin's powers of inspiration in the understanding of runes and the craft of poets extend beyond the world of warriors, but came to be associated with it. The poets who were also followers of Odin developed and communicated the imagery of Valhalla. We do not know how far a cult of Wodan among the Germans provided for the needs of men and women outside the demands of warfare and the fortunes of the royal dynasties, but it seems clear that the power of the god increased as the king became the central figure in the community. Both Odin and Lug were themselves seen as rulers; Lug led the other gods to victory, while Odin ruled Asgard, in spite of the far-reaching powers of Thor and Freyr. As has been seen, there is little evidence for local shrines devoted to Odin's worship (p. 57), and such centres as existed seem to have been associated with royal dynasties. It is not surprising that we hear comparatively little of the god in Iceland, although the appeal to him as the god of poetry by skalds like Egil Skallagrimsson kept the heroic imagery alive, since poets were often fighting men as well as skilled in word-craft. As Snorri realized, it was scarcely possible for young Icelanders to understand their native poetry without considerable knowledge of Odin's powers and mythical exploits.

THE CULT OF THOR

While Odin was singled out for worship by kings and warrior leaders and fighting men on expeditions abroad, he was evidently of less importance for those living on the land, depending on hunting, fishing and farming. Both Freyr and Thor, on the other hand, had worshippers among members of the local community. Thor's ring was used for the swearing of oaths, and he presided over the Assembly, which opened on his day, Thursday, in Iceland, while his image apparently stood in the Assembly Place in Sweden, since Adam of Bremen (97, lxii) tells of a Christian missionary breaking it up with an axe and being killed by the angry crowd. Another symbol of the thunder god in forest countries was the oak, although this would mean little to Icelanders. St Boniface cut down a great oak called the Oak of Jupiter in Hesse, which the people held in high regard (Robinson 1916:63), and Jupiter is usually equated with the thunder god on the continent (p. 47).

Images of Thor are mentioned more often in the literature than those of other gods. Whether there was really a figure of the god in his wagon at Thrandheim which could be pulled along (*Flateyjarbók* I, 268:320) is doubtful, but the noise of his wagon bringing thunder is emphasized in myths and poems, and this may have been acted out in ritual; Saxo refers to hammers in Thor's temple in Sweden used to imitate the noise of thunder, removed by Magnus of Denmark in 1125 (XIII, 5). The popularity of the hammer sign and the uses it was put to in the Viking Age indicate the strength of the cult of Thor in Norway and Iceland (Figure 28). It was used to mark boundary-stones, was raised over a new-born child as a mark of its acceptance in the community, and according to the poem *Thrymskviða* was brought in at weddings to hallow the bride, and laid on her lap. It was also depicted on memorial stones for the dead, to whom Thor's protection extended, while the conception of the hammer restoring the dead to life is found in the myth of Thor raising his goats to life after they had been killed and eaten (p. 81).

Thor's link with the home was indicated by the use of his image on carved pillars in the hall on either side of the central seat, probably those supporting the roof. The pillars were clearly of symbolic importance, and are mentioned several times in *Landnámabók* and the sagas. It is possible that in Norway they were found in shrines of the god rather than in the hall. Settlers arriving in Iceland from Norway were said to bring them along and to throw them into the sea as

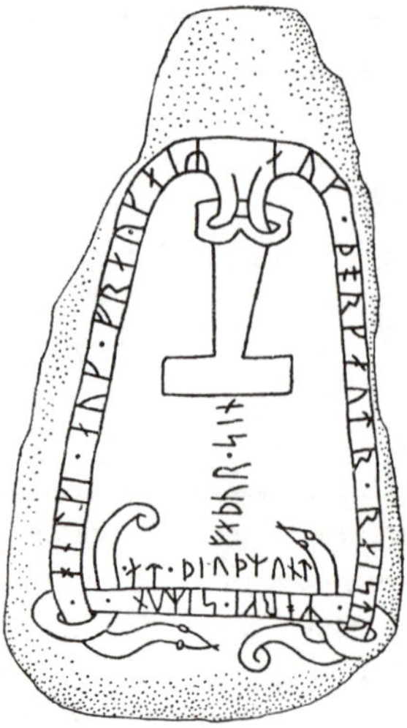

Figure 28 Stone from Svenkista, Sweden, showing Thor's axe-hammer (after Simpson).

they approached the coast; in one case this is said to be so that Thor could determine where his home was to be (*Eyrbyggja Saga* 4), and the settler in question, Thorolf of Mostur, had previously consulted Thor as to whether he should leave Norway for Iceland. The phrase used in *Eyrbyggja Saga* for enquiry of the god is *gekk til fréttar* ('went to enquire'), and comparison may be made with the Scots dialect-word *frete*, meaning, according to *Craigie's Dictionary*, 'belief in omens, an omen, or a foreboding'. Thor as god of the sky, was evidently often called upon when making a voyage; Helgi the Lean, who had been brought up a Christian, nevertheless 'called upon Thor for seafaring and difficult decisions, and matters he considered of greatest importance' (*Landnámabók* H, 184). Thorolf of Mostur, on the other hand, was wholly dedicated to Thor, whom he called his *ástvinr* (his 'beloved friend'). When he had found the site for his house, he marked out the boundaries of his land with fire – another rite presumably connected with Thor, who guarded boundaries and was associated with fire because of his power over the lightning. At the point where Thor had come ashore, the local place of assembly was marked out, and this had to be kept holy and free from pollution by blood or excrement. When later there was an act of deliberate desecration by Thorolf's neighbours, and blood was shed in the fighting, a fresh assembly-place had to be found, since 'the field had been defiled by blood shed in enmity, so that now the earth was no holier there than elsewhere' (*Eyrbyggja Saga* 10). Thorolf also built a temple for Thor, in which were kept the sacred ring on which oaths were sworn and the bowl holding sacrificial blood. This saga was probably written at the Augustinian monastery established at Helgafell in AD 1184 (Mabire 1971), which became one of the intellectual centres of western Iceland by the thirteenth century, and local tradition that it preserves regarding the early worship of the god seems likely to be reliable.

Thor is the only god with poems surviving in his praise. Some of these describe a picture of Thor's exploits on a shield or a carving in a hall, and visual representations of Thor were evidently popular: we have several examples on stones surviving from the Viking Age (p. 50). Some of these myths may conceivably have been acted at festivals (p. 86). Tales of Thor in the later literature represent him as a loved and popular deity. In spite of the terror evoked by his red beard and flashing eyes, which represented the power of the storm, his huge appetite and quick way of dealing with troublesome adversaries endeared him to his worshippers, contrasting favourably with the wiliness of Odin and the more dubious aspects of Freyr. Thor figures above all in the literature as protector of gods and mankind, supporting law and order and the good of the community more wholeheartedly than any other god.

THE CULT OF FREYR

There are examples of men in the saga transferring their loyalty from Thor and Odin to Freyr, or forsaking Freyr for another god. There is a good example of this in *Víga-Glúms Saga*, where Freyr in the end proves victorious. Holtsmark (1933) showed very convincingly that here the family of the hero, Glum, was originally devoted to Freyr, owning a share in a field sacred to the god, which was expected always to bear a good crop. Glum's father died while he was still a boy, and his mother was cheated of her rights by greedy relatives and neighbours; Glum then went to visit his grandfather in Norway, proved himself a successful fighting man by a contest with a bear, and returned home with a cloak and sword, which are symbols of Odin. He killed one of the troublesome neighbours in the sacred field of Freyr, arousing the god's hostility against him. In the end Glum had to forfeit his land, finding Odin no protector against the anger of Freyr, for all his successes as a warrior. This is an example of narrative writing, and no clear statements are made about the change to the cult of Odin, but Holtsmark's interpretation appears to be a valid one, and the picture of Freyr's hostility is clear. Those who looked on Freyr as a special protector were likely to be closely linked with the land or guardians of a sacred place under the rule of the deity, associated with his shrine, and the mention of a number of Icelanders bearing the title *Freysgoði* in *Landnámabók* indicates that they had some priestly connection with the cult of the god. In Sweden Freyr was worshipped by the royal family at Uppsala, who as indicated in *Ynglinga Saga* traced their descent from him, and the cult of Freyr seems to have spread from Sweden to Norway and then out to Iceland. There is a reference in a late saga of Olaf Tryggvason to two wooden men, presumably images of the god, being taken from Freyr's mound: one was kept in Sweden while the other was sent to Trondheim in Norway, where a cult centre existed in the tenth century (*Flateyjarbók* I, *Óláfs Saga Tryggvasonar* 323:403).

A well-known character among these priests or leading worshippers of Freyr in Iceland was Ingimund, a man from western Norway who came out to Iceland and settled in Vatnsdale in the east. According to *Landnámabók* (S. 179), a silver amulet of Freyr that he kept in his pouch disappeared, and was later found in Iceland, in the place where he came to live and where he built a shrine for the god (Davidson 1990:29). Ingimund's grandfather was a jarl in Gautland, not far from the centre of Freyr's cult. Another *Freysgoði* was Thorgrim Thorsteinsson, grandson of Thorolf of Mostur who was devoted to Thor, and father of Snorri *goði*, the main character in *Eyrbyggja Saga*. Thorgrim's death is related in *Gísla Saga*, and it is said that after he was buried Freyr kept his mound free from frost and snow, since 'the god was unwilling to let frost come between them' (18). His son Snorri, however, showed no interest in the cult of Freyr, and became guardian of the temple of Thor that his great-grandfather had set up at Helgafell. Another Freyr worshipper was Ingjald, who built the temple mentioned in *Víga-Glúms Saga*. He was the son of Helgi the Lean, brought up as a Christian but said to put his main trust in Thor (p. 102). The impression left by the two last examples is that worshippers of Freyr were individuals who broke away from the family tradition.

The reference to Thorgrim's mound is in keeping with the link between burial mounds and Freyr in Sweden, indicated in *Ynglinga Saga* 10, where it is said that offerings were brought to Freyr's own mound after his death. There seems, indeed, a possibility that early Swedish kings were identified with Freyr after death. Another characteristic of places sacred to Freyr in Sweden and Norway was that sacred horses were kept there. In a late tale in *Flateyjarbók*, Olaf Tryggvason is said to have ridden a stallion at Trondheim intended for sacrifice to Freyr, while he afterwards destroyed the wooden image of the god (*Óláfs Saga Tryggvasonar* I, 322:401). In *Hrafnkels Saga* there is an account of a sacred horse belonging to the hero, which no one was permitted to ride on pain of death because it was dedicated to the god; the horse was named Freyfaxi (Mane of Freyr). This picture of Freyr's cult in iceland used to be accepted as a genuine tradition from pre-Christian times, but Nordal in 1958 gave convincing reasons for regarding it as a late fictitious saga. There is no firm evidence for any Hrafnkel Freysgoði in this part of Iceland, or for the historical existence of other characters in the story. Here we have a good example of the difficulties in assessing the value of literary sources, for in this brilliant short saga careful efforts have been made to render the story convincing by the inclusion of local details and vague genealogies. The idea of horses dedicated to a god, which is undoubtedly ancient, may have been given new interest by the account of the temple of the Wends at Ancona, destroyed by the Danish king Valdemar in AD 1169, which is given by Saxo Grammaticus in Book XIV of his history. Here sacred horses were used for divination, and there is mention of a white horse that none might ride. The name 'Freyfaxi' may have come from the tradition of the horse in *Vatnsdœla Saga* belonging to the family of Ingimund, a known worshipper of Freyr. The horse-fights known to be popular in Scandinavia may originally have been associated with Freyr's cult, and perhaps the horse sacrifice also, although in *Víga-Glúms Saga* an ox is the offering made to the god.

It is tempting but perhaps time-wasting to pay too much serious attention to the robust comic tale of Volsi in *Óláfs Saga helga* in *Flateyjarbók* (II, 265:33 ff.). When an old farmhorse died, it was decided to use it for food 'as do heathen men'. A thrall cut off the horse's male organ, here said to be called *vingull* by the ancient poets. The mischievous son of the house ran indoors with it to shake it at the women, with appropriate jests, and his sister told him to take the disgusting thing away. However, the old mother dried it, wrapped it in linen and herbs and kept it until the autumn, when she brought it out for worship. Each in turn spoke a verse over it, addressing it as 'Volsi', and ending with the words: 'May Mornir receive this sacrifice (*blæti*)'. News of this reached St Olaf, and he came to the farm in disguise. When the usual ceremony took place and he was given the Vǫlsi, he spoke a verse, and then threw it to the farm dog.

Much learned ingenuity has been expended on this tale, and it has been suggested that the 'Mornir' were fertility goddesses, or that this was a name for Skadi, the wife of Njord (Ström 1954). A close parallel, however, has been pointed out in the custom still known in the Faroes, called the 'Drunnur'. The tail-bone of an ox or sheep, decorated with ribbon, was passed round at a wedding feast, and whoever received it had to compose a short verse in rhyming couplets before delivering it to the next victim. The verse was usually an insulting one, full of sexual innuendo. Something similar went on at harvest feasts in Scotland and Bavaria, and it seems that earlier the dried penis of an animal was used as in the Icelandic tale (Coffey 1989). The Faroese word for the tail-piece is *drunn*, apparently Celtic in origin. The passing round of an obvious phallic symbol at weddings and harvests was therefore likely to have been a practice known to the story-teller and his audience, but the joke might lie in the link made between such ribald games, familiar to Christians, and the pagan gods, and we cannot assume that we have memories here of a formal pre-Christian ceremony. There are, however, various hints about disreputable practices associated with Freyr, such as Saxo's reference to 'womanish bodily movements, the clatter of actors on the stage and the soft tinkling of bells' at Uppsala (VI, 185), and Christians showed special disapproval of rites connected with the Vanir.

In *Ynglinga Saga* Freyr is represented as a divine king, continuing to bless his people from his mound. There are also Danish traditions of a king being carried round among his people after death, as was one of a series of rulers called Frodi in Saxo (V, 171); this name, which might be translated 'fruitfulness', may be a title rather than a personal name. Freyr himself is called *inn fróði* in the poem *Skírnismál*. The Anglo-Saxons had a memory of Ing and his wagon, mentioned in the *Runic Poem*, and this name too is associated with Freyr, sometimes called Ingi-Freyr. One of the difficulties in understanding the cult of the Vanir deities, Freyr and Freyja, is the variety of names under which both seem to have been remembered. A ceremony connected with Freyr in the literature is the bringing of the god's image in a wagon to bless the land in the spring. There is a celebrated account of such a ritual for a goddess in Tacitus (*Germania* 40), said to take place in Denmark in the first century AD (p. 133). In *Flateyjarbók* (*Óláfs Saga Tryggvasonar* I, 277:337 ff.) we have another comic tale in which Freyr's image is similarly taken round the farms in Sweden, in a wagon drawn by oxen, attended by a young woman called his wife. The humour depends on a young Norwegian taking the place of Freyr's image, deceiving the simple-minded Swedes and delighting them by being able to eat and drink at their feasts, and finally getting his wife pregnant. Evidently such journeys of the god were known to go on in Sweden, and are mocked at here by the Christian story-teller. Another brief reference to a god in a wagon who may be Freyr is found in *Flateyjarbók* (*Óláfs Saga Tryggvasonar* I, 467:579), where the wagon of Lytir (otherwise unknown) is used for divination, and said to become heavy when the god is within. It was drawn to the royal hall, and the king put questions to Lytir. Such journeys may be seen as divination ceremonies, when omens were observed to discover if the harvest would be good, or questions put concerning the future of the kingdom or of individuals in the coming season.

Freyr, god of the land, could be evoked by the Swedes as a god of battle also, since his emblem, the boar, was set on shields and helmets and was a favourite symbol for warriors. He is called in poetry 'ruler of the hosts of the gods' (*Skírnismál*), while battle is called 'sport of Freyr' in a poem quoted in *Heimskringla* (*Haralds Saga Hárfagra* 15). The early kings of Uppsala were said to possess great helmets as battle treasures, bearing names like *Hildisvin* (Swine of Battle), and some helmets pictured on helmet plates from the Vendel graves (Stolpe and Arne 1927) appear almost like boar-masks. It is conceivable that the king put on such a helmet in order to be possessed by the god, and it may be noted that in one of the Edda poems, *Hyndluljóð*, a young prince who worshipped Freyja was disguised as her boar when he went down to the underworld to learn about his ancestry. The world of battle was closely linked to that of death, and Freyr is connected with both these worlds, as was Odin.

Odin, Thor and Freyr are the only three gods who emerge from the written sources as actively worshipped in the Viking Age. A number of others are mentioned in the literature, but no definite information is known about their cults. This applies to such familiar names as Loki, Njord, Tyr, Balder, Heimdall, Mimir, Ull, and the mysterious twin deities mentioned by Tacitus known as the Alcis. Many theories have been put forward as to the significance and importance of these various deities in the periods before the Viking Age, but here we are confined to conjecture and speculation. However, there is some definite information in the literature concerning the worship of the goddesses, and this will be discussed in the following chapter.

5

Goddesses and Guardian Spirits

Freyja kept up the sacrificing, for she alone lived on after the gods.
(*Ynglinga Saga* 10)

It would be a mistake to neglect the goddesses in this survey, since there is good reason to believe that their cults were important in everyday life, and were by no means confined to women and children. They were of considerable importance also among the Celtic peoples – even though we have little evidence as to how they were worshipped – for traces of powerful female divinities may be found in many Irish tales. One reason for our limited knowledge is no doubt because most of our records were written by men, and usually by monks, who would be unlikely to know much of the lore and practices of mothers, wives and unmarried girls who turned to the female deities to help them to achieve a good marriage or to give them healthy children; nor were they likely to give such matters their approval. Christian writers tended to condemn fertility rites, such as were usually associated with the female deities. Moreover, confusion is caused by the practice of giving many different names to one goddess, so that it is often assumed that these are separate divinities. It seems also that the goddesses were often worshipped in small local cults rather than in established public rituals like those of Thor or Odin. Sometimes they were represented as a group, receiving worship in Scandinavia as the Dísir, while the norns,valkyries and various female spirits of the Vanir are often introduced as groups of beings in the tales. In Ireland there is often a trio of goddesses under one name, as in the case of the Irish Brigid. Again, it is sometimes difficult to distinguish between goddesses and giantesses; a goddess might be conceived as huge or even monstrous in stature, while a giantess from the underworld might become the bride of a god.

The importance of the goddesses is indicated by their frequent appearance on carved stones of the Roman period in both Germanic and Celtic regions, and it may be noted that many of these stones were raised by men, including individuals of importance in the Roman army. Some outstanding female deities have already been mentioned in earlier chapters. There is the Germanic goddess Nehalennia depicted on many carved stones recovered from the North Sea coast in Holland (p. 49) and the Celtic goddesses Epona and Rosmerta, popular both in Britain and on the Continent (p. 46). The inscription to Sulis Minerva at Bath shows that the temple there was dedicated to a Roman goddess identified with Minerva, who must have been associated with a sacred spring (p. 129). Many goddesses, such as Coventina, guardian of the spring near Carrawburgh on Hadrian's Wall (p. 131), and Sequana, the deity worshipped at the source of the Seine, were of sufficient importance for their worship to be taken up by the Roman officials so that their names have survived. The reason for this seems often to be the healing properties of a spring over which the goddess presided, but many of these enigmatic figures had evidently other powers to do with fertility and divination.

THE CULT OF THE GREAT GODDESS

Clearly there was a multiplicity of local goddesses, but the literary sources also tend to give the impression of one supreme and powerful goddess, who might be regarded as wife or mistress of her worshipper. If he were a king, her cult would become part of the state religion, and she would receive official worship along with the leading gods. In Scandinavian tradition the main goddess appears to be Freyja, sister and perhaps also bride of Freyr; the names of these two Vanir deities are really titles, meaning 'Lord' and 'Lady', and Snorri tells us that Freyja had many other names. There is also the goddess Frigg, wife of Odin and therefore Queen of Heaven, who figures in the myths as the weeping mother, lamenting the fall of her son Balder and later that of Odin, her 'second woe', as *Vǫluspá* expresses it. It seems as if these two figures with similar names may indeed be two aspects of the same deity. Sometimes it is Freyja who is paired off with Odin in the tales, and she too is represented as a weeping goddess, shedding tears of gold; her tears serve as a favourite poetic symbol for gold in the kennings. Why Freyja weeps is not altogether clear; she is said to be searching for her husband, of whom we know nothing, but since he is called Óðr he may be a doublet of Odin.

Other possible representations of the main goddess under different names are Idun, the guardian of the golden apples of youth (p. 72), Gerd, the radiant maid of the underworld who meets Freyr as his bride in the poem *Skírnismál* (p. 71), and Gefion in Danish tradition, who according to *Ynglinga Saga* 5 ploughed the island of Zealand out of the land of Sweden, leaving a large lake behind. Additional names given by Snorri to Freyja are Mardǫll, suggesting a link with the sea; Hǫrn, thought to be related to *hǫrr*, 'flax'; Gefn, which like Gefion is related to the verb 'to give'; and Sýr, 'Sow'. All these names are relevant for the understanding of her cult, for she was connected with water and the sea, and flax was an important crop for which her blessing was sought; she was regarded as a giving goddess, bringing bounty to the fields, animals and mankind, while the sow was the female counterpart of Freyr's symbol, the golden boar.

There are various myths in which the gods strive to protect Freyja or rescue her from the giants who long to possess her; she is represented as the desired one, universal lover of gods and men. Her love-dealings with various gods are referred to in outspoken language in the poem *Lokasenna*, where Loki accuses her of accepting most of the gods as her lovers. In Irish literature we have parallels in figures like Medb, the queen of Connacht, with her constant stream of lovers, who shows no hesitation in granting her favours to any handsome hero who will give her help when needed (Bower 1975). Freyja takes her lover Ottar, who is of royal lineage, down into the underworld in the poem *Hyndluljóð* so that he may learn his ancestry; this is one of the occasions where she might be seen as a supernatural bride of the ruler of a kingdom. She had also dominion over the dead, and was said in *Grímnismál* 14 to possess half the slain while half passed to Odin. There is some indication that women were welcomed by Freyja after death, possibly after a sacrificial death; in *Egils Saga* 78 a woman who was proposing to commit suicide declared that she would eat nothing more until she came to sup with Freyja. It is possible that while in the figure of Frigg we see the great goddess ruling in the heavens, looking down with Wodan upon earth or sharing Odin's high seat (p. 79), in Freyja we see rather the goddess as queen of the underworld, at home in the land of the dead.

Freyja is represented as possessing a famous necklace, Brisingamen, if indeed it is a necklace and not, as some have claimed, a girdle or an amulet of some kind. One early skaldic poem refers to Loki and Heimdall fighting over this in the form of seals, so that evidently one of the exploits of Loki the arch-thief was to steal it; he does this again in one of the late legendary sagas, *Sǫrla þáttr*. A necklace is a symbol associated with the goddess from the earliest times of which we have record (Gimbutas 1982:44), so there are probably valid reasons for retaining it; the underworld maiden won by the hero in a late poem *Svipdagsmál* is called *Menglǫð*, 'Necklace-glad', which may be another of Freyja's many names. Hoever, the meaning of the name Brisingamen (?necklace of the Brisings) and its possible link with a splendid neck-ornament in *Beowulf* (1199) called 'necklace of the Brosings' remains an unsolved problem. Another precious possession of Freyja was her 'feather-form', which enabled her to fly as a bird; this she lent to Loki in *Thrymskviða* so that he could fly to the land of the giants, and again, according to Snorri, when he went to rescue Idun. Frigg apparently possessed a similar bird-form, since in an early kenning she is called 'mistress of the hawk's plumage' (*Skáldskaparmál* 1, 18). The link between birds and goddesses is strong in both Scandinavian and Celtic tradition, and seems to go back to early times, judging from the importance of the bird symbol in Celtic art. Again, Freyja is associated with precious metals; her tears are of gold, and she is a giving goddess, bringing prosperity and riches like her brother Freyr and her father Njord.

However, we hear little of rich goddess-images in temples in Norway or Iceland. The only goddess figure described as richly adorned in a shrine is that worshipped by Jarl Hakon of Halogaland in the late tenth century. The jarl was for some years virtually king of Norway, and was a determined opponent of Christianity, finally overthrown by Olaf Tryggvason. In a number of tales he is said to have worshipped Thorgerd, called *Hǫlgabrúðr* (presumably 'Bride of

Helgi'); he showed her great devotion, and she was known as his wife. In the Saga of Olaf Tryggvason in *Flateyjarbók* (I, 326:408), Olaf is said to take Thorgerd's image from the temple at Trondheim, strip it of its fine robe and gold and silver adornments, drag it along at his horse's tail and finally break it up and burn it along with the image of Freyr. The title 'Bride of Helgi' might be accounted for if Helgi were the mythical founder of the kingdom of Halogaland; the goddess could be seen as his wife, who became the bride of his various successors in turn. When he destroyed her image, Olaf declared that now she had lost Hakon, her husband, 'who was very dear to her', and added that the chiefs of the land had been loyal to her in turn, and had given her high praise.

Although such accounts are late, they are consistent in stressing Hakon's devotion to the goddess, and there is one earlier reference of the tenth century in a poem of Tine Hallkelsson which refers to Hakon in the arms of Gerd. The account of Hakon offering up his young son Erling, 'by such rites as were customary' (*Flateryjarbók*, *Óláfs Saga Tryggvasonar* 1, 154:191) sounds suspiciously like propaganda against the pagan jarl, but other tales are more sympathetic. Particularly impressive is the description of Thorgerd with her sister Irpa sending down a terrific hailstorm against the jarl's enemies, who saw Thorgerd as a monstrous being shooting arrows with great skill and rapidity. After a second hailstorm, the two goddesses appeared again on Hakon's ship, like the huge trollwomen said to be seen in dreams by men who took part in the Battle of Stamford Bridge (Davidson 1988:95). Dream imagery of this kind from the Icelandic sagas can provide valuable evidence for pre-Christian traditions; evidently it raised no objections from Christian writers as long as it was presented in dream-form.

In another tale of Thorgerd (*Flateyjarbók* I, 114), Sigmund from the Faroes visited Hakon, and was taken by the jarl to a shrine in the woods surrounded by a fence with gilded carving, holding images of the gods. Among the figures was one of a woman splendidly adorned, sitting on a bench, and Hakon threw himself on the ground before her, remaining like this for a long while. He then told Sigmund that they must make her an offering, and put down some silver; if she accepted it, he said, the ring on her finger would become loose. However, he failed to get it from her hand, whereupon he threw himself down again and wept; then he tried again, and was able to remove the ring. This he gave to Sigmund, in return for a promise never to part with it. Here no prejudice against Thorgerd enters into the narrative, and it is possible that in such tales we catch a rare glimpse of the cult of the northern goddess seen as the wife of the ruler.

The name 'Thorgerd', rather than 'Gerd', which is used in the early poem, may be due to confusion with one of Hakon's many wives. She was an historical character called Thora, daughter of Skagi Skoptason, and bore Hakon three children (N.K. Chadwick 1950). Gerd is one of the possible names for the goddess, used in *Skírnismál.* The vivid and haunting tale of Hakon's end given in *Heimskringla*, when he was hidden in a pit in the earth, and a herd of swine driven over it to conceal him, might be a misunderstanding of some reference to

Gerd, and to the boar or sow that was the emblem of the Vanir deities. The picture of Thorgerd with her bow is less suggestive of Freyja, but she may have had some link with a goddess of the Saami, the Lapp peoples, in Halogaland, with whom Hakon was in close contact (Davidson 1990). No doubt the dominant goddess with her many names varied in character according to the background against which her worship took place in different regions of Scandinavia.

It has been claimed that the cult of the Great Goddess was a powerful and important one in Scandinavia, and that the later cult of Odin in the Viking Age took over some of its ritual and symbolism (Ström 1954). However, the evidence we possess hardly justifies such sweeping assumptions. It is vague and suggestive merely: for instance, a series of verses on the early kings in the poem *Ynglingatal*, composed in the tenth century by Thjodolf of Hvin, tells how a number of Swedish kings met their deaths by drowning, burning or hanging, brought about by their wives. Such 'wives' could be references to the goddess viewed as wife of each king in turn, and when Snorri used the poem in *Ynglinga Saga*, he may have rationalized a record of sacrificial deaths. Here we are in the realm of speculation, since the verses are puzzling and obscure. It can only be said that a strong tradition of the goddess as the wife of the reigning king survives in Scandinavian literature, and that this is related to the last pagan ruler of Norway, Jarl Hakon, at the end of the tenth century.

This offers an interesting comparison with the territorial goddess in Irish tradition, who in the early literature is described as proffering a cup to the man destined to be king (MacCana 1955–8). In Irish literature we have the king appearing as a representation of human society, and the goddess as the divine power manifested in nature (McCone 1990:129 ff.). McCone points out that such an image of divine power in the natural world has biblical parallels and could therefore be accepted and developed by Christian monastic writers. A similar development of the ideals of kingship may be seen in the work of Saxo Grammaticus in the late twelfth century, when he uses native tales and poems in which protective guardian spirits assist princes to attain sovereignty; this is to support current theories concerning the virtues and vices of kings in his own time (Johanneson 1981). Here again, then, it is necessary to bear in mind the difficulties in attempting to reconstruct the thought-patterns of an early religion from the works of sophisticated writers of medieval Christian times.

Some of the evidence from early Irish literature, taken into consideration together with popular tradition, shows memories of beliefs in a major goddess. In a detailed study of legends about Cailleach Bearra or 'Hag of Beare', Ó Crualaoich (1988) suggests that on one level she appears to represent a version of 'a Mother Goddess emanating from the worlds of Indo-European and even old European cosmology'. She is linked with the image of a female guardian of the wild and also with that of the Sovereign Queen, and these two aspects are recognizable in the ninth-century 'Lament of the Old Woman of Beare' (Murphy 1953). Ó Crualaoich suggests that there may be Norse influences behind her associations with wild nature, while other important links are with the cow, and with reaping contests in harvest time. In the 'Lament', the Hag is identified with an elderly Christian nun, looking back on a glamorous past as the bride of kings; this is strengthened by the use of the word *caille* for a nun's veil. The Hag is linked with the Beare peninsula in south-west Ireland, but Wagner (1981) has suggested that earlier names given to her might be derived from titles of the *Magna Mater* from much earlier times.

Another side of the Cailleach Bearra is that of a Hag of war and death, and she shares such characteristics with various war-goddesses of Irish tradition (Ross 1973:155 ff.). Legends concerning her are by no means confined to one part of Ireland, and are also known in Scotland. In some of these she can be represented as Creator and Shaper of the landscape, suggesting the figure of Divine Mother. She is said to have taught the people how to thresh corn, and to have put to death a number of men who could not overcome her in a reaping contest. Similarly, the Irish goddess Ána/Aine is said to have been overcome by Lug in a harvest-contest. Such scattered but valuable evidence for a powerful creator goddess emerges when brief glimpses of such a figure in the literature are studied in the light of local legends.

Another powerful Celtic goddess who was more than a local deity and possessed far-ranging powers is indicated by the rich traditions associated with the Irish Brigid. Here we have a good example of a former deity transformed very successfully into a popular and revered Christian saint. It has been thought that the Minerva mentioned by Julius Caesar as the chief goddess in Gaul who inspired craftsmanship (*Gallic War* VI, 17) might be the same goddess, known as Brigantia to the Romans, who gave her name to the Brigantes, a tribe that came originally from central Europe (Joliffe 1941:37 ff.). A third-century inscription on Hadrian's Wall identifies Brigantia with Dea Caelistis, thus exalting her to the highest rank of divinity. The Romans also saw Brigantia as a goddess of victory and with powers of healing. Joliffe suggested that the Romans deliberately promoted Brigantia into a major deity for political reasons, but the wide-ranging powers of Brigid were echoed in the cult of the saint. In Cormac's *Glossary* Brigid had two sisters of the same name, daughters of the Dagda, one of whom specialized in healing and one in the craft of the smith. She was associated with such crafts as dyeing, weaving and the brewing of ale, and with the welfare of flocks and herds, as well as with the art of poetry, and with traditional learning, divination and prophecy, so that her powers extended into many aspects of the life of the community.

The Christian Brigid was said to have been the Abbess of Kildare, and references to her go back to the seventh century. She had the power to increase the milk-yield and to help with butter-making, to change water to ale and stone to salt, and was called 'the All-Giving'. She was fed by a cow which seems to be a creature of the Otherworld, and her festival was on 1st February, the ancient spring festival associated with the rearing of young animals (p. 89). There is, however, no firm evidence for the Abbess as an historical figure (Ó Cathasáigh 1982:82 ff.). There seems good reason to believe that here we have scattered traces of a once-powerful goddess, whose cult was important for the community as a whole.

THE LOCAL GODDESSES

Nevertheless, the goddess figure is not really an isolated one; Snorri in the Prose Edda is certainly under the impression that there was a large company of female deities. In reply to the query as to who were the gods, the High One gave the number as twelve, and his companion added: 'No less holy are the goddesses (*ásynjurnar*) nor are their powers less' (*Gylfaginning* 19). There are references to worship of the Dísir, another word for female deities generally used in the plural, although *día* is occasionally used of a single goddess such as Freyja or Skadi. It is said that sacrifices were offered in the hall of the Dísir at Uppsala, and there are also references to feasts in their honour in the autumn taking place in Norway, as in *Víga-Glúms Saga* 6 and *Egils Saga* 44. The former of these was held in the hall of the hero's grandfather in western Norway, and the latter on one of the king's estates, attended by Eirik Bloodaxe and his queen. It is not clear whether this was a feast held separately from that of the gods, since it seems to have taken place at the same time of year, in the period of the Winter Nights (p. 88). It is generally assumed that the Dísir were family guardian spirits, closely associated with particular localities, to whom sacrifices were made for the luck and fertility of the land and those owning it, and thus at the highest level connected with the royal dynasty.

They may therefore be linked with the group of supernatural beings known as land-spirits, who were closely connected with the land itself. Some interesting traditions have survived in *Landnámabók* about help given to early settlers in Iceland who made a voluntary contract with such local spirits (Davidson 1988:103 ff.). A number of these were female, and traditions survive up to recent times of stones in Iceland sacred to the *land-dísir* which had to be left undisturbed, so that the grass remained uncut round them, and children were forbidden to play games close by, in case the protective spirits were offended (Turville-Petre 1963). A number of places in Norway and Sweden were also named after the Dísir (de Vries 1957–8:II, 298). The land-spirits, male and female, were said to promote the increase of livestock and maintain the prosperity of the farms, as well as giving good luck in hunting and fishing, and bringing helpful counsel in dreams.

Memories of such figures may be found in traditions of female supernatural beings in Sweden, such as the *sjörå* and the *skogsrå* (Lindow 1978:39), the first associated with lakes and rivers, and the second with forests. In Irish literature there is also evidence of female guardian spirits who were connected with certain families. In her study of the Irish Banshee, the death-messenger, Lysaght came to the conclusion that such a spirit was associated with families of early origin (Lysaght 1986:53 ff.). Parallels can be found in the Scottish Highlands, where, as in Sweden, there are legends of supernatural women who looked after both the animals on the farm and the wild creatures in the forests and hills. One name for such a being is *Glaistig*, and they were closely linked with particular places. The Glaistig of Glen Duror, for instance, protected cows, while the Maiden of Callart guarded the deer on the hills. She once gave a wonderful dog to an old hunter, whose own dog was growing old and could no longer run fast, and she promised that the hound would never fail to run down any four-footed creature that he pursued. When his master died, the dog disappeared into a cave in the rocks and was never seen again (MacDougall 1978:53ff.). Two mountains called the Maidens were said to be named by him after the two supernatural women who appeared to the hunter. It seems that the protective spirit, like Jarl Hakon's Thorgerd, had a 'sister' with her when she appeared, although only one of the pair offers a gift.

The family guardian spirit, who brought prosperity to the land but was also concerned to protect the women and children of the family and ensure the succession, is also found in the Scottish Highlands. One instance is the Fairy Wife of Clan MacLeod, said to have given Ian Keir, the Chief who died in 1390, the Fairy Banner still to be seen in Dunvegan Castle, promising to protect the Clan as long as it remained in the family's possession. A story is told of how she was once seen nursing the baby who was the heir, and wrapping him in the banner, when his nurse had left him alone, while she sang a lullaby still preserved in the family (MacGregor 1937:20 ff.). She also gave a chanter to Iain Og MacCrimmon, a young man who afterwards became the hereditary piper to the Chief (MacGregor 1937:34 ff.). There are many other examples of tales of this type, such as that of the spirit Nic Gilmichael, a maiden attached to the Campbells of Glen-Faochan, who looked after the servants and punished them if they neglected their work. When the estate was sold, it was said that at night she could be heard lamenting among the trees around the house (MacDougall 1978:47).

The giving of a hunting dog to an unnamed 'gentleman' in the story from Callart recalls various instances of gifts of animals from the land-spirits in Iceland. In one case the gift of a goat resulted in the increase of the farmer's herd (Davidson 1988:103). Just as the dog vanished into a hill when his master died, so a flock of sheep that prospered through help from a land-spirit plunged into a waterfall on the death of the farmer (Davidson 1989b:107). Similarly, there are stories from Wales about women who come out of a lake bringing wonderful cattle with them, become the wives of farmers, and then return taking the animals with them when the husband does not keep his side of the contract. The most famous of these is the tale of the Lady of Llyn y Fan Fach, a mountain lake near Llandeusant (Rhys 1901:I, 2 ff.). The widespread distribution of such legends is a testimony to the established belief in a local female spirit of land or water, who might be viewed as a local goddess (Wood 1992). Such figures in the tales often possess a dual nature; they can be benevolent and generous, showing great loyalty to the families to which they are attached and saving individuals, including the children of the house, from danger; but if angered or humiliated they may prove dangerous and formidable powers.

There seems good reason to believe that such beliefs among the country people in both Celtic and Germanic areas went on for many centuries, and they give some idea of the part played by local goddesses in the community in the period before Christianity. Here we are left with a host of legends, to which one can hardly give the name of 'myth', but which were passed on in local tradition, surviving because they were often associated with natural features such as lakes, springs and mountains. The many representations of the Mothers on stones of the Roman period suggest a similar attitude to female protective spirits of this kind (p. 48).

Another group of minor goddesses may be seen in figures associated with both the plough and the spinning-wheel in Germany, Austria and Switzerland. Jakob Grimm had noted them as possible memories of pre-Christian goddesses (Grimm 1883:265 ff.), and Waschnitius published a rich collection of such traditions in 1913. They bore names such as Holde, Frau Holle, Perht and Berta, spelt in various ways in different regions, or less frequently, Frau Gode, St Lucia and other names. Some of these might be titles: Holde seems to come from an adjective meaning 'merciful', 'benign', and Perht and Berta from one meaning 'bright' or 'glorious'. Holde and Perht were closely associated with spinning, and legends about them circulated in the spinning-room where women and girls worked. They approved of good spinners, but punished those who were lazy and slovenly, setting fire to their distaffs or tangling and breaking their thread (Waschnitius 1913:20, 33, 56, 65, 89 etc.). They were also angered if anyone worked at her wheel at forbidden times, such as the days between Christmas Eve and Twelfth Night, or on Saturday evening, Sunday or the evenings of various festivals, while spinning at night was also prohibited. In extreme cases they were said to cut open the stomachs of offending ones and put in chopped straw, or sweepings from the floor. Naughty children who did not eat up their food might be threatened with similar treatment, or told that Perht would stamp on them in the night, or Frau Holle would carry them off in her sack.

However, in spite of such sinister threats, they were evidently regarded as the guardians of children. There were legends in some families that Birta as a White Lady would rock the cradle when the nurse fell asleep, and that Frau Holle would draw children to her pond and reward good ones generously. They also helped young women and brides: Frau Berta in the Tyrol would visit them, give them thread and yarn and help them with their spinning, while in Thuringia Frau Holle, appearing as a grey-haired woman with long teeth, might leave a gift by the distaff, or bring children presents in her wagon on New Year's Eve. They might also be present when a bride's chest was taken to her new home, while young women who bathed in Frau Holle's pool hoped to become healthy and fertile wives.

There is also mention of such women driving wagons, and of those who helped them when the wagon broke down being rewarded by chips of wood which turned into gold (Motz 1984). They were also said to travel with a plough, attended by a troop of tiny children. Sometimes these are said to be the spirits of those who died unbaptized, or infants who had been carried away leaving changelings in their place, but it seems possible that at one time they were thought to be the souls of the unborn, since in some districts babies were said to come from Frau Holle's house, or from her pool. The association with the plough is interesting in view of later Plough Monday ceremonies, since the period associated with these female spirits extended to about 6 January. Motz (1984) has argued that these various beings represented an earlier Germanic winter goddess, but this hardly seems to be borne out by the evidence Waschnitius collected, and spinning is not confined to winter. However, they certainly visited homes at Christmas, when tables might be laid for them or milk left with spoons crossed over the bowl; the position in which the spoons were found when the family returned from church would foretell the future of members of the household in the coming year, while the milk might be given to the hens to help them lay, or to the cows (Waschnitius 1913:36, 48, 57, 62). Records of such visits go back to early sources, which refer to a troop of children accompanying the goddess, and those who tried to get a glimpse of them being smitten with blindness. Special cakes or prepared dishes would be eaten on the feast-days of such beings, while the day might also be celebrated by bands of masked or disguised youths waving whips and chasing passers-by or visiting houses; sometimes the local goddess might be carried about, represented as a grotesque or monstrous figure (Waschnitius 1913:37, 57, 73).

There is no doubt of the link between such spirits and the natural world. Frau Holle was said to be making her bed or turning her mattress when snow fell; fog was the smoke from her fire, and thunder caused by her reeling her flax. Holle might bring flowers and fruit from her beautiful garden, and she was said to go round the fields to make them fruitful, like Nerthus in Denmark much earlier (p. 133) and to awaken the apple trees in spring. Waschnitius suggested that her connection with spinning arose from her link with the growing of flax, but it may be noted that there is also a widespread and ancient link between a spinning goddess and human destinies (p. 138). Again, the dual nature of these goddesses is very marked; the local spirit might appear as a benign White Lady rising from her pool or as an ugly monster. There is also folklore from the British Isles connected with supernatural helpers who use a spinning-wheel, such as the tale of Habetrot, where an old woman who lives under the earth with a company of other spinners befriends a feckless girl who hates spinning and ensures a splendid marriage for her (Briggs 1970:303).

Such legends are a valuable source of evidence for the nature of the belief in the protective goddesses who especially helped women and children. Parallels to those customs noted by Waschnitius may be found in records of local traditions in many parts of north-western Europe, for instance those associated with St Brigid in Ireland. Her festival is 1st February, and on that day spinning was forbidden, and sometimes ploughing and smithying also. The saint was said to travel round the countryside on the eve of her festival, and buttered bread or a dish of porridge might be left on the window-sill for her, or the table set with food as for the German visitants. Images of Brigid might be carried round, or a girl dressed in white might represent the saint. A wild group of youths in fantastic costumes, known as the biddies, might also visit houses and terrify the children (Danaher 1972:13 ff.).

There is also a tradition found in France of a travelling goddess fleeing from her enemies who made the corn sprout and grow with miraculous rapidity. This later became attached to legends of the Virgin Mary fleeing with the Christ Child to Egypt, and to various female saints. Berger (1988) has shown that it can be traced back to medieval times. Another striking example of the transference of earlier rites to Christian tradition is given by Thevenot (1968:191). He describes pilgrimages to the shrine of Notre-Dame-de-la-vie in a remote district north of Lyon, which continued as late as 1960. Gifts such as cereals, cheese and butter were brought in large quantities to the little chapel of Belleville, where there was a sacred spring, and gifts of sheep and cattle sold by auction. A small stone figure there is said to represent the Virgin, and this is clearly of considerable age; Thevenot thinks it may even date back to Roman times. According to local tradition, it originally represented a pregnant woman, but was mutilated some time in the last century because this was felt to be improper. The figure wears a hood and holds an object like a muff, apparently a symbol of the spring whose waters were believed to have healing powers. Women in particular came for healing, bringing cloths to dip in the water and apply to afflicted parts of their bodies, and there are records from the seventeenth century of dead babies being temporarily restored to life when brought there, so that it was possible to baptize them.

Clearly, there is a considerable amount of material provided by folk tradition and legend that can add to our understanding of the cults of local goddesses in pre-Christian times, and a great deal remains as yet unexplored. From the pre-Christian period archaeology provides us with a few hints only. In Scandinavia locks of hair, gold rings and various women's ornaments have been found at offering-places in use before the Viking Age, and also traces of flax, together with instruments for beating it (Arbman 1945). In the sixth century Gregory of Tours refers to offerings of cheese, wax, bread and spices of various kinds, 'which would take too long to enumerate' (Hagberg 1967:67). A good deal of work has now been done on offerings of weapons thrown into lakes or swamps, but we know little about the kind of offerings that might have been made to the goddesses, and such objects as cheese or bread would leave little trace in earth or water. Written sources may help to fill the gap here, and remind us of the constant link between female spirits and the work done on the farms in stable, kitchen or dairy, while the value of popular tradition in filling the gap must not be underestimated.

GUARDIAN SPIRITS

It becomes apparent that the mythical world must be extended beyond the company of the powerful individual gods to that of supernatural guardians and protectors of a lesser kind, with whom a covenant might be made. It is not always easy, however, to draw a clear line of separation between them and the leading gods. Worshippers of Thor or Freyr in the sagas might similarly make a covenant with their favourite deity and receive help in making decisions and planning a course of action (p. 102), and certain families apparently chose to worship one particular god, usually Thor or Freyr, in this way.

There are also examples, however, of local guardian spirits, either male or female, attached to a family, and the valkyries, originally spirits of battle associated with the war god, may also function in this way, appearing in poems and stories as the guardians and brides of young heroes. Such beings are found in the early books of Saxo's *History*, usually appearing in a small group, and again in the Helgi poems (Davidson 1988:93 ff.). Besides giving help and victory in battle to their protégés, and receiving them after death, as would be appropriate for a battle spirit, they may also present a young prince with a weapon and even give him a name.

Together with the norns and the Dísir, they appear to determine the destiny of an individual and may be present at the birth of a child. The norns are represented in the poem *Vǫluspá* as three powerful women who 'cut on wood'; Holtsmark has explained this expression by the custom in Norwegian farmhouses as late as the nineteenth century of recording important dates or numbers of months or years by notches cut into a plank in the wall, often above a window (Holtsmark 1951:85 ff.). In the poem the three are named Urd, Verdandi and Skuld. Urd is the name of the being representing fate who sits by the spring under the World Tree, and she might therefore be linked with the time of birth when an individual's fate is decreed. Verðandi comes from the verb *verða* (to become) and could stand for the time of life on earth; while Skuld (something owed) could be linked with death, the debt which all must pay (*Njáls Saga* 119). It has been suggested that this concept of three fates has been borrowed from classical mythology, but if so it seems to have been thoroughly absorbed into native tradition. In the first of the Helgi poems in the Poetic Edda the norns are described in a cosmic setting, 'with power weaving the web of fate', and fastening the golden threads of the young prince's destiny 'in the midst of the hall of the moon'. In the Icelandic Sagas, however, the norns have been transformed into local wise women, journeying round the farms and uttering words of prophecy concerning the destiny of small children. Here we have certain echoes of the Mothers of an earlier period, with their rolls of destiny and infants in their arms or at their knees.

Again, there is some confusion between such figures who determine the fate of mortals and the Dísir, sometimes represented as supernatural beings attached to one particular family. In an early poem of Bjorn of Hitdale, he refers to foreseeing Dísir, who are summoning him to death, and there is a reference in the Edda poem *Atlamál* to Dísir seen in a dream summoning the king to join them, which means that he is about to die. In a series of verses attributed to Gisli Sursson in his saga, thought to have been composed after his lifetime however, perhaps in the twelfth century, there are references to two women who visited him in his dreams when he was living a lonely life as an outlaw. One of these was destructive and hostile, while the other was compassionate and welcoming. The threatening woman foretold his death by violence, but the other promised to receive him into her dwelling. Two companies of women, one dressed in dark clothing and armed like valkyries and the other in shining white, appear in the tale of the death of Thidrandi told in *Flateyjarbók* (I, 418 ff.). The dark women are said to be the Dísir of the family, angry because Hall and his household had accepted Christianity, while the women in white are the Dísir of the new faith, as yet too far away to be able to prevent the slaying of Thidrandi as an act of vengeance by the family spirits (Davidson 1988:140 ff.; 106). In both cases we have what appear to be memories of an earlier belief adapted to fit into a Christian setting.

The term *fylgja* ('following one') is another used occasionally for a female spirit in the literature. It can refer to an animal form, which may represent someone in a dream, or be visible to a person with second sight as it accompanies its human partner (Davidson 1978a). However, the *fylgjukona* ('following woman'), seen by those with the poet Hallfred at the time of his death, is evidently an attendant spirit of the family, who is received by Hallfred's son after the poet's death (*Hallfreðar Saga* 11). She may be compared with the spirit seen in a dream by Glum on the death of his grandfather in Norway (*Víga-Glúms Saga* 9). In the verse describing her, she is called a goddess, but in the prose account she is said to be the *hamingja* of the dead Vigfuss. This word can be used for good fortune and strength, such as a powerful king possessed, and she seems here to represent the good luck of the family, which was now to pass to the hero.

Among the land-spirits attached to the countryside, there are many male spirits also, sometimes called 'rock-dwellers' in the Icelandic sagas (Davidson 1988:103). One of these visited Goat-Bjorn in a dream, according to a tale in *Landnámabók* (S, 329; H, 284:330), and offered to enter into partnership with him. Another spirit said to dwell with his family in a great stone (*Kristnis Saga* 2; *Þorvalds þáttr* 2) is called both *ármaðr*, 'harvest-man', and *spámaðr*, 'one who foretells the future'. He was driven out by the Christian bishop with prayers and holy water, and the farmer regretted his departure, since, he said, 'he tells me beforehand many things that will happen in the future, he guards my cattle and gives me warning of what to do and what to avoid, and therefore I have faith in him and I have worshipped him for a long while'. Another rock-dweller is Bard of Snaefell, a mountain spirit who helped people in need and protected them against evil beings, whose story is told in a half-legendary saga *Bárðar Saga Snaefellsáss*. He lived high in the mountains, and is described as wearing a grey cloak and hood, with a belt of walrus-hide round his waist, and carrying a long staff like a shepherd's crook with a two-pronged handle and a spike to help him across the glacier. He also had a family which included a number of daughters, some of whom might visit local farms, but remained hidden from sight, like household guardian spirits. He is called the 'god' (*áss*) of Snaefell, and there are references to other such beings on Svinfell (*Njáls Saga* 123), and Dovrefjell in Norway, where the giant Dofri was said to have fostered and helped Harald Fairhair (Ellis 1943).

The land-spirits were held to be offended and alarmed by violence. In one place in southern Iceland where a settler was murdered by his thralls, it was said that no one for a long while dared settle in this area 'on account of the land-spirits' (*Landnámabók* S, 330:333). It is recorded that no ship was permitted to enter Icelandic waters with a threatening figure-head on the prow, because this would alarm the land-spirits (*Landnámabók* H, 268:313). This should not, however, be taken as an indication that the hard-headed Icelanders had a naïve, childish belief in such spirits. Land-spirits were a symbol for them of their independence, as may be seen in the tale of the wizard sent by a Danish king to Iceland in the form of a whale who was frightened away by the land-spirits who appeared on every side, since 'all the mountains and hills were filled with land-spirits, some great and some small' (*Heimskringla*, *Óláfs Saga Tryggvasonar* 33). This is a jesting tale mocking at the pretensions of the ambitious Danish king, but on the other hand there was a strong assumption that was anything but naïve that the spirits of the land must be in harmony with their rulers to ensure prosperity (Davidson 1988:107).

The figures of such protective spirits appear to resemble those depicted on carved votive stones of the Roman period in England, known as the *Cucullati* or 'Hooded Ones' (Figure 29). They are found near Hadrian's Wall in the north and

Figure 29 Three hooded figures from Romano-British carving, Cirencester. Drawing by Eileen Aldworth.

also in the Cotswolds, and appear to be male, usually depicted in groups of three; they wear a hood and a cloak that reaches either to their knees or down to their ankles. Sometimes they are pictured in company with one of the Mother Goddesses, and like her they may carry symbols of plenty, such as fruit or eggs. Sometimes these little beings are depicted in naturalistic Roman fashion, while other carvings are clearly the work of native artists. The votive tablets indicate that both soldiers and civilians took an interest in these protective spirits, and belief in them evidently flourished among the Celtic people of Britain, as some of the stones were set up on country estates (Davidson 1989b).

Such traditions did not wholly die after the coming of Christianity, since there is a rich store of tales about brownies and other house-spirits recorded in many parts of the British Isles. They might be attached to certain families, and they helped with the hard work of the farm, such as harvesting and threshing, with the care of the animals, and also in the dairy and kitchen. They protected the women and children, and sometimes helped over childbirth. In return for their labours they asked little more than a supply of fresh creamy milk, left on the hearth or outside the house; if cheated over this, or treated with disrespect, they could be both mischievous and dangerous, and there are many amusing tales of how they turned the tables on those who made them unwelcome. They were known under various names, such as Hob, Puck, boggart, *grogach* in Ulster, *bwca* in Wales, and *fenodoree* on the Isle of Man. There was much local tradition about them in the sixteenth and seventeenth centuries in England, as we learn from Shakespeare's *Midsummer Night's Dream* and Milton's *L'Allegro*, and many references in plays and verse. Such guardian spirits brought good luck to the household, and took it away if they left. They were generally male, but occasionally had female companions (Davidson 1989b).

Such humble spirits need to be borne in mind along with the greater gods when striving to reconstruct the lost religion of northern Europe. Close parallels to the British spirits are found in other European countries, and it seems probable that half-serious, half-mocking beliefs of this kind formed a familiar part of the supernatural in earlier times, contributing to the general picture of the Otherworld. Their comparatively humble status helped them to survive the hostility of the Christian church and to linger on in folk tradition. In the Viking Age they may have been part of the company of the Vanir. We often hear of the Æsir and Vanir, and also of the Æsir and the elves in the poetry of the Edda. The earlier conception of elves differed from the tiny creatures of modern children's tales, and one of the Norwegian kings who was said to benefit his people after he was laid in his mound was called the Elf of Geirstad (p. 122). Elves were also linked with Freyr, said to dwell at Alfheim. This group of lesser beings, then, must not be discounted in any study of the divine world of pre-Christian tradition, and here we have an example of the value of folk tradition in helping us to reconstruct the past, even though our ideas of the way in which this was preserved and developed may differ greatly from those of earlier scholars like the Grimm brothers.

THE CULT OF THE DEAD

The attitude to the dead in northern religion is by no means easy to define. Many of the tales that have found their way into the Icelandic sagas express a primitive attitude towards the dead, who are viewed as hostile to the living, grudging them life and desirous to deprive them of it. A terror of the dead is expressed in tales of those who refuse to lie quiet, and who as *draugar*, animated corpses of great strength and ferocity, become destructive beings who lay waste whole districts in the long winter nights. The only means of dealing with the restless dead was to overcome them by force, cut off their heads, and finally destroy the bodies by burning (Davidson 1981b). Archaeology provides us with examples of mutilated and sometimes headless bodies with the head included in the burial, which might be the result of such fears of the dead walking out of the grave (Simmer 1982:43 ff.).

However, in spite of this deep-rooted fear of the dangerous dead, there is some indication that the dead might also be regarded as guardian spirits, helping and supporting the living. For this reason they must not be forgotten in any consideration of such spirits in the family or community. The Celtic custom of treasuring the heads of dead enemies seems at least to have been partly based on the belief that this brought strength and good fortune to the victor. Graves of former kings were regarded as sacred places, and also as centres of inspiration. It was of importance to know where kings of the remote past were buried, and the poem on the Swedish kings composed in the tenth century, *Ynglingatal*, which was used by Snorri in *Ynglinga Saga*, shows the emphasis on death and the place of burial in the case of these semi-mythical figures. There are references to offerings of gold, silver and copper at Freyr's mound (*Ynglinga Saga* 10), while the Norwegian king Olaf known as the Elf of Geirstad was said in *Flateyjarbók* (*Óláfs Saga helga* II, 6:7) to be worshipped after death; this was the king held to have a special link with his descendant Olaf II, the Saint. The story goes that the younger Olaf could not be born until the sword of the earlier king was brought from his burial mound, together with the sword-belt and a gold ring, and the belt put round the mother, while the name 'Olaf' was afterwards given to the newborn child. There is a strange account of St Olaf's men asking him if he had been buried in the mound of the earlier king, whereupon he became angry, denying that his soul could ever inhabit two bodies, 'either now or on the Resurrection Day', since this was clearly contrary to Christian teaching.

The use of the term 'Elf' for the dead king is of particular interest here. It is also said of this Olaf's brother, Halfdan the Black, that many different regions of the kingdom wished to possess his body after death, 'for they thought if they could obtain it it would bring them prosperous seasons' (*Heimskringla*, *Hálfdanar Saga* 9). There seems to have been an assumption also that the remote, unknown dead of an earlier period might still be able to help the living. Archaeological evidence shows that sacred places such as Tara in Ireland and Tynwald in the Isle of Man were situated on earlier burial grounds, while the holy centre at Uppsala in the Viking Age was surrounded by many grave-mounds large and small, some of which go back at least to the Migration Period.

The importance of the burial mound is confirmed by extensive archaeological evidence for rich burials, apparently necessitating elaborate funeral ritual and expensive provision of valuable grave-goods (p. 21). The great Scandinavian ship-burials must have been planned with deliberate use of religious symbolism, and one contemporary account by an Arab writer of the early tenth century certainly confirms this. In Ibn Fadlan's detailed account of a cremation funeral on the Volga by Swedish merchant-adventurers in 921, we find reference to complex funeral rites, including songs, ritual actions and animal and human sacrifice (Smyser 1965). Of especial interest is his description of the ceremony where the girl who was to be offered up as a sacrifice as the bride of the dead chief was made to look through a frame into what appears to represent the Otherworld; she described it as green and fair, claiming to see her husband and her dead kinsfolk awaiting her.

The welcome by ancestors and kindred in the Otherworld is remembered too in Icelandic literature. According to *Eyrbyggja Saga* 11, Thorstein Thorolfsson, while still a young man, was drowned along with his crew when out fishing one night. He and his companions were seen by a shepherd entering the holy hill Helgafell, which his father had chosen as a sacred place when he settled in Iceland (p. 102). Inside, it was bright with lights and men were sitting drinking, as his father from the world of the dead welcomed his son, and he was led to the seat of honour. There could not have been many inside the hill, since Thorolf, the drowned man's father, had been one of the first settlers to come out to this part of Iceland, but it seems as if the concept of ancestors dwelling in a hill was already established. Another relevant passage is from *Víga-Glúms Saga* 26, where the hero, who had offended the god Freyr, had a dream. He is said to see Freyr sitting on a chair near the river, while many people thronged about him, and was told that these were his own dead kinsfolk, who had come to beg Freyr not to let him be driven from his land. Here Freyr is seen in company with the dead of one particular family, and Glum's forebears strive to help him to escape the god's anger, although without success.

Another reason for seeking the help of the dead was to receive inspiration. In a tale from *Flateyjarbók* (*Óláfs Saga Tryggvasonar* 174:214), a shepherd called Hallbjorn is said to have sat on the burial mound of a dead poet called Thorleif while minding his sheep. He wanted to make a poem in praise of the dweller in the mound, but was not skilled in word-craft and could get no further than the opening line: 'Here lies a poet ...' One night he dreamed that the mound opened, and a huge man came out and sat beside him. He thanked Hallbjorn for his efforts, and told him that he was going to recite a verse to him, and that if Hallbjorn remembered it after he woke up he would become a famous poet. After this Hallbjorn found no difficulty in composing poetry; he is remembered as a poet at the Danish court and later at that of King Sverri in Norway, although his work has not survived. This tale offers an interesting parallel to that of the gift of poetry given to Caedmon as related by Bede in his *Ecclesiastical History* (IV, 24). Caedmon was inspired by an angel, who appeared to him in the stable and taught him a verse, while Hallbjorn got his inspiration from the dead poet. There seems no reason why the Icelandic tradition should not be an independent one, and indeed a much later Icelandic poet of the nineteenth century claimed to have learnt a verse from a dead poet in a dream in a similar way (Turville-Petre 1966).

There are further instances of dreams caused by sleeping on burial mounds. When King Halfdan the Black wanted to have meaningful dreams, by which he probably meant dreams foretelling the future, he was told by a wise man that he himself would sleep in 'the dwelling of swine' when he needed to dream. N.K. Chadwick (1968:41) suggested that this might mean that the seer used to sleep on a burial mound, since the pig was the symbol of Freyr and the Vanir, and Freyr was specially associated with mounds; this idea might have arisen from a kenning. Another story in *Flateyjarbók* (*Óláfs Saga Tryggvasonar* I, 206:253) tells of a dream of Thorstein Ox-Foot which resulted in the recovery of his mother's power of speech. When he was a boy aged 10, he was out with a servant when they came to a great burial mound. He declared that he was going to sleep on it, and ordered the thrall not to wake him, however he behaved in his sleep, 'for I believe that much depends on it'. He was very restless while he slept, but the man did not wake him. Next morning he told his dream, and how a man in red, of great size, had come out of the mound and invited him in. There he saw eleven other men in red and twelve in black, with an evil-looking leader of the black men who bullied the rest. Thorstein was told that this man possessed a ring that could heal his mother, who was dumb, so he attacked him with an axe, and battle broke out. The wounds dealt by the men from the mound had no lasting effect, but those of Thorstein did, and so with his help the men in red were victorious, and Thorstein obtained the ring. The man in red then entreated him to pass on his name to a son, so that the dead might 'come under baptism'. Here a Christian slant has been given to the tale, but the idea of the dream on the mound and the healing obtained as a result seems likely to have come from an earlier world of belief. The two contrasted pictures of the dead – one of hostile beings and the other as helpers with whom a contract could be made – are characteristic of the attitude to the dead as a whole in Norse tradition.

Dead men may also appear in dreams, like the land-spirits, to give needed information. In *Flóamanna Saga* a man learns in a dream how he can overcome a berserk in a duel. In *Sturlunga Saga* 136 a dead man who had fallen in battle is said to appear in one of the many dreams mentioned in this saga, a gruesome figure with his head half-sliced away, to foretell violence to come. Another dream-figure in the same saga is said to be the famous Gudrun of heroic tradition, who declared she had come from Hel, the abode of the dead, to give warning of a coming battle to a girl aged 16, whose name is given. Sometimes the dead appear to complain of being disturbed by the living, like the dead seeress in *Laxdœla Saga* 76 whose grave lay under a church, or Asolf in *Landnámabók* (H, 21:63) who objected to a girl herding cattle wiping her muddy feet on his mound. His bones were afterwards dug up, whereupon he appeared in a dream to the man who had disturbed his peace, threatening to make his eyes start out of his head if he did not leave him alone. Asolf had always been a difficult character: he was one of the few Christians to settle in Iceland early on, had not got on with other people and finally retired to live alone as a hermit, but was remembered as a man with special powers. The strength of the dream tradition and the conviction that many have the power to 'dream true' still persists in Iceland, and dreams clearly formed an important link both with the dead and the land-spirits.

It is evident that the guardian spirits of the pre-Christian religion cannot be easily arranged in clearly defined compartments. It is important to recognize their complexity, and also how such concepts continued to develop in Christian literature because of their power as symbolic images. Many of these guardian spirits belonged to local or family tradition, so that there was much that was spontaneous and individual about them, and we are fortunate that in Iceland some pre-Christian beliefs and practices have been remembered and recorded. If we are to understand the religion of the past, it is essential to investigate such evidence, to gain some idea of what such traditions meant to those who preserved or added to them. Some understanding of how folklore traditions evolve and are passed on, often with the help of written literature, is a valuable clue towards the interpretation of a religion never fully organized or governed from a powerful centre. After the change to Christianity, the figures of the guardians became increasingly blurred, as one image influenced another. It may be noted that comparatively few of them have personal names, with the exception of the known dead and the valkyries, many of whose names were probably invented by poets of the Viking Age.

Belief in such spirits was evidently linked with the cults of the gods, and a variety of different beings, male and female, were apparently included in the group known as the Vanir, led by the god and goddess associated with fertility. The saga-tellers make frequent use of tales about them to enrich their plots, and the number of helpful spirits mentioned in *Landnámabók* in a casual way gives some idea of the richness of the material on which they could draw. They formed a link also with the older heroic legends, such as we find in the Helgi poems and Saxo. Further back in the Germanic and Celtic past, the vast number of votive stones and representations of guardian beings of various sorts that have survived into our own day in England, France, Germany and the Netherlands shows that such traditions played a part in the lives of the rich and influential as well as in those of simple folk. In Christian times similarly we find an enormous amount of material concerning local saints and their shrines, including hymns in their honour, carved stones in churches and gifts and votive inscriptions left by those who received help and healing. Some of the earlier guardian figures, such as Brigid, took on new life in the character of Christian saints. As the saints had their place in the structure of the Christian church, so the spirits were linked with the more powerful gods, and thus found entry into the world of mythological poems and tales used by Snorri when he looked for material for his Prose Edda and histories of the early kings. In any account of the pre-Christian supernatural world, it is evident that this popular element must not be forgotten, since it was one that was very real to the men and women of the Viking Age and earlier, and they perceived no clear line of separation between such spirits and the cults of the greater gods.

6

Contacts with the Otherworld

> Far have I fared, much have I dared,
> oft have I tested the Powers
>
> (*Vafþrúðnismál* 3)

The surviving evidence for the pre-Christian religion in north-western Europe leaves us with a confused but lively impression of a world-picture now lost, which once inspired an abundance of tales and legends, as well as a vigorous pictorial and symbolic art, even though very little of this has survived. Much of the art was carved in wood, and the examples that have come down to us, like those from the Oseberg ship from southern Norway in the ninth century, show complex skills in artistic expression, as well as a plentiful use of symbolism. Another source of art almost wholly lost is that of designs and narrative scenes on narrow panels of tapestry or embroidered pictures, which were set up in halls on festive occasions, or on board ships in harbour. Isolated examples like the Bayeux tapestry and the roll from the Oseberg ship with its medley of supernatural figures (Figure 30) reveal how rich a source this could have been. A number of references to such pictures of mythical or heroic subjects in Old Norse poetry indicate that this kind of work, carried out by aristocratic women, may have had a considerable influence in preserving religious traditions, especially since tapestries could easily be transported from one area to another.

We rely mainly on carved stones to put alongside the written sources, together with metalwork of the pre-Christian period. Some prove to be in surprisingly close agreement with the later literary accounts, although the carving may be older by some centuries than the written sources. The picture of the bound Loki on the Gosforth Cross, for example (p. 50), or representations of Thor fishing for the World Serpent (p. 52), indicate that some motifs have altered little over a considerable period of time. However, more perplexing pictures like the plates on the Gundestrup Cauldron (p. 25) or tiny scenes on the gold bracteates (p. 41) show us how little of the symbolic language of the past we really understand, and remind us that the chances of survival may lead us to overvalue the trivial and neglect the symbols of greater importance for those who worshipped the old gods and goddesses.

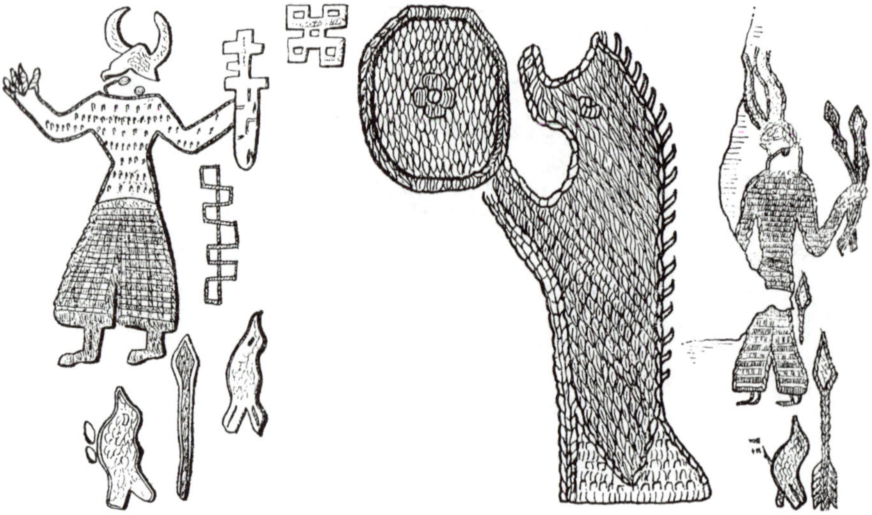

Figure 30 Figures on tapestry found in Oseberg ship burial.

It is worth reviewing the scattered material at this point, to see if there is any hope of building up a coherent scheme of the relations of men and women with the supernatural world in a pre-Christian society. Here it is necessary to distinguish between evidence for religious rites and customs on the one hand, and the content of the myths on the other. In this chapter it is intended to survey what appear to be the outstanding characteristics of the religious life of the Scandinavians before the conversion, putting this against the vaguer background of our picture of the Celtic and Germanic past.

THE EARLY CENTURIES

Early accounts of the Celts and Germans from outside observers stress the use of sacred places in the open air, rough wooden figures of the gods, and the practice of animal and human sacrifices, as well as the leaving of offerings in water or in the earth. Such archaeological evidence as we possess consists mainly of isolated sites within some kind of enclosure. Graves often in association with such sites offer some chance of dating, but those discovered before the Roman period are usually too isolated in time and space to allow firm conclusions to be drawn about the religious rites for which they were intended. Lucan in the first century BC refers to 'grim-faced gods, uncouthly hewn by the axe' (*Pharsalia* III, 411–13), and wooden figures that accord with such a description continued to be set up as late as the Viking Age, proving very difficult to date. However, the Celts in southern Gaul who came into contact with the Greeks and Romans were able to produce impressive male figures in stone considerably earlier than this. In the sanctuary of Roqueperteuse in southern Gaul there are two memorable Janus heads facing in opposite directions, perhaps of the third century BC or even earlier. Another two-faced figure that must surely represent a god is the sandstone pillar from Holzgerlingen, which stands 2.3 m high and is topped by a formidable head with a face on either side, under the remains of a horned or moon-shaped crown (Sandars 1968:248). The towering statue of a grim warrior figure from Hirschlanden which stood on a mound and has been generally taken as a funerary memorial may go back to the sixth century BC (Megaw 1970:47); from about the third century we have the line of figures seated cross-legged in the sanctuary at Entremont along the sacred way (Benoit 1975). Thus there are indications of powerful divine beings, whether gods or ancestors, occupying a place in the Celtic world-picture at an early date, but we depend on a few chance survivals only to give us hints of the nature of the Celtic Otherworld.

A ritual that goes back to the Bronze Age and was continued by the Celts is the deposit of offerings and sometimes sacrifices of animals placed in deep shafts or pits in the ground (Figure 31). It is hard to be sure in some cases whether these might simply be rubbish or storage pits with no religious purpose, but the presence of a number of dog skeletons and occasional human ones, the trunk of a cypress sapling in one pit, and finds of carved human figures, indicate that some at least were intended to hold offerings and presumably that they were viewed as possible entries to the underworld (Green 1986:132 ff.). Groups of such shafts have been found both in Britain and on the continent, and a large number in the area around Chartres may have been associated with the centre where druids were said to meet (Ross 1978–80). The problems involved in assessing this type of evidence for ritual practices have been discussed by Wait (1985:51 ff.). In a survey of a number of such shafts from the Iron Age and the early Roman period in Britain, he emphasizes the large investment of time and manpower in making such shafts, and also notes an apparent shift in the later examples from offerings connected with local fertility to those of 'more personalised material objects of wealth' (Wait 1985:82).

The period from the first to the fifth century, when the Romans were occupying Gaul and much of Britain, gives us more evidence on which to draw. There is indication of a flourishing religion among the native population with beliefs in many supernatural beings, male and female, and of sacred places on hills and islands, in woods and beside springs and lakes. We have a vast number of altars and votive stones surviving from military and domestic sites which have been set up in honour of Otherworld powers. Some Celtic sacred places were taken over by the Romans and developed as popular centres for pilgrims. One outstanding example is the temple of Sulis Minerva at Bath, where the sacred hot-springs must already have been associated with a goddess who was identified with the Roman Minerva. What had apparently been an open pool was roofed in with great skill by Roman engineers, so that visitors to the shrine could look through three large windows at the water rushing out of a cavern through a stone arch. The mist and steam rising from this must have made it an impressive place, and groups of statuary were placed at water-level, while baths were provided as

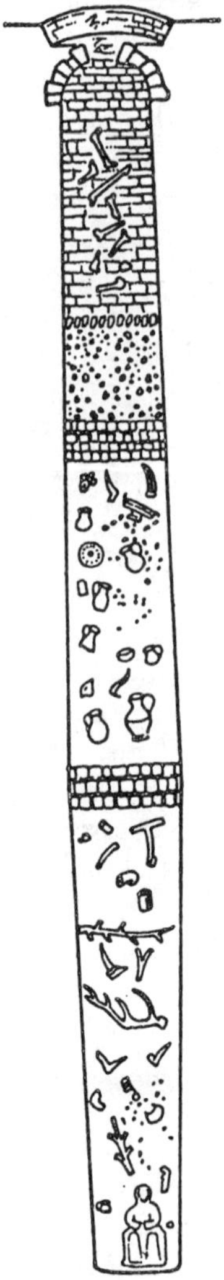

Figure 31 Ritual shaft from the Vendée, France (after Piggott).

another means of making use of the sacred waters. There seems to have been a deliberate attempt to add to the romantic mystery of the place, and parallels can be found from other Roman sites (Cunliffe 1986:4). One can but wonder whether this added to the reputation of the goddess among the local people, or whether they felt saddened to have her taken over by their new rulers. Certainly the temple was a commercial success, attracting rich pilgrims, to judge from the valuable gifts recovered from the spring, including coins, jewels, inscribed gems and fine metal vessels. Some of those who visited it must have been people of importance from various parts of the Empire, but there are also clues as to the simpler rites offered to the guardian goddess of the spring before the Romans developed it. As well as rich gifts and money, there are two military items, suggesting requests for help in a campaign or gratitude for its success, one a piece of harness decoration and the other a washer from a model ballista.

There is also the somewhat depressing collection of curses written on lead, calling down the wrath of the goddess on some unknown person (though possible suspects are named) who had stolen from the worshipper or injured him in some way. This process had been organized in typical Roman fashion, with a set formula provided, and a temple scribe supplying an approved form of invocation that could apparently be copied out by the applicant (Cunliffe 1986:10), but again it strongly suggests a more spontaneous approach to such a deity linked with the natural world, in a place where there seemed to be an opening into the underworld, before the Romans came.

A similar place of offering on a smaller scale is Coventina's Well, now only the site of a former spring in marshy ground near the Roman fort of Carrawburgh on Hadrian's Wall between Chesters and Housesteads (Allason-Jones and McKay 1985). In Roman times a small shrine and carefully constructed well were made there, and the well may have served as the centre of the shrine, left open to the sky. When the site was excavated in 1876, inscribed stones bearing the name Coventina were found; in this case we do not know if she was a local goddess or was perhaps brought into Britain by German troops manning the fort. The well yielded a large number of coins, together with objects of bronze, bone, pottery, glass, lead, leather, jet and shale, as well as the boar-tusks, deer-horns and animal bones which unfortunately were not retained. We have no evidence here for curses offered at the shrine, but gifts seem to have been made in gratitude for benefits received. The history of the well shows the problems of interpretation facing the investigators. It is now apparent that various published references to the finds have been misleading: for instance, there was only one pin recorded, while the attractive model of a small dog, claimed along with finds of many pins to prove the existence of a healing cult, seems not to have been found at the spring at all. However, the fact that the water from the well continued to be valued by local people until the spring was destroyed by lead mining in the last century confirms the importance of the water from this source, and this is emphasized by the carving of three nymphs with jars on one of the stones found at the site, and another of a reclining figure on a stele holding a water-plant. Such a centre by a spring for a local cult is in accordance with many other sacred wells and springs on Celtic territory. Humble offering places of this kind must have been common among both Celtic and Germanic peoples before the Roman occupation and again after they left.

There are many tribal deities mentioned in inscriptions on votive stones and altars who were fitted into the existing Roman system as far as was practicable, and sometimes given a Roman name alongside the native one, as in the title Sulis Minerva at Bath, or in place of it. In the later evidence from the literature of the

British Isles, we have vague indications of powerful Celtic deities which may be strengthened by the earlier material. It is important that neither the evidence of the monuments nor that of the literature should be considered in isolation, provided always that gaps in time and in geographical space are taken into account.

There is little support now for O'Rahilly's theories (1946) of one supreme deity of the Celts, put forward with much vigour and determination earlier in this century. On the other hand, there were certain powerful gods like Lug and the Dagda, whose cults evidently extended over a wide area.

On the Germanic side, it seems as if at least three main deities, equated by the Romans with Jupiter, Mars and Mercury, were already established by the time the Romans reached the Rhineland. Among the Germans also there were recognized goddesses, some of whom, like Sulis and Brigantia, were deliberately developed by the Roman authorities, for their own purposes. Clearly, one of the most fruitful ways to discover more about the early religion of these peoples is to make more use of the rich material available from the provinces under Roman rule. Here we find many protective deities, some apparently of local importance only and others with an influence over a wide area by the time the Roman establishment showed an interest in them. Their powers included support in battle, help in travel and in the winning of wealth, as well as power over the weather, the fruitfulness of the land and the prosperity of crops and animals. Help might be sought from such powers by means of dreams, as is indicated by some of the inscriptions in temples, where altars are said to have been set up at the command of some deity (Henig 1986:161). This is in agreement with the later accounts of communications from supernatural beings in Scandinavia, including both the major gods such as Thor and Freyr and also local spirits linked with the land.

Reliance on messages received from dreams, signs and omens, and various forms of divination is indicated in the written sources, and continued to be of importance throughout the Viking Age. Tacitus noted this practice among the Germans in the first century AD, and in *Germania* 10 gives an account of the casting of lots, either by a priest on behalf of the community or by the father of a family on private occasions. One important use of the Germanic runic symbols in early times may have been in such ceremonies (Davidson 1988:153). He tells us also of sacred horses consulted by those desiring to discover the will of the gods, since these animals, he declares, were in the confidence of the divine powers, whereas the priests and nobles were merely the gods' servants. This is a striking observation, indicating the value placed on horses as animals linked with the supernatural world, and helps to explain the wide popularity of the cult of the goddess Epona (p. 47). Another means of discovering the future was by observing the movements of birds and animals: thus Boudicca before the opening of her revolt against the Romans released a hare and observed the direction in which it ran, according to Dio Cassius (X, 2). A similar reliance on the movements of animals as a help in making decisions continued into the Viking Age, to judge from a reference in *Landnámabók* (S, 68, H, 56:96). Here a family chose to build their house in Iceland in the place where their mare lay down for the first time with her load on her back.

It seems that methods of divination played an important part in the organized religion of gods and goddesses as well as in private life, and those with special gifts of second sight possessed considerable influence in the community. Of particular interest are the seeresses among the Germans in the Roman period, of whom we learn from Tacitus and others. The best-known of these is Veleda, an influential figure in the tribe of the Bructeri in the Rhineland, who played a leading part in political life and was one of the arbiters when an agreement was made between the Romans and the people of Cologne. She is said to have sent her decisions by a messenger, while she remained in a high tower (Davidson 1981a:127 ff.). Among the Celtic peoples of Gaul and Britain, the druids had considerable influence in the Roman period, and aroused the curiosity of the learned Roman world. They encouraged and preserved religious learning, and were also associated with divination and prophecy. They undoubtedly played an important political role also, thus paving the way for their own suppression, but it was difficult in any case in the pre-Christian era to separate the religious and secular sides of life.

There is early evidence for the ritual progress of a deity around the countryside to visit farms and bless crops and households. Tacitus describes the journey of the goddess Nerthus in Denmark in *Germania* 32, and there are references to such processions in Roman Gaul, as well as in Scandinavia in the Viking Age. Gregory of Tours describes how a goddess, whom he calls Berecynthia, was drawn through fields and vineyards 'according to the wretched custom of the pagans' to bring them prosperity, while the people sang and danced before her (*Liber in Gloria Confessorum* 77). Two skilfully made processional wagons thought to date back to the late second century BC were recovered from a peat-bog at Dejbjerg in Denmark, with a little alderwood stool which could have been used as a seat (Brøndsted 1938–40:III, 52 ff.), and there may be links here with earlier wagons of the type discovered in the Vix tumulus (p. 14), in which a woman of importance was placed. Later literary evidence links the processional wagon and the journey round the countryside with the fertility god as well as the goddess (p. 106), and the practice may be seen continuing into the Christian period when statues of the Virgin Mary or a saint were carried round to bless the fields (Berger 1988).

Another ritual reported to Tacitus in the first century AD was that of the annual gathering in a sacred wood by various tribes of the Semnones to witness a human sacrifice. He describes this in *Germania* 39, alluding to the Semnones as the oldest and noblest of the Suebi, and may have received his information from Masyos, a king of the Semnones who visited Rome in AD 92, or one of his followers. Anyone entering this wood had to be bound with a cord as a sign of submission, and might not get to his feet again if he fell. The wood is said to have been the place where this people had their origin, and was evidently the sacred centre, standing for the place of creation. Here they worshipped the god said to be the ruling deity (*Regnator omnium Deus*). Many attempts have been made to identify him; one suggestion is that he was Tîwaz, the early sky god, and another that he was Wodan, on account of the symbolism of binding. Whatever the name of the deity worshipped, there is significance in the emphasis on the great sanctity of the place.

FUNERAL SYMBOLISM

Much of the evidence for religious symbolism comes from graves, and while it is often impressive, it is not easy to interpret. It does not seem possible to explain wagon- and ship-graves simplistically as always signifying a belief in a journey after death. Again the practice of putting food and drink in the graves, and providing an array of dishes, drinking vessels and flagons, as well as cauldrons, large bowls and firedogs to hold logs for the hearth, cannot be dismissed as a practice based on a naïve belief in life continuing within the grave. The idea of the Otherworld feast, and its link with some kind of belief in continued life with the ancestors in another realm, has left many traces in later literature. In any case it is reasonable to suppose that such customs meant different things to the various families who practised them; family funeral traditions were of great importance, and could account for one particular custom found in a series of graves but not throughout a whole cemetery or locality. A distinction needs to be made also between the disposal of certain objects that might be felt to belong to the dead by right, such as weapons and jewellery, and offerings placed in the grave for the use of the dead, possibly based on some concept of the after-life (Young 1976:36). Some grave-goods again might be viewed merely as accessories of costume, or possibly as indicating rank.

It does not seem possible to lay down any rule as to why inhumation or cremation was chosen as a funeral rite. It must be remembered that cremation is only possible when there is an ample supply of wood; it was a natural means of disposing of the dead in forest areas, but one would not expect to find it practised in Iceland. In Anglo-Saxon England it was likely to depend on family custom and local tradition brought from their former homelands by the Germanic settlers. The great Germanic cremation cemeteries of the Roman period on the continent indicate only the simplest of burial rites, with the ashes placed in a simple urn and deposited in the ground, but we lack any information concerning the funeral rites that went on while the body was reduced to ashes. The symbols used on funeral pottery later became increasingly complex and interesting, and included animal symbols such as boars, horses and birds, as well as axe-heads or possible lightning symbols, found on a number of Anglo-Saxon urns (Myres and Green 1973:60 ff.; Myres 1977:63 ff.). Recently there has been much valuable study of the lay-out of cemeteries, and of the customs associated with death and burial. Nevertheless, as far as beliefs in the after-life are concerned, we have not progressed much further since Cumont published his study of the Roman beliefs about death in *Lux Perpetua* (1949), where he pointed out that concepts of the soul residing in the tomb could be held at the same time as those of the dead joining their ancestors in an underworld kingdom, or escaping to some kind of celestial paradise. No common consensus as to the fate of the dead can be expected, and varying concepts, as Cumont demonstrated, could exist side by side, and be given expression in religious imagery.

Looking back on the customs and beliefs of the early centuries, we are inevitably being influenced by what we know of those of the Irish and Scandinavians of later times, when the existence of written sources helps to interpret the evidence of archaeology and iconography. This is bound to be so even though the sources themselves may be misleading and difficult to assess. Whatever the problems, it is impossible to escape the conclusion that there is much continuity in religious concepts in the attitude towards the dead, just as in attempts to learn the future, methods of consulting supernatural beings, and ways of worshipping the gods. Undoubtedly, the funeral rites of kings and important people must have formed an important part of religious ritual in which the whole community participated. Spectacular funeral ceremonies, for which we have ample evidence both from archaeology and written sources, must indeed have been memorable occasions, passed down to later generations by those who witnessed them. The Anglo-Saxon heroic poem, *Beowulf*, generally dated back to about the eighth century but certainly composed in a Christian period, contains impressive accounts of pre-Christian funeral rites. There is one passage describing the burning of slain warriors on a funeral pyre after a battle, and another concerned with preparations for the funeral of the hero, who is also cremated on a huge pyre, the ashes of which are covered by a great burial mound to perpetuate his memory. There is a ruthless realism in the account of the mass funeral of the warriors (1119 ff.). Heads melt and break up in the heat as the flames roar upwards, old wounds reopen on the bodies, until finally the greedy fire devours all. A woman chants a dirge as the bodies are consumed in front of the burial mound that is to receive the ashes. Armour is burnt along with the corpses, while more treasures are brought 'from the hoard' to be placed with the ashes. When Beowulf's time comes to be cremated, we are told that wood was collected from various parts of the kingdom, and of the enormous pyre, hung with shields, helmets and coats of mail. Once more as the great fire roared upwards, a woman sang over and over again a dirge to the dead ruler who had saved his people by his battle with the dragon. After the burning, it took ten days to build a mound on the headland to cover the ashes, and afterwards twelve of the leaders of the people rode around it, chanting a lay in honour of the hero which concludes the poem (3110 ff.).

Archaeological evidence suggests that such passages were not wild flights of fancy on the part of the poet or imitations of classical models far removed from actual experience. Great cremation funerals certainly took place at Uppsala in the period before the Viking Age, from evidence gained from the excavations of three great mounds believed to be the burial places of three Swedish kings of the sixth century. The construction of the pyre seems to have been in the form of a kind of wooden shelter like a charcoal-burner's hut with a pointed top, inside which the body was placed (Lindqvist 1936:148 ff., 339), and the cremation was clearly on a grand scale. At Asthall in Oxfordshire, much nearer home, a mound had been built over a cremation burial of the seventh century, and a wall put up round it (Leeds 1924). We now know that there were several cremation burials under mounds in the cemetery at Sutton Hoo (Carver 1992:367–9), which it may be assumed would involve elaborate funeral ceremonies, since these were burials of important people. There is no doubt as to the riches of inhumation burials in the pre-Christian period, of which the famous ship-grave at Sutton Hoo (p. 20) and the great Scandinavian ship-graves of the Viking Age furnish impressive examples. Earlier scholars like Stjerna were perplexed by the fact that such archaeological evidence as was known did not correspond to the literary accounts in every detail, but now that we know of the many local variations and separate family fashions for the disposal of the dead, we no longer expect agreement and uniformity.

The funeral ceremony of a king as described in *Beowulf* must indeed have been a memorable experience, and when it was over the great mound was left to be, as he had promised before he died, 'a memorial to my people'. The importance of the mound as a symbol of the powerful dead and as a link with the cults of the gods has already been discussed (p. 122). Moreover, knowledge of such graves formed a framework around which history could be reconstructed. Like the kings of ancient India (Gonda 1956), the Scandinavian kings, even those minor rulers who possessed only small kingdoms, were regarded as the protectors of their people, representing them in relations with the gods, so that the god of the king was the god of his people also. He formed the link between human and divine worlds, and this helps us to understand the importance of the royal funeral in pre-Christian religion.

COMMUNICATION WITH THE OTHERWORLD

Not surprisingly, the ruler also played a major part in the feasts held regularly throughout the year which dominated the calendar, including sacrifice and drinking in honour of the gods (p. 88). In the main religious centre the king presided over this whenever possible, while in Iceland the *goði* of each district appears to have been responsible for its organization and the hallowing of the sacrificial meat and the drink. This was the main way in which the community could meet together and seek the blessing of the divine powers as a whole. There were also many ways by which a family or an individual could communicate independently with the divine world. The literature leaves the impression of a constant search for hidden knowledge, which included information as to events to come, revelation of where concealed people or animals might be, counsel as to what course of action to take, and reassurance about the coming season or the result of a campaign or enterprise. The study of signs and omens and the use of prophecy, as well as deliberate inducement and interpretation of dreams, appear to have played a considerable part in religious practice.

The position of wise men and women, seers and poets, is hard to define, but as in the Roman period their influence is unmistakable. The Scandinavian peoples had their seers and seeresses, as well as interpreters of dreams and omens. There are memories in the literature of a ceremony known as *seiðr*, which Snorri in *Ynglinga Saga* 7 associated with Odin and the goddesses. Some of the accounts of this show striking resemblances to shamanistic practices in northern Europe and Asia in more recent times. The most detailed account, which includes a description of the costume worn by the seeress and the high seat on which she sat and from which she delivered her replies, is found in *Eiríks Saga rauða* and represented as taking place in Greenland. It seems most unlikely that this was possible in a new colony at so late a date, and more probable that this is a tradition from northern Norway transported to the Greenland scene (Davidson 1990). Here we have yet another illustration of the difficulties of using saga literature in assessing evidence for religious practices. Nevertheless, the concept of the *vǫlva* on her high seat seems to be firmly established in Norse tradition, and this may be something that developed in the north from the consultation of the seeresses in Germany centuries earlier (p. 133). The practice of *seiðr* may have been influenced by northern divination ceremonies in Halogaland, but the priestesses of the goddesses further south may also have been consulted about the future when they went round on their visits to the country districts, leaving vague memories in the Icelandic sagas.

There is no lack of evidence in the written sources of the important part played by signs and omens in everyday life. This was especially so in warfare, a time when instant decisions had to be made with imperfect knowledge of the facts. Rimbert in his ninth-century *Life of Anskar* (XIX) tells of the retreat of an armed force of Vikings from the defenceless market-centre of Birka in Sweden, because when challenged to cast lots to see whether the gods were in favour of an attack after ransom-money had been paid, they received a negative answer with a directive to move on and make an attack elsewhere. Not surprisingly, the writer saw this as a miracle, but there seems no reason to doubt the basic facts of the account, or the statement that the Scandinavians were accustomed to accept such messages from the gods and to act accordingly; and Rimbert was writing not long after the event took place (C.H. Robinson 1921:xix, 65 ff.).

In early Irish literature there are references to frequent consultation of the natural world, relying on the movement of clouds, or flames, or the sea, to provide clues for action (Davidson 1988:150 ff.). The Scandinavians also used the sea (pp. 101–2), and in both literatures there are references to observation of bird-flight and behaviour as a way of gaining information or reaching a decision. The understanding of bird-omens is among the skills taught to young warrior leaders; in *Rígsþula* in the Poetic Edda it is mentioned as part of the lore taught to a young prince, while in *Reginsmál* and *Sigrdrífumál* it is included in advice given to the young hero by Odin and a valkyrie. The reference in *Reginsmál* 20 to a dark raven on the road counting as a good omen may be compared to a passage in the early *Life* of St Gregory (*English Historical Documents* I, 688) relating how King Edwin of Northumbria on his way to church stopped to listen to a crow cawing 'with an evil omen'; his Christian bishop Paulinus told a servant to shoot the bird, and later brought it into the hall to prove that since it did not foresee its own death it could not prophesy death for others. Ravens and crows were associated with Wodan, Odin and the Celtic Lug, and had close links with the battle-goddesses who might appear in this form.

There is no doubt of the awareness of fate in the mythological literature of the north, and this must have strongly influenced the attitude of the people towards the divine world. The picture of the battle-spirits under Odin's command governing the fortunes of war, and of the norns determining the destiny of the new-born (p. 118) indicates the general acceptance of the concept of an overruling destiny. It is this that gives force to the tales of kings and heroes who go down fighting, and of Odin himself unable to avert the fate that he foresees. There are some indications that a powerful goddess was associated with destiny, and the suggestion has been made that a female figure with weaving implements shown on certain bracteates of the sixth century might represent such a power (p. 41). Weaving swords have been found in women's graves in Germany in the vicinity of place-names associated with the gods, making it possible that emphasis on fate formed part of the cult of the main goddess (Enright 1990). It is the awareness of fate that gives depth and irony to the finest of the Icelandic Sagas, and to *Brennu-Njáls Saga* above all. This saga at many points seems to have its plot deliberately shaped to recall the myth of Ragnarok. Njal, wise father and elder statesman though he is, cannot avert the doom threatening himself and his sons, even while he foresees it. The innocent foster-son whom he loves is struck down by his foster-brothers in a harvest field, just as Balder was slain. This strong emphasis on fate must be taken into account in any attempt to reconstruct the religious world-picture that preceded the Christian one.

HOLY PLACES

Finally among aspects of religion affecting daily life we must include holy places and shrines. The local centre where the king was inaugurated appears to have represented the original centre of creation; sites such as Tara in Ireland were holy places, where sacrifices could take place and people assemble in times of crisis. The halls where feasts to the gods took place were likely to be at or near such centres, while in Scandinavia law cases could be held there and new laws proclaimed. Beside such main centres as Uppsala or Thingvellir, there were many local holy places, the centres of small communities. There were also the many spots in the countryside and on the farms associated with land-spirits and supernatural beings who could bring fertility and give help and protection to their worshippers. A settler in a new area such as Iceland might deliberately choose a holy place in a spot marked by some striking natural feature, like the little rocky hill of Helgafell in Snaefellsness in western Iceland (p. 102). There is a superb view from the top of Helgafell on a clear day, extending far over land and sea in all directions, and this is characteristic of holy places. There are many such in Celtic areas that are high, with a good view over the land, and the custom of climbing up to some of these on feast-days lingered on in Ireland up to modern times, as MacNeill has shown in her *Festival of Lughnasa* (1962). Thus the countryside had an abundance of holy places, some private, some enclosed, and others in the open spaces far from human habitation. These were reminders of the divine world, and usually places of offering, sometimes marked by signs of burning, or animal bones; occasionally some ceremonial object has been abandoned there, as in the marshes and peat-bogs of Denmark and northern Germany. Other sacred spots were in forest clearings, and sometimes such places have left a record in local names.

There must presumably have been a number of small shrines and temples, although evidence for the existence of large elaborate buildings of this kind is lacking, apart from those, like the temple at Bath, enlarged and developed by the Romans (p. 129). Individuals built small shrines for their private use, and there were evidently temples of some kind at important centres like Uppsala, the centre of a kingdom. Here the sacred treasures of the gods would be kept, like the ring of Thor, or the bowl for sacrificial blood (p. 102). As to the appearance of such shrines, one possible clue might be seen in the striking and unusual stave churches of Norway (Figure 32), built in wood by much the same method as the great Viking ships (Lindholm 1968). As many as thirty-one survive in Norway, although many have been largely rebuilt and the earliest only go back to the eleventh century, since the wooden bases and walls of the building, packed in with stones, could not last very long. With their series of roofs decorated with elaborate carvings, rising up to a central point, and their dark, mysterious interiors with carved heads whose grim outlines show little link with Christian tradition, these churches are very different from early church buildings in Anglo-Saxon England or Germany. Their structure depends on the number and arrangement of their 'masts', the wooden pillars supporting the roof which rest on a 'ground-sill', formed of four massive lengths of timber arranged on the ground to form a square. There may be as many as six different levels from the ground to the central roof in a large stave church such as the one at Borgund, and the roofs at different heights are grouped round the central sanctuary. Thus the importance of the centre is emphasized, while a covered way runs round the outside of the building, enclosed by a low wall with an arcade above. Such a structure would be in keeping with the pattern of the divine world in the mythology, and figures of the gods or some sacred object could be kept in the heart of the building under the central roof.

After the Reformation it seems that some of the carved wooden figures from the stave churches were taken out and kept by some of the families in Setesdal and Telemark up to the eighteenth and nineteenth century (Bø 1989). They are said to have been honoured with simple ceremonies such as receiving a bowl of ale at the Christmas feast, or being given gifts of food, eaten by mice and rats,

Figure 32 Stave church at Gol, Hallingdal, Norway (after Lindholm).

and to have brought good luck to the farm (Lid 1928:158 ff.). Earnest Protestant pastors and some scholars assumed that these were indeed pagan 'gods' that had been preserved from the pre-Christian period, but the evidence is against this. However, it is an interesting example of how a secondary development could take place, and Christian figures whose origin had been forgotten could turn into protective symbols not unlike those recorded in northern tradition. If, indeed, shrines similar to the early stave churches existed in Scandinavia before the coming of Christianity, they would presumably have been fairly small, and no definite archaeological evidence for them has been found. There were evidently pre-Christian buildings under the medieval churches at Uppsala in Sweden, Jelling in Denmark and Maere in Norway (Lidén 1969), but the evidence is insufficient to give us a convincing plan of an early temple.

Much work has been done in recent years on the small temples and shrines set up in Britain and Gaul in the period of Roman occupation, some of which are now believed to have pre-dated the coming of the Romans (A. Ellison 1980; Rodwell 1980). Some of those excavated consisted of a central area, usually square, known as the *cella*, which might be left open to the sky or roofed over with a small tower (Figure 33). Some sacred object or symbol might occupy the *cella*, and in one temple in Gaul this contained an enormous stone menhir (Wilson 1980:5). The temple might be enclosed outside by an ambulatory, like the stave churches, by means of which visitors and pilgrims could look into the sacred place through an opening. The amount of classical influence on these buildings has long been a subject of debate, but it has been claimed that it was on a limited scale only, and that the use of the traditional native form of building probably continued under the Romans (Horne and King 1980). It seems that in some areas, such as the valley of the Somme, these little temples may have been as plentiful as parish churches in Christian times, although it is often not easy to identify them, or the smaller shrines which certainly existed (Wait 1985:156). The majority from pre-Roman times in Britain were isolated from domestic sites, but found in or near places with a concentrated population, perhaps by some natural feature such as river or forest; in some cases simple shrines were later replaced by temples (Wait 1985:173). In the case of the Celtic temples, the ground-plan generally survives, whereas the wooden shrines in Scandinavia could leave few or no traces behind. It may be reasonably assumed, however, that a number of shrines sacred to supernatural powers existed in both Germanic and Celtic areas, and this would serve as yet another reminder to the people of the part played by religion in their daily life.

Figure 33 Reconstruction of a Romano-British temple (from Yorkshire Museum Guide, 'Roman Life').

FITTING THE PIECES TOGETHER

The general picture of religious observance throughout the year, and of the individual cults of the gods, is one that holds together reasonably well. Moreover, the evidence from Germanic and that from Celtic sources has a good deal in common. It was hardly a demanding faith with stern requirements from those who practised it, in either statements of belief or the faithful following of ritual. We are not likely to hear of converts to this kind of religion; rather, the ritual was there for those who desired to take part in it, and there was no inbuilt hostility towards other forms of belief and practice. It may be seen as providing a framework holding the community together, by regular feasts and sacrifices, appeals to the divine powers for prosperity at home and victory against enemies, and emphasis on the ruling king acting as intermediary between the people and the gods, bringing blessings on the realm that could continue after his death. Beside the cults of the main gods, there was a strong tradition of a powerful goddess, both at the aristocratic level and throughout popular tradition. While the regular sacrificial feasts at points in the calendar and appeals to the gods for guidance provided a support for living, the elaborate funeral ceremonies and the rich symbolism of a journey to the Otherworld, of the dead king joined with the gods, and of the beneficial influence of the ancestors, together with the welcome of the goddess or of protective female spirits into the world of the dead, provided a possible framework for the acceptance and recognition of death.

For many, this background of religious observance, linked with lively local beliefs in lesser beings belonging to the natural world who could give luck and protection, an elaborate system of omens and portents, and the possibility of enquiry into the future in various ways, was no doubt sufficient. Although undemanding, it was a faith constantly brought to mind by set festivals, holy places and a wealth of tales about supernatural beings. There are references in the literature to men who trusted in their own strength and might, and it is probable that then as now many pursued their own objectives without spending much time or thought on assistance from the divine powers. There would be no penalty for or condemnation of such an attitude. The test of beliefs and practices was how far the individual who held to them proved lucky and successful, for a fortunate man or woman was felt instinctively to be in tune with the powers governing the world, and it was prudent not to swim against the current. There are few certainties here, it would seem, to induce a person to die for his faith, and yet a number certainly died at the hands of Olaf Tryggvason and others. We have no knowledge of whether they were resisting the greater demands Christianity would make of them, or how much they believed faith in the old gods to be satisfactory and right. There was certainly no condemnation of the faiths of others, but rather a willingness, it seems, to accept new gods into the pantheon that governed their world, if it could be shown that faith in them proved profitable.

For those desiring a deeper insight into the supernatural world and the divine order, there was the possible pursuit of wisdom, divination and the learning of the past that had come down by oral tradition from previous generations. Of this, unfortunately, we can expect to recover little, but there is no doubt that it formed an important part of the old religion that must not be ignored. It was probably those most familiar with it who held back from entry into the Christian church. On the other hand, as suggested by Bede's account of the conversion of Northumbria, one attractive alternative offered by the new faith was entry into greater certainty, a system of rewards and punishments, and a wide field of fresh learning, including that of the extensive written literature available for those who became converts.

Much of the religious life of the pre-Christian era in northern Europe is hidden from us now for ever, and we can do no more than offer tentative suggestions as to the strengths and weaknesses of a world-picture that proved acceptable to warrior peoples over a period of many centuries. Apart from the ritual, the fixed customs marking out the year and protective practices available in times of impending danger and threat, we have also the mythical tradition in the fragmented form in which it has reached us, better preserved in Scandinavia, for all its incompleteness, than elsewhere in north-western Europe. Many scholars have worked with industry and enthusiasm in attempts to understand the significance of these myths, and their various attempts to interpret them will be examined in the final chapter.

7

THE INTERPRETERS

Our little systems have their day and their hour; as knowledge advances they pass into the history of the efforts of pioneers.

(Letter of Andrew Lang to the widow of Max Müller)

THE MEDIEVAL CHRISTIAN VIEWPOINT

No religious system can exist in a vacuum. It grows and develops subject to outside influences, which are apparent in the religious art of the period and in the surviving myths and legends. Beliefs and practices change according to the changing needs of those familiar with them, while they are subject also to certain general laws. Those interested in the history of religions are constantly trying to determine the patterns of myth which survive from the various religions of the past. However, fashions of interpretation change according to the current mode of thought, and the emphasis varies in each generation. In the early centuries of Christianity, when the cults of the pagan gods still flourished in certain areas and had not been forgotten, the usual reaction was to regard such gods as devils, part of the forces of evil battling against the kingdom of Christ. This was, however, by no means the only attitude open to the medieval scholar with an interest in antiquity.

Saxo Grammaticus in the early thirteenth century distinguished between three species of wizard, in which he claimed that the northern peoples had previously placed their trust (I, 19–20). First, there was the powerful race of the giants, second that of the gods, 'masters of the Delphic art' who overcame the giants, and then a third race which emerged from the union of the first two, with lesser powers than the gods but still viewed as divine by the foolish populace. Snorri Sturluson, however, writing at about the same time, saw the matter differently. According to him, the men and women who peopled the earth after the Flood forgot the creator God who had preserved Noah, but when they gazed on the wonders of the world, they realized that some almighty power must have created it. They gave various names to this deity, and in Scandinavia hailed him as Odin. Thus Snorri viewed the pre-Christian religion as a groping attempt to discover the truth about the divine world, and felt able to consider the beliefs of his forefathers objectively and without condemnation (Faulkes 1983). At the same time, according to theories of contemporary scholarship also familiar to Saxo, he could see Odin and the other leading gods as originally human beings, whose great achievements led poets and story-tellers in the course of time to invest them with divine qualities (Bætke 1950).

With his customary ingenuity, Snorri set the myths into a narrative framework, presenting them as information given by three of these so-called divine powers in reply to the questions of a Swedish king Gylfi, who was an earnest seeker after knowledge. This allowed him to bring in another favourite theory of the time, namely that demons delighted to lead mortals astray; this freed him from any personal responsibility for the tales and information about the divine world that he was setting before his readers. He was accordingly able to enjoy the material about the old gods, presenting it with wit and imaginative appreciation. Indeed, any medieval scholar brought up on the classics was likely to take an interest in stories of divine beings, which they would meet in the works of Ovid and other favourite texts. The gods of the Greeks and Romans were sufficiently far removed in time and space to be regarded with detachment, while their own native deities fell into in a somewhat different category. Nevertheless, the rich heritage of their early poetry made it impossible to ignore these traditions, and thus a treasury of popular lore about the gods and tales of their exploits came to be passed down both among the learned and the illiterate in Iceland, and we depend largely on Icelandic tradition for our knowledge of the mythology of the north.

THE FIRST COLLECTORS

The first serious attempt in modern times to make a systematic study of Germanic religion was that of Jakob Grimm in Germany. He and his brother Wilhelm began collecting folk-tales early in the nineteenth century, and their first book of 'Nursery and Household Tales' (*Kinder- und Hausmärchen*) was published in 1812, after six years of work. They differed from earlier retellers of popular tales in seeing them not merely as entertainment but rather as remains of earlier myths, reflecting past beliefs and customs; they thus offered a means of investigating the Germanic past that Jakob in particular found so fascinating. He continued to work on the laws of language and on the beliefs of earlier times all his life. The brothers set out intending to record the tales as nearly as possible in the words of the narrator, but their first efforts proved unsuitable for children's reading, and Wilhelm carried out a good deal of rewriting and polishing to avoid adverse criticism (Tatar 1987:3 ff.). The story of Evald Tang Kristensen's struggles in Denmark later in the century to record songs and tales from poor country-folk without 'improving' them, and the resistance he met from established scholars, illustrates the obstacles that lay in the path of those who tried to record oral traditions as they received them from the tellers (Rockwell 1981:88 ff.).

Jakob's work was not confined to folk-tales, and in 1825 he completed his *Deutsche Mythologie*. The final edition of four volumes produced in English by Stallybrass (1883–8) still proves a treasure-house of odd and surprising information, much of it collected locally. Grimm put together all he could find about the names of gods and other supernatural beings, as well as cult practices, sayings and legends from various parts of Germany. He has references to such varied subjects as swan maidens, encounters with the devil, heroes asleep in hills, and the like, as well as to early Germanic laws, the folklore of nature and weather, and much more. Even if some of his learned etymology is no longer acceptable, there is still much that is of great value in his recognition of a possible mythological basis in popular traditions. He deliberately left the Scandinavian material alone in an attempt to concentrate on the rarer evidence from the continent, as he explains in his introduction, so as to 'gain clearness and space and to sharpen our vision of the Old German faith, so far as it stands opposed to the Norse or aloof from it'.

In a later preface of 1844 (Grimm 1883: III, xxix) he comments on the recent interest shown in Celtic antiquities by scholars, 'insisting that this downtrodden race, which once occupied wide tracts of Germany, shall receive its due'. Serious work in early Welsh literature had been done in England and Wales from the seventeenth century onwards, but the idea of a Celtic religion had not been taken seriously. Irish manuscripts were still virtually inaccessible, and Scots and Irish regarded as barbaric foreigners (Piggott 1967:14). Then came the romanticizing of the druids in the eighteenth century to confuse the position still further (Piggott 1968). It was to be some time before the possibilities of archaeological finds, the impressive monuments from the early period, and the rich store of carved stones from the Roman provinces, were seen as a means of throwing light on the peoples who produced the early literature of Celtic Britain, and on the rich assortment of native gods and goddesses whom they once worshipped.

THE SOLAR MYTHS

As the evidence increased, it became obvious that there were resemblances between the myths of different European cultures, and various theories of mythology evolved. Our interpretation of the religion of Germanic and Celtic peoples has always been influenced by the prevailing theories of the time, and must be judged in the light of contemporary thought. As we look back on early theories now from a different viewpoint, they seem awkward and exaggerated; but it is important to consider how they shaped our present conception of mythology, also doomed in time to become outdated. The years of debate between Frederick Max Müller and Andrew Lang and their followers in the second half of the nineteenth century resulted in an increase of interest and curiosity among scholars and the general public alike concerning earlier religious beliefs, and much profitable work was done in the course of the controversy. Müller was a formidable German scholar studying the science of language and early Indian religion at Oxford, while Lang was a Scottish historian, poet and journalist, with very wide interests and considerable knowledge of anthropology. Both were prolific writers and good speakers and debaters, able to express their ideas in such a way as to catch the interest of a wide public. They produced lengthy books and innumerable articles, although they wasted much energy in what now seem vain repetitions and attempts to score points against one another. Both wanted to account for the savage and barbaric elements in Greek myths, and found different ways of doing so.

Müller discovered a philological link between the names of Greek gods and heroes and Sanskrit names in Vedic literature, and then found that this also applied to names of some of the deities in European tradition. He claimed that *Dyaus pita*, the Vedic sky god, as well as the Roman Jupiter, could be linked with the Greek Zeus, and that these names could be traced back to the Indo-European form **dyeus pater*, which might be translated 'Father Sky', standing for day and the bright heavens, whom he saw as representing the earliest sky god. Another major deity **perkumo* was seen as the god of thunder and storm and patron of war, and from his name Müller derived those of the Indic rain god Parjanyas, the Slavic Perun, and the mother of the Norse Thor, Fjörgyn (Mallory 1989:129).

Müller's essay on Comparative Mythology was published in 1856, and brought a new approach to the religions of early Europe. He claimed that the Germanic god *Tîwaz was derived from the same root as Zeus and other names for sky deities, and that he must therefore have been the chief Germanic sky god. As well as seeing an Indo-European origin for many myths, Müller believed that his new approach helped to explain much that was puzzling in the mythological literature, due to earlier attempts to interpret poetic symbols literally. The solar basis of our myths, he argued, had left an indelible mark on our legends and traditional language: 'Every time we say Good Morning we commit a solar myth.' Indeed, as a general rule, myth arose out of 'the disease of language', the tendency to take poetic metaphor literally; taking a humble example from a folk-tale, he suggested that Dick Whittington's cat could have come into being owing to misunderstanding of the French word for 'trade', *echat*.

Much of this is unsatisfactory, as was immediately apparent to Lang, who once remarked that the history of mythology was 'the history of rash, premature and exclusive theories'. He pointed out that there was no general agreement as to the interpretation of the names of various gods; other philologists, for instance, derived Tyr's name from a word for god represented by Latin *deus*, Iranian *deva*, and Old Irish *día*. As for savage and fantastic elements in Greek myths, Lang provided a different answer, finally expressed in two volumes entitled *Myth, Ritual and Religion*, published in 1887. He turned to evidence for beliefs and customs recorded from undeveloped communities in various parts of the world, and showed how such myths might seem appropriate to their way of life. For him, then, myths preserved traditions from an earlier phase of human development. He was much influenced by the work of E.P. Tylor and the evolutionists, and in this differed from Müller, who had a higher respect for the mentality of the so-called primitive savage than had the early anthropologists. Thus while Müller explained the myth of Cronos devouring his children as evolving from a poetic description of the sun devouring the clouds, Lang saw it simply as based on memories of a time when cannibalism was a common practice among savage tribes.

The controversy dragged on for about thirty years, and distinguished scholars at the London Folklore Society debated it with passion and eloquence, for this was the main centre for the arguments that aroused interest throughout Europe (Dorson 1958). In the course of time Lang yielded some ground, since he recognized that some early myths must be based on the forces of the natural world of storm, rain and the return of the sun after the winter dark in the north. It was his approach, nevertheless, that became the generally accepted one, since it offered more chance of development than that of Müller, while it was very much in agreement with the current theories of evolution. The death of Müller in 1900 robbed Lang of his most redoutable opponent, but Müller's years of research and exposition were not in vain. Out of his solar theories developed the conception of the supreme sky god, recognized in the myths of various European cultures. Thomas O'Rahilly, for instance, saw the sun as the Divine Eye of heaven, and therefore represented in Irish mythology by the one-eyed god Balor, who was slain by Lug (p. 72). He linked lightning with the sun, and interpreted the spears of Lug and Cú Chulainn as lightning weapons, together with that of the hero MacCecht, even though this was said to be dark and oozing with blood. Famous swords of Celtic legend were placed in the same category, such as Caradbolg, the weapon of the hero Fergus, which became the Excalibur of Arthurian legend. O'Rahilly battled with other theorists, however, like Sir John Rhys, who saw Lug and his son Cú Chulainn as sun gods, as well as with such distinguished Celtic scholars as Eleanor Hull and Alfred Nutt.

Indeed, one of the fascinations but also the weaknesses of solar mythology was the number of possibilities available when choosing characters and objects to identify with the sun. Other scholars preferred to stress the importance of thunder and lightning, which obviously played a prominent part in Germanic mythology, while sky gods such as Zeus clearly wielded the thunderbolt as their weapon, and there is little doubt that Thor's invaluable hammer-axe was regarded as a thunder weapon, shattering rocks and bringing down fire from heaven. Others, such as Zimmer and Mogk, sought to interpret Odin as a god of the storm, stressing his association with the Wild Hunt and attempting to connect his name with the Indian *Vata*. Many of these theories were abandoned after a time, because of objections to the derivation of names, or more often because fuller investigation into the character of the god showed that such an interpretation was inadequate. On the other hand, the importance of the natural world for the northern peoples made it likely that such imagery was employed in their myths and reflected in the character of their dominant gods.

RITUAL AND MYTH

Towards the end of the century a new approach to myth was developed as there was increased interest in early ritual and its importance in religious life. The writings of James Frazer, making up the various sets of volumes that appeared at different dates under the title of *The Golden Bough*, had for many years an enormous influence on the interpretation of early religion. His first two volumes were published in 1890, and were based on Frazer's extensive knowledge of the classics gained at the University of Glasgow. When he moved to Cambridge he came under the influence of the Old Testament scholar Robertson Smith, while at the same time he, like Lang, was convinced by the evolutionists. In spite of his strict Christian upbringing – or perhaps as a result of it – he saw religion as an inevitable but limited stage in human development, which was to be replaced by science. For him customs and myths were a survival from the past, and he became increasingly fascinated by the way humanity had progressed in facing the various problems posed by conditions on earth. He spent many years in untiring amassing of evidence from books, drawing on reports from the Mediterranean countries as well as Greek and Latin literature, together with evidence from Germany and the British Isles, although he made little use of Scandinavian material. Beginning with the tradition of the slave who reigned as king in the sanctuary at Nemi until overcome and slain by his successor, he finally built up a monumental structure, of which the focal point was the sacrifice of the king at a certain stage in his reign, while he also concentrated on the distribution and significance of the custom of totemism. In considering the northern gods, he returned to some extent to the medieval theory that they were originally outstanding leaders, as he brings out in his volume on Balder the Beautiful, based on the Scandinavian myth. For him, myths were essentially early and misguided attempts to give a scientific explanation of the world, as wizards attempted to win control over the forces of nature (Ackerman 1987:231 ff.).

There has been a strong reaction against Frazer's work in recent years, since anthropologists felt that he relied on second-hand material and travellers' accounts which were often of dubious value, doing no fieldwork of his own. He made no distinction between different types of evidence, mixing sophisticated poetry like that of Virgil with naïve works of fiction written for entertainment, or with modern accounts of village ceremonies in remote places; he lacked historic sense, and a critical approach to sources. He viewed undeveloped societies and those of early times as primitive and credulous, with their ritual organized by wizards who were largely charlatans, deceiving their hearers. He looked back pityingly from the achievements of his own time, and such a negative attitude as this was hardly likely to result in the understanding of early religious thought. The reason for Frazer's enormous success was partly due to his undoubted ability to perceive underlying patterns that had not been previously recognized, and his confident explanation of strange myths in a way more satisfying than those of Müller and Lang. He could supply an enormous amount of material to convince his readers, and the connections are undoubtedly there, even though he remained blind to the power and importance of symbolism and the imaginative and mystical possibilities of myths and ceremonies. Along with the religions of the past, he explored the folk-customs of his own time, and, like Lang, saw these as part of the general evolutionary picture. He also offered, as it seemed to many, a new freedom of thought, and an escape from religious domination. He made no overt attack on Christianity, and in fact aroused less hostility from the churches than Robertson Smith, whose attitude to the religion of Old Testament times was not nearly as destructive to Christian thought and belief.

For all its limitations, Frazer's approach brought an advance in the understanding of myths, as he showed how the new patterns he had revealed prevailed over a huge area of mankind. Two theologians, S.H. Hooke and E.O. James, were able to benefit from his work in their study of the religions of the Near East, although they differed profoundly from him in their view of myth and belief. They saw myths as the spoken part of religious rituals, the uttered word possessing, in Hooke's words, 'the efficacy of an act' (Hooke 1933:3). For him the original myth, in a symbolic fashion, was 'seasonally reenacted in the ritual'. In their work on the early religion of the Hebrews and their neighbours in the Near East, both Hooke and James viewed the various religious systems as coherent totalities, and not merely as examples of a common pattern (Porter 1977:139). They also established the concept of the sanctity of kingship, including the rite of the sacred marriage, and this part of their work was later confirmed by the discovery of new texts not known in their time. Although their research was not directly linked with the religions of north-western Europe, it is clearly of importance for our better understanding of ritual and practice.

Another classicist, contemporary with Frazer at Cambridge, was Jane Ellen Harrison, who produced brilliant and exciting studies of Greek ritual and mythology, culminating with *Thetis* in 1912. She showed how Greek myth could arise out of ritual, and survive the rite that gave it birth, so that it is often hard to understand it when it appears in later literature. She also showed how myths, once freed from their ritual origin, may be subsequently attached to historical events and people. Meanwhile A.B. Cook, also at Cambridge, had been working for many years on the concept of Zeus as sky and thunder god, and tracing this further afield in northern Europe. He was one of the first to make serious use of iconography as well as written sources.

These various theories of myth all have their weaknesses if pushed too far, as tended to happen among later followers of those who originated the theories. Lord Raglan, for instance, carried the ritual theory to absurd extremes, making dogmatic assertions that myth could originate in no other way. For him there was also one central ritual, the periodic sacrifice of the king, which he believed spread from the Near East throughout the world; before that no myths had formed a part of religious teaching. The new advances, which proved so exciting and disturbing at the outset, gradually became established as the accepted way of thought in studying past religions, until they in turn were thrust aside by later explorers and treated perhaps with unmerited scorn by the next generation of scholars. Where many theorists tended to go astray was in assuming that one set of rules only must be accepted, and that religious development must have followed a single path. Another common weakness was the habit of ignoring previous theories, assuming that all was chaos until at length the new thinker saw the light (Strenski 1987). Charlotte Burne, an outstanding folklorist in the early years of this century and the first woman President of the Folklore Society, saw more clearly than most the danger of rigid conformity to one path only. In a wholly admirable review of *The Golden Bough* in 1901, in which she praised Frazer's skill in managing such varied material, she observed shrewdly: 'The fate of the solar mythologists should be a warning to us. There is no master key' (Burne 1901:240).

Another scholar who was to have a wide influence on the study of religion, and who, like Frazer, brought together material from many parts of the world and studied the patterns which emerged, was Mircea Eliade, a Romanian scholar who for many years worked in the University of Chicago. His view of myth was very different from that of Frazer. He saw myths essentially as tales revealing how the world or some custom or ritual first came into being, and he claimed that when such myths were narrated, the purpose was to reorientate those who listened, by letting them return to their own creative beginnings. The creation of the world and of the first gods and giants, the making of the initial human pair, the establishment of order and of the calendar, and the introduction of various crafts and skills, were clearly regarded as important in both Germanic and Celtic mythology, as far as can be judged from surviving written sources. Eliade believed also that the sacred centre in each kingdom represented the original centre where the work of creation began. For him this explained the meaning of the wild orgy that often accompanied important religious festivals; just as creation meant the establishment of order out of chaos, so this time of frenzy before returning to the familiar ordered world brought back something of the power and energy of the beginning, and provided briefly an escape out of time.

In his *Patterns in Comparative Religion*, published in 1958, Eliade showed the persistence of certain symbols used in many regions of the world as expressions of divine power. They are often taken from the world of nature, and include sun, moon, wind and water, stones, plants and trees, as well as many living creatures. According to Eliade:

> Each must be considered a hierophany in as much as it expresses in some way some modality of the sacred and some moment in its history; that is to say, some one of the many kinds of experience of the sacred man has had.
>
> (Eliade 1958:2)

In this Eliade was following Rudolf Otto, who in *Das Heilige*, published in 1917, first translated as *The Idea of the Holy* in 1923, claimed that religion rose out of an independent form of experience. He sought to make clear the 'extra' in the meaning of holy, that something that makes it 'above and beyond the meaning of goodness', and he coined the term 'numinous', which has proved of great value in the understanding of religious experience (Otto 1952:6 ff.). Eliade learnt much also from the work of Carl Jung in depth-psychology. Jung had found in the dreams of his patients images and symbols resembling those used in myth and legend, even though they were apparently unacquainted with these from their reading. Symbols in dreams such as dragons and monsters, the horse, the hare and other animals, the tree reaching to heaven, the flying steed or the supernatural helper, convinced him that there is a basic need for such images. He believed that certain of these were archetypal, part of the human inheritance from early times, and consequently they offered a clue to the regaining of wholeness for those whose minds were disturbed. For Jung, as for Frazer, historic evidence for the evolution of the various symbols was unimportant, but his work proved helpful to Eliade in emphasizing the importance of myths and the reason why certain images are so readily welcomed into religious systems.

Eliade has been criticized for his unscientific approach, for putting too much reliance on depth-psychology, and for making claims for myth impossible to verify (Strenski 1987:106 ff.). Even if we do not follow him all the way in his pattern of 'timeless' myths, it should be recognized that his work has been of great importance for the better understanding of symbols in early religion, and that the major symbols may be included in ritual, but are by no means wholly dependent on it. Eliade's survey is on a world-wide scale, so that only a part is directly connected with Germanic and Celtic religion, but there is much that is relevant for this study in his writings. His work helps to explain the persistence of certain patterns hard to understand, and the long life of certain symbols in literature and art.

THE STRUCTURE OF MYTH

Yet another ambitious scheme which ranges over myths from many parts of the world is that of Claude Lévi-Strauss, which has been claimed to offer a more scientific approach than that of Eliade and his followers. Lévi-Strauss argued that the confusion over the understanding of myth resembles that formerly facing those working on the development of language. At first in comparing different languages they found nothing but confusion, until they realized that it was not the individual sounds but the combinations of sounds that provided the significant data. Myths like languages are made up of units, and need to be broken down into these if we are to comprehend their true significance. Instead of attempting to determine the original or 'true' form of a myth, he believed that it was necessary to get together all available versions and subject these to structural analysis. To some extent this is an enlightening approach, the main difficulty being the enormous amount of material that needs to be collected and stored in the case of the more important myths. Nor is it always easy to agree on the essential features of a myth in its various versions, particularly in the more complex and fragmentary tales. One helpful discovery that has emerged from this approach, however, is that of the importance of polarity and contrast in myths, with light opposed to darkness, life to death and so on. Another is the insistence by Lévi-Strauss on the creative thinking of human beings, even in the earliest times of which we have record. He insisted that so-called 'primitives' were in no way inferior in their thought processes to modern men and women, pointing out that a stone axe and a steel axe may be equally well made and the only reason that the second is superior as a tool is because steel is a different material from stone (Lévi-Strauss 1958:66). Consequently his work has resulted in a higher appreciation of early myths and legends, and proved a much-needed corrective to Frazer's contemptuous approach to the religious thinking of those following a simpler mode of life and an oral tradition.

THE APPROACH OF DUMÉZIL

The work of Georges Dumézil is of more immediate relevance for the understanding of the beliefs and traditions of the Germanic and Celtic peoples, because he is primarily concerned with the patterns that emerge among those peoples whose language indicates descent from the Indo-Europeans. He has introduced new meaning into strange myths like that of an early battle between two companies of the gods (pp. 71–2), and his explanation of this has 'the not inconsiderable merit of recovering order and purpose from apparent chaos' as MacCana puts it (1970:61). He starts with the figures of the main gods of the various pantheons rather than attempting to deal with myth as a whole, claiming that among peoples of the Indo-European group there were three main social divisions, reflected in the nature of the main gods whom they worshipped. He finds this tripartite division among the gods of Ancient India, and again among those of Ancient Rome, and goes on to apply the same pattern to other mythologies, including those of the Germans and the Celts. The first of the 'three functions' that he believed was apparent in their mythical world was that of the ruler, showing itself in the control of magico-religious power on the one hand and of law-giving on the other, sometimes represented by a pair of powerful gods. The second function was that of physical force, expressed by the warrior class in society. The third was concerned with the fertility of the earth and that of animals and mankind, represented by a number of deities, male and female; this was associated with the farming class and the country people in general, as opposed to aristocrats and rulers. In Ancient India, the first function was embodied in the brahmin caste and the second in the warrior caste. The gods of the first function he took to be Varuna and Mitra, while the second function was represented by Indra. The third class of farmers and workers on the land was represented by the Ashvins and other deities, a group of supernatural beings rather than single outstanding ones, and including the goddesses.

When he examined Scandinavian tradition, Dumézil saw the first function as represented by Odin and Tyr (Germanic Wodan and Tîwaz). The first stood for power by magical and religious ceremonies, since Odin was a leader of the gods skilled in magic, while Tyr stood for rule by law. He saw Thor as resembling Indra in many ways, particularly in his use of force, represented by the thunder-weapon with which he attacked the enemies of the gods. The third function would be represented by the fertility powers, under the leadership of Freyr and Njord. Dumézil also used historical legends, such as those concerning the early kings of Rome or those of Denmark as recorded by Saxo Grammaticus, to extend the area of his search. Rather surprisingly, he and his followers have made little use of possible evidence from iconography or archaeology, which might have helped to establish his tripartite model (Mallory 1989:132).

A major difficulty in accepting Dumézil's theories as applied to the systems of belief among Germans and Celts is that of complications in the case of the major gods. Among the Scandinavians, Odin was undoubtedly the god of kings and warriors, even though Thor was admittedly the champion of the divine world. Thor, on the other hand, was the acknowledged patron of law and justice; one might argue that he took over this function from Tyr, but there is little firm evidence for this. On the Celtic side, the work of Sjoestedt has clearly demonstrated that the Celts regarded their deities as many-skilled, so that it is hardly possible to divide them satisfactorily according to their separate functions, as can be done with the gods of Ancient Rome. Her interpretation is based on the evidence of the sources themselves and not on any dominant theory, and she has given us one of the most illuminating studies of early Celtic religion. She felt that it was not possible to assume that there had once been a clearly defined Common Celtic religion, with easily recognizable gods and goddesses, declaring that 'What we know of the decentralized character of society among the Celts, and of the local and anarchical character of their mythology and ritual excludes that hypothesis' (Sjoestedt 1982:4). The same impression of confusion and variety, making it difficult to fit the Germanic gods into the required slots, is gained from the detailed survey of Germanic religion from the historical viewpoint which has been presented by de Vries (1957–8).

A further problem that Dumézil at first left unsolved was that of the goddesses, since to include them all vaguely with the deities of the third function was clearly unsatisfactory. However, he gradually became aware of the importance of the goddess who was related to the gods of all three functions, and he defined her position in 1970 as 'a goddess who synthesizes these functions, who assumes and reconciles all three' (Dumézil 1970:300). In a recent study, *Archaic Cosmos* (1990), Lyle suggests a further development of the work of Dumézil on the possible framework of early European religion. Dumézil deliberately omitted space and time from his system of triads, concentrating on the application of this to social groups, but other scholars have extended his scheme and this she finds rewarding. The division into four as well as into three was evidently of significance in the early European world-picture, as has been pointed out by the Rees brothers (1961:112 ff.). Lyle suggests that the fourth division was taken as standing for the whole, and this was presided over by the goddess, who would thus function as the deity of the entire people and not just of one particular social group (Lyle 1990:2).

The division of horizontal space into four, each with its appropriate colour, had already been suggested by the Rees brothers and others. In Ancient India the colour of the brahmin class was white, and that of the warrior class red. Lyle suggests that yellow was the colour of the food-producers, not black as had been previously suggested, and that the dark colour blue/black was that of the goddess. If she indeed stood for the country or kingdom as a whole, this would account for the importance of the symbol of the sacred marriage, since on becoming king the ruler had to detach himself from the interests of any one class of society, and see that all three were justly represented (Lyle 1990:16). Again, it might be possible to equate three seasons of the year, spring, summer and winter, with the three gods, while the fourth, autumn, would belong to the goddess who was linked with all of them. At the main feast at the beginning of the new year at Samain or the Winter Nights (p. 88), the gods were honoured as a whole, and it was at this time also that the feast to the goddesses was celebrated (p. 113). While Dumézil insisted on the importance of his system for Indo-European peoples, Lyle suggests that it may not have been limited to them but was possibly an archaic feature retained by the Indo-Europeans more fully than the rest.

The importance of the goddess in early religion is emphasized from another angle by Gimbutas. She sees the Indo-Europeans as dominated by male warrior gods, but also as influenced in their beliefs by the earlier religion which she calls that of Old Europe, where the goddess was the most powerful deity, dealing out life and death. She claims that this earlier system, the existence of which she attempts to prove by archaeological evidence and symbolism, prevailed over a large part of Europe for a very long period of time (Gimbutas 1982:9 ff.; 1989:316 ff.). The weaknesses of her case and of other recent attempts to establish the goddess as the dominating figure in early religion have been pointed out by Hutton (1991:39 ff.). Clearly, it may help in the search for a lost religion if we take into account some of the hypothetical theories for the structure and development of early religions in north-western Europe that have been put forward; but it is essential also for any real understanding of a lost religion not to neglect the historic approach, arising out of the patient study of sources and of the social background of the peoples whose religion we seek to recover from the past.

OUTSIDE INFLUENCES

It was usual for those interested in the literature and religion of the past in the nineteenth century to have been trained in the classics, and to have first encountered gods and goddesses and religious cult practices in the literature and art of Mediterranean countries. Consequently it has proved difficult to escape from the assumption that the same pattern of mythology must have prevailed among Germans and Celts. Frazer began as a classicist, and so too did Hector Munro Chadwick, whose careful work was to have considerable influence on the study of early religions in northern Europe. His book *The Heroic Age*, published in 1912, broke new ground in showing the striking resemblances between the subject-matter of the heroic poetry of the Germanic peoples and that of Homer, in spite of the wide gap in time and the geographical distance between Ancient Greece and northern Europe. The reason for this was that the way of life and the ideals of men grouped in small warrior-bands under aristocratic leaders, and trained in the use of weapons for close fighting, was similar in both cases, and thus produced the same kind of literature. This was in general oral literature, recited at the courts of kings or noblemen; this, however, might later come to be written down and to inspire more written literature of a similar kind when the time of upheaval and constant warfare was being replaced by settled kingdoms, and writing had been introduced by the Christian church.

With his wife Nora, Hector Chadwick went on to study the main characteristics of oral poetry in different parts of the world, the result being the three large volumes making up *The Growth of Literature*. Much of the literature they studied belonged to non-Christian cultures, and was bound to include treatment of the supernatural world relevant for the study of early religion. Indeed, two early studies by Chadwick of Germanic and Scandinavian gods, 'The Cult of Odin' in 1899 and 'The Oak and the Thundergod' in 1900, showed how much could be achieved by a fresh survey of written sources, including what was reported by Greek and Latin writers of the religious practices of the northern barbarians. He made no attempt to begin from any theory of myth, or to fit the evidence into the Roman pattern, nor did he assume that reports by Greek and Latin writers were necessarily reliable. This critical approach with an open mind is a great contrast to that of Frazer, whose findings Chadwick mistrusted because he had paid no attention to the varying nature of the sources which he used.

Chadwick was ahead of many of his contemporaries in his readiness to use local history and archaeological evidence along with early written sources. His *Origin of the English Nation*, published in 1907, was the first serious study of the Anglo-Saxons in Britain before the coming of Christianity to include a survey of their religious beliefs. He recognized that the powers of the main deities in northern Europe were not clearly defined, and that the position was very different from that in the Roman Empire, where a sophisticated state religion had been established for the highly literate ruling class with a simple framework for the working populace. To look for a similar framework among Germans and Celts might well lead us astray. As Sjoestedt pointed out some years ago:

> When we are tackling a strange mythology, we seek instinctively an Olympus where the gods abide, an Erebus, kingdom of the dead, a hierarchy of gods, specialized as patrons of war, of the arts, or of love. And, seeking them, we do not fail to find them.
>
> (1982:2)

In her work on the Celts, she decided to proceed as though no Greek or Roman had ever visited Celtic territory, but to examine what they themselves had to say of their past. Since Ireland never came under Roman rule, this was easier than it might be in England or Gaul. Nevertheless, it cannot be denied that the influence of Rome meets us at every point. Deities have been presented on carved stones mainly in Roman fashion in the pre-Christian world of north-western Europe, while in Scandinavia the little bracteates with their protective magic based on the lore of the gods were imitated from Roman designs (p. 39). The sacred boar was a favourite Roman emblem, since it was the symbol of the Twentieth Legion. The great silver dishes in the Sutton Hoo treasure with figures from classical mythology were found alongside what seem to be sacred symbols of Germanic kingship, reminding us how motifs from southern Europe must have inevitably influenced northern artists when they ornamented gifts or booty, and suggested new treatment of their own native themes. On the literary side, the work of that ardent scholar Saxo Grammaticus, well-grounded in the latest teaching of European universities of the twelfth century, is a warning of how minor Latin works may have influenced the presentation of native legends. His story of the golden statue of Odin in his first book, for instance, could well have been suggested by his familiarity with the work of Valerius Maximus, who refers to men stealing gold from statues of the gods (Davidson 1980:32). At the same time it is important to remember that such borrowings may have been prompted in the first place by a resemblance already existing between the native and the classical tradition.

It can be seen from the subjects of the pictures selected for the Franks Casket, the little box of whalebone ivory thought to have been made in the seventh century in Northumbria, that in the early Christian period the Anglo-Saxons deliberately compared native legends with tales from classical or Christian sources. On the box we are shown Romulus and Remus suckled by a she-wolf, the despoiling of the temple at Jerusalem by the Romans, and the nativity of Christ, with the arrival of the Wise Men bearing gifts. These are joined with other scenes from native tradition: there is Egil the archer, a scene in a smithy which appears to portray the legend of Weland, and a strange group including a horse and a burial mound and what seem to be supernatural figures (Davidson 1969). Heroic scenes from foreign sources would naturally have a strong appeal, and in the case of the panel illustrating the Weland tale of ruthless vengeance, which resulted in the birth of a semi-divine child, the picture of the Christ Child with his mother receiving the gifts of the Magi may have been deliberately placed beside it for contrast. New Christian traditions must have influenced the telling of the old myths, and indeed some scholars like Sophus Bugge and Karl Krohn attempted to derive all the main Scandinavian myths from Christian origins. Evidence available from archaeology and iconography is sufficient now to convince us that this was not the case, but subtle Christian influences may often have affected the presentation of old tales, just as appears to have happened in the early literature of Christian Ireland (McCone 1990:56). In recent years the emphasis in Beowulf studies has increasingly fallen on possible influences from learned Christian sources recognizable in the poem, so that less attention has been paid to it as a rich source of pre-Christian myth. On the other hand, the evidence for knowledge of cremation funerals, the bear-like characteristics of the hero, the ship as a symbol of departure to another world, and the supernatural figures from beneath the lake of Grendel and his mother, all of which are found in the poem, need not be rejected as without value for our knowledge of native tradition.

Once learned material from foreign sources is recognized, however, it becomes increasingly difficult to sort out early religious traditions. The early history of Ireland and traditions about invasions and the coming of the gods have been deliberately blended with Old Testament events and the history of Greece and Rome, until it has become well-nigh impossible to unscramble it. In a less ambitious scheme writers of the *Anglo-Saxon Chronicle* trace back their line of kings to Noah's Ark or to Adam, much of this work being carried out by antiquarians of the ninth century (Sisam 1953), who also bring in the pre-Christian gods for good measure. At the end of *Vǫluspá* the mighty ruler who is to come may or may not be the Christian Christ, while ideas of the Christian heaven and hell seem to have left their mark on the picture of the cosmos that it gives. Resemblances between native and Christian tradition were certainly obvious to the people responsible for raising memorial crosses in some early Viking settlements in Britain, where scenes from Ragnarok and the crucifixion of Christ were shown side by side (p. 50). The obvious similarity between Christ on the cross and Odin hanging on the tree does not mean, however, that the Odin tradition cannot be an independent one. The only way to test this is to trace the motif in the north, and see how the idea of a sacrifice hanging on a tree is likely to have formed part of the Odin cult. We have to recognize the power and long life of certain mythological symbols and motifs, which may be found in very different settings, since, as Jung claimed, they are instinctively welcomed by the imaginative mind.

Once we reach the Viking Age, we have also to be prepared for tales and motifs from abroad being imported by Scandinavians returning from their travels to their homelands. The strong links that existed in the tenth and eleventh centuries between Scandinavia and south-eastern Europe, in particular, meant that many tales and art motifs might be brought back by those who had spent years in the Greek army or navy, travelling in the Caucasus area, or meeting other travellers in the eastern markets including Constantinople. Certain motifs like the bound Loki, writhing beneath great rocks and causing earthquakes, or the great interest shown in the last great battle when the gods met the giants and the monsters and all were destroyed, may have been partially influenced by traditions from that region of Europe (Davidson 1976:313 ff.). Germans or Celts who came to Rome in the earlier centuries and to Constantinople in the Viking Age found themselves confronted by conflicting religious teachings and practices, while they would encounter a rich series of pictures and statues associated with the supernatural world. The Scandinavians were such gifted story-tellers that they could introduce foreign plots and motifs into their sagas very skilfully, placing them in a convincing native setting, so that they seem like genuine Scandinavian traditions (Strömbäck 1971).

Yet another possible direction from which influences might reach the religion of Scandinavia is from the north, since they were in close contact with the Saami and other Finno-Ugrian peoples further east. The central tree is one possible motif that may have been influenced by the beliefs of such neighbours (p. 69). Certain elements in Scandinavian tradition suggest the influence of shamanic beliefs and practices in the idea of travel between different worlds and of taking on animal form. Again, some of the tales of women practising divination in the sagas have marked resemblances to accounts of shamanic ceremonies recorded in later times in northern Europe and Asia (p. 137). Such ideas may have come into Halogaland at the time when it was under the rule of Jarl Hakon, the last pagan ruler of Norway, in the late tenth century. The progress made in the study of shamanism in recent years has made this a possibility worth considering.

When we survey the possible complications and varied influences which could have affected pre-Christian religion in northern Europe, it is evident that such 'scientific proof' as Strenski desired in his criticism of the theories of Eliade (p. 152) is hardly possible to provide. Nor is it yet possible to reach firm conclusions as to the religious beliefs and myths of the Indo-European peoples from whom the Celts and Germans are descended. If the difficulties appear frustrating, we can at least comfort ourselves with the thought that new and valuable insights will undoubtedly be gained as the search goes on. Many new ways of approach have been explored and fought over in the past, and there is every hope of fresh understanding of the divine world of our ancestors emerging from continued investigation of the written sources together with careful study of pictures, symbols and archaeological finds. There is much left to discover.

Conclusion

It is clear that there can never have been one simple period in early religion to which we can confidently look back, a golden age of well-established ritual shared by all communities in the early days, as scholars once believed (Davidson 1963). There cannot be one simple key to the understanding of systems of belief; all religions must be subject to change and development over a vast period of time, influenced by both enemies and neighbours, and by the differing needs of the people as their way of life changed, and roving warrior-tribes gradually settled into established kingdoms. A detailed historic survey is necessary to check the tendency to depend on one prevailing theory, for the world of beliefs is a complex one, however far we go back in time, and we are limited to the confused and often contradictory evidence of fragments of literature, art and language, vague memory of former customs, and the rich confusion of local legends. Because this is to a large extent uncharted territory, there is a temptation to oversimplify wildly, to assume direct links between horned figures or sacrificial rituals kept apart by centuries of time and changing methods of living. One method of approach, favoured by both Frazer and Eliade, is to see how the same patterns constantly recur, and to assume that therefore definite outlines can be traced. Another is to proceed by detailed and honest investigation of the sources, like Chadwick and de Vries, with the realization that nothing is ever simple and that tentative conclusions must bring fresh questions and uncertainties in their wake.

Still, even if we have a long way to go before beginning to understand the thought-processes of those who told the myths and left us a handful of images of their supernatural world, the purpose of this survey has been to show how much material has in fact been left us to study, and the various ways in which we may go about it. The world of thought with which we have been dealing is that belonging to the religion of the peoples of north-western Europe in the course of the Migration Period and the Viking Age, following the collapse of the Roman Empire and the formation of new kingdoms in western Europe, with occasional glimpses of religious practices in earlier periods. The peoples under scrutiny were subject to constant movement and turmoil, and this was bound to affect their religious thought and imagery. The predominating pattern is of a religion that has developed in a warrior society, with the king holding the dominant position both in the human world and also in relations with the gods. We know less concerning the other side of religious tradition, that represented by the wise men, poets and diviners, sometimes supporting the royal power and sometimes opposed to it. Nevertheless, there is weighty evidence for their influence on religion, and here the work of N.K. Chadwick on the early literature of Scandinavian and Celtic peoples is of great value in restoring the balance.

There is no doubt that certain patterns predominated, and were expressed in ritual and legend, varying according to local conditions and the chosen methods of religious expression. The replacement of the familiar patterns by the framework of the centralized Christian church must have been disrupting and painful to many. We know comparatively little of this revolution in thought and organization, with its appeal to central authority and refusal to tolerate other forms of belief, since it is Christians for the most part who have left us the records. Obviously, there was always some possibility of continuity in the new faith, as wise teachers like Pope Gregory realized and encouraged. Friendly saints might replace the land-spirits, and guardian angels the protective beings of the families; a calendar of Christian feasts, some on the same dates as the former ones, continued to relieve the hard monotony of everyday life; less comfortably, the threat of Judgement Day succeeded that of Ragnarok. Christ might be seen in a familiar guise as the young child coming from another world to save his people, or as a young warrior demanding allegiance, and his death as lamented by the natural world, as with the old fertility gods. While the oral wisdom of the wise men and law-givers passed away in a few generations, those who desired to have contact with ancient wisdom were now offered entry into the past world of written learning and the thoughts of holy men and women stored in manuscripts, as well as the recorded learning of past civilizations.

Meanwhile on a more popular level, the story-tellers and poets took over, using the old themes and half-recollected tales and legends of their forebears. Much of the former body of traditions and beliefs had been at that level in any case, and could therefore survive, disorganized but stimulating, with comparatively little alteration under the new establishment. The church periodically condemned various superstitious practices, indicating their continued life. Yet even the serious-minded John Milton in the seventeenth century was able to enjoy, along with imaginative pictures of the classical world of legend, more homely tales of hobgoblins and spirits of the countryside without feeling guilty or disloyal to his demanding creed. While folk tradition constantly develops and changes, and must no longer be assumed to lead back in a direct line to a pre-Christian past, it shows us how certain customs and traditions could quietly continue, along with the new store of approved teaching about religion to which men now turned for enlightenment.

So the search for a lost religion goes on, using of necessity a variety of approaches and many different roads. There were tales in Ireland of ancient heroes recalled from the dead to answer questions about the past, while Snorri

Sturluson in Iceland searched the work of earlier poets to find information about the realm of the Æsir, and the quest has continued unceasingly. It is useless to attempt to recreate it as a living way of faith, as some have attempted to do, relentlessly shutting their eyes to the problems and striving to see the old religion in clear lines and bright colours. The attempts of Nazi Germany to recreate a non-existent Aryan religion belonging to the heroic past and its hideous consequences should be sufficient warning against such attempts to catch a fallen star and restore it to the heavens again. But such wisdom and sense of the numinous as can be found in any religion that has satisfied the aspirations and imaginative needs of men and women for thousands of years, and held communities together in a way that our divided faiths often fail to do, is surely worth seeking after, however long and arduous the quest.

Bibliography

Ackerman, R. (1987) *J.G. Frazer: His Life and Work*. Cambridge.

Allason-Jones, L. and McKay, B. (1985) *Coventina's Well: A Shrine on Hadrian's Wall*. Chesters Museum.

Almqvist, B. (1965) *Norrön Niddiktning: Traditionshistoriska studier i versmagi* I (Nordiska Texter och Undersokningar 21). Uppsala.

Amira, K. von (1922) *Die germanischen Todesstrafen* (Abhandlungen der Bayer. Akad. der Wissenschaften (Philos–Philol) 31(3)). Munich.

Arbman, H. (1945) *Käringsjön: Studier i halländsk järnålder* (Kungliga Vitterhets Historie och Antikvitets Akademiens Handlingar 59). Stockholm.

Bætke, W. (1950) *Die Götterlehre der Snorra-Edda* (Berichte Verhandlungen der sach. Akad. der Wissenschaften zu Leipzig (Philos–Hist) 97(3)). Berlin.

Barnard, S. (1985) 'The *Matres* of Roman Britain', *Archaeological Journal* 142, 237–45. London.

Benoit, F. (1975) 'The Celtic Oppidum of Entremont, Provence', in R. Bruce-Mitford, ed., *Recent Archaeological Excavations in Europe*, 227–59. London.

Berger, P. (1988) *The Goddess Obscured: Transformation of the Grain Protectress from Goddess to Saint*. London.

Biddle, M. and Kjølbye-Biddle, B. (1985) 'The Repton Stone', *Anglo-Saxon England* 14, 233–92. Cambridge.

Bosanquet, R.C. (1922) 'On an Altar Dedicated to the Alaisiagae', *Archaeologica Aeliana* 19 (series 3), 185–92. Newcastle upon Tyne.

Bourriot, F. (1965) 'La tombe de Vix et le mont Lassios', *Revue Historique* 234, 285–310. Paris.

Bower, C. (1975) 'Great-Bladdered Medb: Mythology and Invention in the *Táin Bó Cúailnge*', *Eire-Ireland* 10(4), 14–34. St Paul.

Briggs, K.M. (1970) *A Dictionary of British Folk-Tales* (4 vols) A.1. London.

Brisson, A. and Hatt, J. (1953) 'Les nécropoles hallstattiennes d'Aulnay-aux-Planches (Marne)', *Revue archéologique de l'Est et du Centre-Est* 4, 193–203. Dijon.

Bronnenkant, L. (1982–3) 'Thurstable Revisited', *Journal English Place-Name Society* 15, 9–19. Nottingham.

Brooks, N. *et al.* (1984) 'A new charter of King Edgar', *Anglo-Saxon England* 13, 137–50. Cambridge.

Bruce-Mitford, R.L.S. (1955) 'The Snape Boat-Grave', *Proceedings Suffolk Institute of Archaeology* 26, 1–26. Ipswich.

—— (1975–83) *The Sutton Hoo Ship-burial* (3 vols in 4). London.

Brøndsted, J. (1938–40) *Denmarks Oldtid* (3 vols). Copenhagen.

Buchholz, P. (1975) 'Forschungprobleme germanische Religiongeschichte', *Christiana Albertina* 18 (n.f. 2), 19–29. Kiel.

Burne C. (1901) Review of James Frazer, *The Golden Bough*, *Folklore* 12, 240–3. London.

Bø, O. (1989) 'Fakses and the Remains of Churches', in R. Walls *et al.*, eds, *The Old Traditional Way of Life: Essays in Honor of Warren E. Roberts*, 14–25. Bloomington, Indiana.

Campbell, J. (1962) *The Masks of God: Oriental Mythology*. London.

Carver, M.O.H., ed. (1986) *Bulletin of the Sutton Hoo Research Committee*, 4. London.

—— (1992) 'The Anglo-Saxon Cemetery at Sutton Hoo: An Interim Report', in M.O.H. Carver, ed., *The Age of Sutton Hoo: The Seventh Century in North-Western Europe*, 343–71. Woodbridge.

Carver, M. and Copp, A. (1990a) 'Excavations in Sector 2', *Bulletin Sutton Hoo Research Committee* 5, 7. Woodbridge.

—— (1990b) 'Inventory of Early Medieval Burials', *Bulletin Sutton Hoo Research Committee* 7, 7–9. Woodbridge.

Carver, M. and Royle, C.M. (1988) 'Moulding Sandmen for Exhibition', *Bulletin Sutton Hoo Research Committee* 5, 20. Woodbridge.

Chadwick, H.M. (1900) 'The Oak and the Thunder God', *Journal Royal Anthropological Institute of Gt. Britain and Ireland* 30, 22–44. London.

—— (1907) *The Origin of the English Nation*. Cambridge.

—— (1912) *The Heroic Age*. Cambridge.

—— (1940) 'The Sutton Hoo Ship Burial VIII: Who Was He?', *Antiquity* 14, 76–87. e.g. Gloucester.

Chadwick N.K. (1950) 'Þorgerðr Hölgabrúðr and the Trolla Þing', in C. Fox and B. Dickens, eds, *The Early Cultures of North-West Europe: H.M. Chadwick Memorial Studies*, 397–417. Cambridge.

—— (1964) 'The Russian Giant Svyatogor and the Norse Utgartha-Loki', *Folklore* 75, 243–59. London.

—— (1968) 'Dreams in Early European Literature', in J. Carney and D. Greene, eds, *Celtic Studies: Essays in Memory of Angus Matheson*, 33–50. London.

Coffey, J.E. (1989) 'The *Drunnur* – A Faroese Wedding Custom', *Arv* 45, 7–16. Stockholm.

Cumont, F. (1949) *Lux Perpetua*. Paris.

Cunliffe, B. (1986) 'The Sanctuary of Sulis Minerva at Bath', in M. Henig and A. King, eds, *Pagan Gods and Shrines of the Roman Empire* (Oxford University Committee for Archaeology, 8), 1–14.

Dalton, O.M. (1915) *Letters of Sidonius Apollinaris* (2 vols). Oxford.

Danaher, K. (1972) *The Year in Ireland: Irish Calendar Customs*. Dublin.

Davidson, H.R.E. (1963) 'Folklore and Man's Past', *Folklore* 74, 527–44. London.

—— (1964) *Gods and Myths of Northern Europe*. Harmondsworth.

—— (1965) 'The Significance of the Man in the Horned Helmet', *Antiquity* 39, 23–7. Gloucester.

—— (1967) *Pagan Scandinavia* (Ancient Peoples and Places 58). London.

—— (1969) 'The Smith and the Goddess', *Frühmittelalterliche Studien* (University of Münster) 3, 216–26. Berlin.

—— (1972) *The Battle God of the Vikings* (University of York, Medieval Monograph Series 1). York.

—— (1975) 'Scandinavian Cosmology', in C. Blacker and M. Loewe, eds, *Ancient Cosmologies*, 172–97. London.

—— (1976) *The Viking Road to Byzantium*. London.

—— (1978a) 'Shape-changing in the Old Norse Sagas', in J.R. Porter and W.H.S. Russell, eds, *Animals in Folklore* (Folklore Society, Mistletoe Books 9), 126–42. Ipswich.

—— (1978b) 'Mithras and Wodan', *Études Mithraïques* 4, 99–110. Acta Iranica. Leiden.

—— (1980) Commentary on Saxo Grammaticus, *History of the Danes I–IX*, (vol. 2). Woodbridge.

—— (1981a) 'The Germanic World', in M. Loewe and C. Blacker, eds, *Divination and Oracles*, 115–41, London.

—— (1981b) 'The Restless Dead: An Icelandic Ghost Story', in H.R.E. Davidson and W.M.S. Russell, eds, *The Folklore of Ghosts* (Folklore Society, Mistletoe Books 15) 155–75. Woodbridge.

—— (1982) *Scandinavian Mythology*. London.

—— (1988) *Myths and Symbols in Pagan Europe: Early Scandinavian and Celtic Religions*. Manchester.

—— (1989a) 'The Training of Warriors', in S.C. Hawkes, ed., *Weapons and Warfare in Anglo-Saxon England* (Oxford University Committee for Archaeology, Monograph 21): 11–23. Oxford.

—— (1989b) 'Hooded Men in Celtic and Germanic Tradition', in G. Davies, ed., *Polytheistic Systems* (Cosmos 5), 105–24. Edinburgh.

—— (1990) 'Religious Practices of the Northern Peoples in Scandinavian Tradition', *Temenos* 26, 23–34. Helsinki.

—— (1992a) 'Human Sacrifice in the Late Pagan Period in North-Western Europe', in M.O.H. Carver, ed., *The Age of Sutton Hoo: The Seventh Century in North-Western Europe*, 331–40. Woodbridge.

—— (1992b) 'Royal Graves as Religious Symbols', in W. Filmer-Sankey, ed., *Anglo-Saxon Studies in Archaeology and History* 5, 25–31. Oxford.

Davidson, H.R.E. and Webster, L. (1967) 'The Anglo-Saxon Burial at Coombe (Woodnesborough), Kent', *Medieval Archaeology* 11, 1–41. London.

Dillon, M. and Chadwick, N.K. (1967) *The Celtic Realms*. New York.

Dorson, R. (1958) 'The Eclipse of Solar Mythology', in T.A. Sebeok, ed., *Myth: A Symposium* (American Folklore Society, Bibliography and Special Series 5), 15–38. Bloomington, Indiana.

Dumézil, G. (1948) *Loki*. Paris.

—— (1970) *Archaic Roman Religion* (trans. P. Krapp, 2 vols). Chicago.

Dumville, D. (1976) '*Echtrae* and *Immram*: Some Problems of Definition', *Ériu* 27, 73–94. Dublin.

East, K. (1984) 'The Sutton Hoo Ship Burial: A Case against the Coffin', *Anglo-Saxon Studies in Archaeology and History* 3, 79–84. Oxford.

East, K. and Webster, L.E. (forthcoming) *The Taplow, Broomfield and Caenby Burials*. London.

Eliade, M. (1951) *Le Chamanisme et les techniques archaïques de l'extase*'. Paris.

—— (1958) *Patterns in Comparative Religion* (trans. R. Sheed). London/New York.

Ellis, H.R. (1943) *The Road to Hel: A Study of the Conception of the Dead in Old Norse Literature*. Cambridge.

Ellison, A. (1980) 'Natives, Romans and Christians on West Hill, Uley', in W. Rodwell, ed., *Temples, Churches and Religion: Recent Research into Roman Britain* (BAR, British series, 77(i)), 305–28. Oxford.

Ellison, N. (1955) *The Wirral Peninsula*. London.

Enright, M.J. (1983) 'The Sutton Hoo Whetstone Sceptre', *Anglo-Saxon England* 11, 119–34. Cambridge.

—— (1990) 'The Goddess Who Weaves', *Frühmittelalterliche Studien* (University of Münster) 24, 54–70. Berlin.

Evans, A.C. (1982) *The Sutton Hoo Ship-Burial* (British Museum), 48.

Evans, D.E. (1982) 'Celts and Germans', *Bulletin Board of Celtic Studies* (University of

Wales) 29(ii), 230–55. Oxford.
Evison, V. (1979) 'The Body in the Ship at Sutton Hoo', in S.C. Hawkes *et al.*, eds, *Anglo-Saxon Studies in Archaeology and History* (BAR, British series, 72), 121–38. Oxford.
Falk, H. (1924) *Odensheite* (Videnskapsselskapets Skrifter (Hist–Filos) 10). Oslo.
Faulkes, A. (1983) 'Pagan Sympathy: Attitudes to Heathendom in the Prologue to *Snorra Edda*', in R.J. Glendinning and H. Bessason, eds, *Edda* (Icelandic Studies 4), 283–314. Manitoba.
Filip, J. (1976) 'Keltische Kultplätze und Heiligtumer in Bohmen', in H. Jankuhn, ed., *Vorgeschichtliche Heiligtumer und Opferplätze in Mittel- und Nord-Europe* (Abhandlungen Akad. der Wissenschaften (Phil–Hist) 3, 74), 55–77. Göttingen.
Filmer-Sankey, W. (1990) 'A New Boat Burial from the Snape Anglo-Saxon cemetery', in S. McGrail, ed., *Maritime Celts, Frisians and Saxons* (Council for British Archaeology Research Report 71), 126–34. Oxford.
—— (1992) 'Snape Anglo-Saxon Cemetery: The Current State of Knowledge', in M.O.H. Carver, ed., *The Age of Sutton Hoo: The Seventh Century in North-Western Europe*, 39–51. Woodbridge.
—— (forthcoming) Report on 1991 boat grave at Snape.
Fitzgerald, D. (1879–80) 'Popular Tales of Ireland', *Revue Celtique* 4, 171–200. Paris.
Flateyjarbók (1860) (3 vols). Oslo.
Flowers, S.E. (1986) *Runes and Magic: Magical Formulaic Elements in the Older Runic Tradition* (American University Studies 1 (Germanic Languages and Literature 53)). New York.
Ganz, J. (1981) *Early Irish Myths and Sagas.* Harmondsworth.
Gelling, M. (1961) 'Place-Names and Anglo-Saxon Paganism', *University of Birmingham Historical Journal* 8, 7–25.
—— (1973) 'Further Thoughts on Pagan Place-Names', in F. Sandgren, ed., *Otium et Negotium: Studies in Onomatology and Library Science Presented to Olof von Feilitzen*, 109–28. Stockholm.
Gimbutas, M. (1982) *The Goddesses and Gods of Old Europe 6500–3500* BC: *Myths and Cult Images.* London.
—— (1989) *The Language of the Goddess.* London.
Gonda, I. (1956) 'Ancient Indian Kingship from the Religious Point of View', *Numen* 3, 36–71. Leiden.
Gray, E. (1980–1) 'Cath Maige Tuired: Myth and Structure (1–24)', *Eigse* 18, 183–209. Kildare.
Green, M. (1986) *The Gods of the Celts.* Gloucester.
Grieg, S. (1954) 'Amuletter og Guldbilder', *Viking* 18, 157–209. Oslo.
Grimm, J. (1883) *Teutonic Mythology* (trans. J.S. Stallybrass, 4 vols). London.
Grønbech, V. (1931) *The Culture of the Teutons* (trans. W. Worster, 2 vols). London/Copenhagen.
Hagberg, U.E. (1967) *The Archaeology of Skedemosse* II (Royal Swedish Acad. (Letter–Hist–Antiq)). Stockholm.
Hald, K. (1965) *Vore Stednavne.* Cophenhagen.
—— (1969) *Stednavne og Kulturhistorie* (2nd edn) (Dansk Historisk Fœllesforenings handboger). Copenagen.
—— (1971) *Personnavne i Danmark* I. *Oldtiden* (Dansk Historisk Fœllesforenings handboger). Copenhagen.
Hauck, K. (1954) 'Herrschaftszeichen eines Wodanistischen Königtum', *Jahrbuch fur frankische Landesforschung* 14, 9–59. Kallmünz.
—— (1970) *Goldbrakteaten aus Sievern* (Münstersche Mittelalter-Schriften 1). Munich.
—— (1972) 'Zur Ikonologie der Goldbrakteaten, I: neue Windott-amulette', in *Fest-*

schrift für Hermann Heimpel III, 627–60. Göttingen.
—— (1985) *Die Goldbrakteaten den Volkerwanderungszeit* (4 vols) (Münstersche Mittelatter-Schriften 24). Munich.
Haugen, E. (1983) 'The *Edda* as Ritual: Odin and his Masks', in R.J. Glendinning and H. Bessason, eds, *Edda* (Icelandic Studies 4), 3–24. Manitoba.
Hawkes, S.C. and Pollard, M. (1981) 'The Gold Bracteates from Sixth-century Anglo-Saxon Graves in Kent, in the Light of a New Find from Finglesham', *Frühmittelalterliche Studien* (University of Münster) 15, 316–70. Munich.
Hencken, T.C. (1938) 'The Excavation of the Iron Age Camp on Bredon Hill, Glos. 1935–1937', *Archaeological Journal* 95, 1–111. London.
Henig, M. (1986) '*Ita intellexit numine inductus tuo*: Some Personal Interpretations of Deity in Roman Religion', in M. Henig and A. King, eds, *Pagan Gods and Shrines of the Roman Empire* (Oxford University Committee for Archaeology, 8), 159–69. Oxford.
Holmqvist, W. (1975) 'Helgö, an Early Trading Settlement in Central Sweden', in R. Brace-Mitford, ed., *Recent Archaeological Excavations in Europe*, 111–32. London.
Holtsmark, A. (1933) 'Vitazgjafi', *Maal og Minne* 111–33. Oslo.
—— (1949) 'Myten om Idun og Tjatse i Tjodolv's *Haustlǫng*', *Arkiv Nordisk Filologi* 64, 1–73. Lund/Oslo.
—— (1951) 'Skáro á skiði', *Maal og Minne* 81–9. Oslo.
Hondius-Crone, A. (1955) *The Temple of Nehalennia at Domberg*. Amsterdam.
Honko, L. (1987) 'The Kalevala: Myth or History?', in B. Almqvist *et al.*, eds, *The Heroic Process: Form, Function and Fantasy in Folk Epic*. Dublin.
Hooke, S. (1933) ed., *Myth and Ritual: Essays on the Myth and Ritual of the Hebrews in Relation to the Culture Pattern of the Ancient East*. Oxford.
Hope-Taylor, B. (1977) *Yeavering* (Department of Environment Archaeological Reports 7). London.
Horne, P.D. and King, A.C. (1980) 'Romano-Celtic Temples in Continental Europe', in W. Rodwell, ed., *Temples, Churches and Religion: Recent Research in Roman Britain* (BAR, British series, 77(i)), 369–555. Oxford.
Hultkranz, A.G.B. (1990) 'A New Look at the World Pillar in Arctic and Sub-Arctic Religions', paper given at IAHR Regional Conference on Circumpolar and Northern Religion, Helsinki.
Hutton, R. (1991) *The Pagan Religions of the Ancient British Isles: Their Nature and Legacy*. Oxford.
Jankuhn, H. (1957) *Denkmaler der Vorzeit zwichen Nord- und Ostsee* (Kulturstromungen und Volkerbewegungen im alten Norden). Schleswig.
Joffroy, R. (1962) *Le Trésor de Vix: Histoire et portée d'une grande découverte*. Paris.
Johannesson, K. (1981) 'Order in *Gesta Danorum*', in K. Früs-Jensen, ed., *Saxo Grammaticus: A Medieval Author between Norse and Latin Culture*, 95–104. Copenhagen.
Johns, C. (1971) 'A Roman Bronze Statuette of Epona', *British Museum Quarterly* 36, 37–41. London.
Joliffe, N. (1941) 'Dea Brigantia', *Archaeological Journal* 98, 36–61, London.
Jones, G. (1968) *A History of the Vikings*. Oxford.
Kiil, V. (1959) 'Tjodolvs *Haustlǫng*', *Arkiv Nordisk Filologi* 74, 1–104. Lund/Oslo.
Klindt-Jensen, O. (1950) 'Foreign Influence in Denmark's Early Iron Age', *Acta Archaeologica* 20, 119–57. Copenhagen.
Kuhn, H. (1938) 'Die Reiterscheiben der Volkerwanderungszeit', *IPEK* (Jahrbuch f. Prähistorische und Ethnographische Kunst) 12, 95–115. Leipzig.
Landnámabók (1968) ed. Jakob Benediktsson (2 vols) (Íslenzk Fornrit I). Reykjavik.
Lang, J.T. (1972) 'Illustrative Carving of the Viking Period at Sockburn on Tees', *Archaeologica Aeliana* (series 4) 50, 235–48. Newcastle upon Tyne.

Larsen, E.B. (1987) 'SEM-Identification and Documentation of Tool Marks and Surface Textures on the Gundestrup Cauldron', in J. Black, ed., *Recent Advances in the Conservation and Analysis of Artifacts*, 393–408. London.

Leeds, E.T. (1924) 'Anglo-Saxon Cremation Burial of the Seventh Century in Asthall Barrow, Oxfordshire', *Antiquaries Journal* 4, 113–26. London.

Le Roux, F. (1953) 'Cernunnos', *Ogam* 25–6, 324–29. Rennes.

Le Roux, F. and Guyonvarc'h, C.-J. (1982) *Les Druides* (3rd edn) (Celticum 14). Rennes.

Lévi-Strauss, C. (1958) 'The Structural Study of Myth', in T.A. Sebeok, ed., *Myth: A Symposium*, 50–66. Indiana, Bloomington.

Lid, N. (1928) *Joleband og Vegetasjonsguddom* (Norske Videnskap Akademi Hist–Filos Kl. 4). Oslo.

Lidén, H. (1969) 'From Pagan Sanctuary to Christian Church: The Excavation of Maere Church, Trondelag', *Norwegian Archaeological Review* 2, 23–32. Oslo.

Liestøl, K. (1946) *Draumkvaede, a Norwegian Visionary Poem from the Middle Ages* (Studia Norvegica 3). Oslo.

Lindholm, D. (1968) *Stave Churches in Norway* (trans. S. and A. Bittleston). London.

Lindow, J. (1978) *Swedish Legend and Folktales*. Berkeley/Los Angeles.

Lindqvist, S. (1923) 'Hednatemplet i Uppsala', *Fornvännen* 23, 85–118.

—— (1936) *Uppsala Högar och Ottarshöge* (Kunglige Vitterhets Historie och Antikvitets Akademiens Handlingar). Stockholm.

—— (1941) *Gotlands Bildsteine* (2 vols) (Kunglige Vitterhets Historie och Antikvitets Akademien). Stockholm.

Linduff, J.M. (1979) 'Epona: A Celt among the Romans', *Latomus* 38(iii) 817–37.

Lyle, E. (1990) *Archaic Cosmos: Polarity, Space and Time*. Edinburgh.

Lysaght, P. (1986) *The Banshee: The Irish Supernatural Death-Messenger*. Dublin.

Löffler, C.M. (1983) *The Voyage to the Otherworld Island in Early Irish Literature* (Salzburg Studies in English Literature (Eliz-Renaiss.) 103). Salzburg.

Mabire, N.T. (1971) *La Composition de la Eyrbyggja Saga*. Caen.

MacCana, P. (1955–8) 'Aspects of the Theme of the King and Goddess in Irish Literature', *Études Celtiques* 7, 76–114, 311–413; 8, 59–65. Paris.

McCone, K. (1970) *Celtic Mythology*. London.

—— (1990) *Pagan Past and Christian Present in Early Irish Literature* (Maynooth Monographs 3). Maynooth.

MacDougall, J. (1978) *Highland Fairy Legends*, ed. G. Calder. Ipswich.

MacGregor, A.A. (1937) *The Peat-Fire Flame: Folk-Tales and Traditions of the Highlands and Islands*. Edinburgh.

Mackeprang, M. (1952) *De nordiske Guldbrakteater* (Jysk Arkaeologisk Selskabskrifter 2). Århus.

Mac Mathuna, S. (1985) *Immram Brain: Bran's Journey to the Land of the Women* (Buchreihe der Zeitschrift f. Celtische Philologie 2). Tübingen.

MacNeill, M. (1982) *The Festival of Lughnasa: A Study of the Survival of the Celtic Festival of the Beginning of Harvest* (2 vols). Dublin.

Magoun, F.P. (1949) 'On the Old-Germanic Altar or Oath Ring', *Acta Philologica Scandinavica* 20, 277–91. Copenhagen.

Mallory, J.P. (1989) *In Search of the Indo-Europeans: Language, Archaeology and Myth*. London.

Megaw, J.V.S. (1970) *Art of the European Iron Age*. Bath.

Meissner, R. (1921) *Der Kenningar der Skalden* (Rheinische Beiträge und Hülfbücher zur germanischen Philologie und Volkskunde I). Bonn/Leipzig.

Motz, L. (1984) 'The Winter-Goddess: Percht, Holda and Related Figures', *Folklore* 95, 151–66.

Müller-Wille, M. (1968–9) 'Bestattung im Boot: Studien zu einer nordeuropaischen

Grabsitte', *Offa* 25–6, 7–203. Neumünster.

Murphy, G. (1953) 'The Lament of the Old Woman of Beare', *Proceedings Royal Irish Academy* 55, 84. Dublin.

Myres, J.N.J. (1977) *A Corpus of Anglo-Saxon Pottery of the Pagan Period* (2 vols) (Gulbenkian Archaeological Series). Cambridge.

Myres, J.N.J. and Green, B. (1973) *The Anglo-Saxon Cemeteries of Caistor-by-Norwich and Markshall, Norfolk* (Reports of the Research Committee, Society of Antiquaries 30). London.

Nordal, S. (1958) *Hrafnkels saga Freysgoða* (trans. R.G. Thomas). Cardiff.

Nylen, E. (1978) *Bildstenar.* Visby.

Ó Cathasáigh, D. (1982) 'The Cult of Brigid: A Study of Pagan-Christian Syncretism in Ireland', in J.J. Preston, ed., *Mother Worship: Theme and Variations*, 75–94. Chapel Hill.

Ó Crualaoich, G. (1988) 'Legends of Cailleach Bhearre', *Bealoideas* 56, 153–78. Dublin.

Ó hÓgáin, D. (1990) *Myth, Legend and Romance: An Encyclopaedia of the Irish Folk Tradition.* London.

Olmsted, G.S. (1979) 'The Gundestrup Cauldron', *Collection Latomus* 162, Brussels.

Olsen, M. (1909) 'Fra gammelnorsk myte og cultus', *Maal og Minne*, 17–36. Oslo.

Olsen, O. (1966) *Hørg, Hov og Kirke* (Årbøger Nordisk Oldkyndighed og Historie). Copenhagen.

O'Rahilly, T.F. (1946) *Early Irish History and Mythology.* Dublin.

Otto, R. (1952) *The Idea of the Holy* (trans. J.W. Harvey). Oxford.

Oxenstierna, Count E. (1956) *Die Goldhorner von Gallehus.* Lidinge.

Paulsen, P. (1967) *Alamannische Adelsgraber von Niederstotzingen* (2 vols). (Veroffenlichungen d. staatliche Amter f. Denkmalpflege (A, Vor- und Frühgeschichte) 12). Stuttgart.

Phillpotts, B. (1929) *The Elder Edda and Ancient Scandinavian Drama.* Cambridge.

Piggott, S. (1967) 'Celts, Saxons and Early Antiquaries' (O'Donnell Lecture). Edinburgh.

——— (1968) *The Druids.* London.

Porter, J.R. (1977) 'Two Presidents of the Folklore Society, S.H. Hooke and E.O. James', *Folklore* 88, 131–45. London.

Powell, T.G.E. (1971) 'From Urartu to Gundestrup: The Agency of Thracian Metalwork', in J. Boardman *et al.*, eds, *The European Community in Later Prehistory: Studies in Honour of C.F.C. Hawkes*, 183–210. London.

Pryor, F. (1990) 'Flag Fen', *Current Archaeology* 119, 386–90. London.

Rankin, H.D. (1987) *Celts and the Classical World.* London.

Rees, A. and Rees, B. (1961) *Celtic Heritage: Ancient Tradition in Ireland and Wales.* London.

Reinach, A. (1913) 'Les têtes coupées et les trophées en Gaule', *Revue Celtique* 34, 38–60, 253–86. Paris.

Rhys, Sir J. (1901) *Celtic Folklore, Welsh and Manx* (2 vols). Oxford.

Richmond, I.A. (1943) 'Roman Legionaries at Corbridge, their Supply-base, Temples and Religious Cults', *Archaeologia Aeliana* 21 (series 4), 127–224. Newcastle upon Tyne.

Robinson, C.H. (1921) *Anskar the Apostle of the North.* Lives of Early and Mediaeval Missionaries. London.

Robinson, G.W. (1916) *Life of St Boniface.* Cambridge, Massachusetts.

Rockwell, J. (1981) *Evald Tang Kristensen: A Lifelong Adventure in Folklore.* Ålborg/Copenhagen.

Rodwell, W. (1980) 'Temple Archaeology: Problems of the Present and Portents for the Future', in W. Rodwell, ed., *Temples, Churches and Religion: Recent Research in Roman Britain* (BAR, British series, 77(1)), 211–41. Oxford.

Roe, H. (1945) 'An Interpretation of Certain Symbolic Sculptures of Early Christian

Ireland', *Journal Royal Society of Antiquaries of Ireland* 75, 1–23. Dublin.
Roman Life at the Yorkshire Museum (1985) Gallery Guide. York.
Rooth, A.B. (1961) *Loki in Scandinavian Mythology.* Lund.
Ross, A. (1967) *Pagan Celtic Britain.* London.
—— (1973) 'The Divine Hag of the Pagan Celts', in V. Newall, ed., *The Witch Figure*, 139–64. London.
—— (1978–80) 'Chartres: The *locus* of the Carnutes', *Studia Celtica* 14–15, 260–9. Cardiff.
Ross, A. and Robins, D. (1989) *The Life and Death of a Druid Prince: The Story of an Archaeological Sensation.* London.
Sandars, N.K. (1968) *Prehistoric Art in Europe* (Pelican History of Art). Harmondsworth.
Simmer, A. (1982) 'Le prélèvement des crânes dans l'Est de la France à l'époque merovingienne', *Archéologie Medievale* 12, 35–48. Caen.
Simpson, J. (1962) 'Mimir: Two Myths or One?', *Saga-Book* 16 (Viking Society for Northern Research, University College). London.
—— (1966) 'Otherworld Adventures in an Icelandic Saga', *Folklore* 77, 1–20. London.
—— (1967) *Everyday Life in the Viking Age.* London.
Sisam, K. (1953) 'Anglo-Saxon Royal Genealogies', *Proceedings British Academy*, 287–348. London.
Sjoestedt, M.-L. (1982) *Gods and Heroes of the Celts* (trans. M. Dillon). Berkeley, California.
Smyser, H.M. (1965) 'Ibn Fadlan's Account of the Rus', in J. Bessinger and R.P. Creed, eds, *Medieval and Linguistic Studies in Honour of Francis Peabody Magoun Jr*, 92–119. London.
Stokes, W. (1903) ed., 'The Battle of Allen', *Revue Celtique* 24, 41–70. Paris.
Stolpe, H. and Arne, J.J. (1927) *La Nécropole de Vendel.* Stockholm.
Strenski, I. (1987) *Four Theories of Myth in Twentieth Century History.* London.
Struve, K.W. (1967) 'Die Moorleiche von Dätgen', *Offa* 24, 33–83. Neumünster.
Ström, F. (1942) *On the Sacral Origin of the Germanic Death Penalties* (Kunglige Vitterhets Historie och Antikvitets Handling 52). Stockholm.
—— (1954) 'Diser, nornor, valkyrjor' (Kunglige Vitterhets Historie och Antikvitets Akademiens Handlingar (Filol–Filos) I). Stockholm.
Strömbäck, D. (1971) 'Uppsala in Old Norse Literature', in P. Foote and D. Strömbäck, eds, *Proceedings Sixth Viking Congress*, 21–32. Uppsala.
—— (1975) *The Conversion of Iceland* (trans. P. Foote) (Viking Society Text Series 1). London.
Stuart, P. *et al.* (1971) *Deae Nehalenniae.* Middelburg/Leiden.
Sørensen, P.M. (1986) 'Thor's Fishing Expedition', in G. Steinsland, ed., *Words and Objects: Towards a Dialogue between Archaeology and History of Religion*, 257–76. Oslo.
Talbot, C.H. (1954) *The Anglo-Saxon Missionaries in Germany.* London.
Tatar, M. (1987) *The Hard Facts of the Grimms' Fairy Tales.* Princeton.
Taylor, T. (1992) 'The Gundestrup Cauldron', *Scientific American* 266(3), 66–71. New York.
Thevenot, E. (1968) *Divinités et sanctuaires de la Gaule.* Paris.
Tierney, J.J. (1959–60) 'The Celtic Ethnography of Posidonius', *Proceedings Royal Irish Academy* 60(c), 189–275. Dublin.
Todd, M. (1975) *The Northern Barbarians, 100 BC–AD 300.* London.
Tovar, A. (1982) 'The God *Lugus* in Spain', *Bulletin Board Celtic Studies* (University of Wales) 29, 591–99. Oxford.
Toynbee, J.M.C. (1976) 'Roman Sculpture in Gloucestershire', in P. McGrath and J. Cannon, eds, *Essays in Bristol and Gloucestershire History*, Bristol and Gloucestershire

Archaeological Society, 62–100. Bristol.
Turville-Petre, E.O.G. (1962) 'Thurstable', in N. Davies and C.L. Wrenn, eds, *English and Medieval Studies Presented to J.R.R. Tolkien*, 21–49. London.
——— (1963) 'A Note on the *land-dísir*', in A. Brown and P. Foote, eds, *Early English and Norse Studies Presented to Hugh Smith*, 196–201. London.
——— (1964) *Myth and Religion of the North*. Oxford.
——— (1966) 'Dream Symbols in Old Icelandic Literature', in K. Rudolph *et al.*, eds, *Festschrift Walter Baetke*, 343–54. Weimar.
——— (1976) *Scaldic Poetry*. Oxford.
Vierck, H. (1967) 'Ein Relieffibelpaar aus Nordendorf in Bayerisch Schwaben', *Bayerische Vorgeschichte Blatt* 32, 104–43. Munich.
——— (1979) 'The Cremation in the Ship at Sutton Hoo', *Anglo-Saxon Studies in Archaeology and History* (BAR, British series, 72), 343–55, Oxford.
Vries, J. de (1933) *The Problem of Loki* (F.F. Communications 110). Helsinki.
——— (1957–8) *Altgermanische Religionsgeschichte* (2 vols) (2nd edn) (Grundriss Germanische Philologie 12). Berlin.
Wait, G.A. (1985) *Ritual and Religion in Iron Age Britain* (BAR, British Series, 149). Oxford.
Wagner, H. (1981) 'Origins of Pagan Irish Religion', *Zeitschrift für Celtische Philologie* 31, 1–28. Tübingen.
Waschnitius, V. (1913) *Perht, Holda und verwandte Gestalten* (Sitzungsberichte Kaiser Akad. d. Wissenschaften (Philos-Hist) 174). Vienna.
Watson, A. (1981) 'The King, the Poet and the Sacred Tree', *Études Celtiques* 18, 165–80. Paris.
Webster, G. (1986) *The British Celts and their Gods under Rome*. London.
Webster, L. and Bakehouse J. (1991) *The Making of England*. London.
Wilson, D.R. (1980) 'Romano-Celtic Temple Architecture', in W. Rodwell, ed., *Temples, Churches and Religions: Recent Research in Roman Britain* (BAR, British series, 77(i)), 5–30. Oxford.
Wood, J. (1992) 'The Fairy Bride Legend in Wales', *Folklore* 103, 56–72. London.
Wrenn, C.L. (1965) 'Some Earliest Anglo-Saxon Cult Symbols', in J. Bessinger and R.P. Creed, eds, *Medieval and Linguistic Studies in Honor of Frances Peabody Magoun Jr*, 40–55. London.
Young, B. (1976) 'Paganisme, christianisation et rites funéraires mérovingiens', *Archéologie Medievale* 7, 5–81. Caen.

Index